Contexts for Hawthorne

CONTEXTS FOR HAWTHORNE

The Marble Faun
and the Politics of Openness
and Closure in American Literature

MILTON R. STERN

University of Illinois Press
Urbana and Chicago

Library of Congress Cataloging-in-Publication Data

Stern, Milton R.
  Contexts for Hawthorne : The marble faun and the politics of
openness and closure in American literature / Milton R. Stern.
    p.   cm.
  Includes bibliographical references and index.
  ISBN 0-252-01819-2 (acid-free paper)
  1. Hawthorne, Nathaniel, 1804–1864. Marble faun. 2. Politics and
literature—United States—History—19th century. 3. Romanticism—
United States. 4. Classicism—United States. 5. Openings
(Rhetoric) 6. Closure (Rhetoric) I. Title.
PS1862.S74 1991
813'.3—dc20   91-8752
                                                                    CIP

For Harriet, Anna, and Alexander
with love

Contents

Preface and Acknowledgments

One central endeavor of this book as an act of literary criticism is a mediation between the two great poles of Romantic and Classicist vision. Those polarities exist in a dialectical interchange, which is what I refer to as politics. Therefore, because this book is concerned with literature and politics, I should indicate, when I say "politics" what this book is not. It is not an investigation of the political affiliations of individual writers, such as has been presented by George Panichas. I do not try to trace the expression of politicalisms as Merle Himmelstein, Donald Gibson, and Daniel Aaron have done. And unlike Joseph Blotner's book, this study is not organized around fiction whose subject is politics—a grand continuum in American letters, from James Fenimore Cooper's *Littlepage Manuscripts* through books such as Henry Adams's *Democracy,* Norman Mailer's *Barbary Shore,* and Robert Penn Warren's *All the King's Men* to Allen Drury's *Advise and Consent* and the latest fictions of political topicality. Neither am I writing about the politics of dealings among writers, agents, editors, and publishers, as Van Wyck Brooks and Perry Miller have done.[1] I am writing about how the radical implications of his choice of vocation by Nathaniel Hawthorne, the conservative, influenced his narrative technique. By becoming a writer of Romances rather than a banker, soldier, statesman, or some other "manly" being necessary and useful to building young America, Hawthorne, in his choice of vocation, challenged the priorities of his society; consequently, he felt a psychological displacement, a withholding of allegiance. His choice was dissent from the expansionist, pragmatic, and yet millennialistic national psyche expressed in the ideologies of the society and its prevailing literary marketplace. By definition, the

pronouncement of belief in and allegiance to the values of an established society are ideologically conservative, and it makes no difference
if the society's rhetoric originally arose from Romantic or Classicist
assumptions. Hawthorne's triple citizenship in the realms of his vocation,
his ideology, and his utopia was a source of psychic disruption, a
citizenship in which Hawthorne constantly belonged somewhere else —
the somewhere elses defining each other. I suppose, for I am uncertain
about neatly distinct categories of criticism, that I am attempting an
applied piece of sociology of literature. Sociologists have tried to define
the subject and literary critics have written theories of it.[2] I am merely
attempting to provide a sample.

The overwhelming crush of scholarly and critical publication on
major authors precludes due reference to all those who have gone before,
except in works whose purposes demand a review of the secondary
literature. This book is not such a work, and although there are many
dozens of references that could have been made to the dismayingly
voluminous Hawthorne scholarship, I have made no attempt to specify
the instances of Hawthorne criticism that touch on the problems I
consider at any given point.[3] I can only acknowledge that although
much that is silly or tedious has been published on Hawthorne, there is
much that one greets with admiration and a collegial sense of respect
and indebtedness.

Inevitably, there are always a few books that for one reason or another
have had special influence, and just as inevitably, although there is
usually a discernible pattern in a list of those books, the diversity of
such lists is a subjective and idiosyncratic matter. Therefore, without
attempting a rationale, I will name some books that, in agreement or
disagreement, helped shape my ideas.

Like all Americanists, I find multiple moments of applicability in
the works of Sacvan Bercovitch. For me, F. O. Matthiessen's *American
Renaissance* remains the great seminal and contextual giant, despite all
the modifications one might make. In that context, I include John F.
Callahan's book (below), on neither Hawthorne nor the period, as an
inspirational example of voice. The sense of voice brings me immediately to a book that at various points is very close to my subject and
whose worth has been so deservedly praised that it needs no further
comment here: Ann Douglas's *The Feminization of American Culture*
(New York: Knopf, 1977). Many, many others could and should be
added, but I could not complete a statement of acknowledgment without especially mentioning Nina Baym's *The Shape of Hawthorne's
Career* (Ithaca, N.Y.: Cornell University Press, 1976) and *Novels, Readers,
and Reviewers: Responses to Fiction in Antebellum America* (Ithaca,

N.Y.: Cornell University Press, 1984); Sacvan Bercovitch's *The American Jeremiad* (Madison: University of Wisconsin Press, 1978); Michael Davitt Bell's excellent *The Development of the American Romance: The Sacrifice of Relation* (Chicago: University of Chicago Press, 1980) and *Hawthorne and the Historical Romance of New England* (Princeton: Princeton University Press, 1971); Richard Brodhead's very useful studies, *Hawthorne, Melville, and the Novel* (Chicago: University of Chicago Press, 1976) and *The School of Hawthorne* (New York: Oxford University Press, 1986); Lawrence Buell's superb *New England Literary Culture: From Revolution through Renaissance* (New York: Cambridge University Press, 1983), which deserves a place of its own; John F. Callahan's *In the African-American Grain: The Pursuit of Voice in Twentieth-Century Black Fiction* (Urbana: University of Illinois Press, 1988); Michael J. Colacurcio's *The Province of Piety: Moral History in Hawthorne's Early Tales* (Cambridge, Mass.: Harvard University Press, 1984); and Edward H. Davidson's *Hawthorne's Last Phase* (New Haven: Yale University Press, 1949).

In the context of this study, it is particularly appropriate to acknowledge Michael T. Gilmore's *American Romanticism and the Marketplace* (Chicago: University of Chicago Press, 1985). I must also add Lawrence Sargent Hall's *Hawthorne, Critic of Society* (New York: Oxford University Press, 1944); Henry James's *Hawthorne* (reprint, Ithaca, N.Y.: Cornell University Press, 1956)—of course; Myra Jehlen's *American Incarnation: The Individual, the Nation, and the Continent* (Cambridge, Mass.: Harvard University Press, 1986); John P. McWilliams's *Hawthorne, Melville, and the American Character: A Looking Glass Business* (New York: Cambridge University Press, 1984); James R. Mellow's *Nathaniel Hawthorne in His Times* (Boston: Houghton Mifflin, 1980); Donald Pease's *Visionary Compacts: American Renaissance Writings in Cultural Context* (Madison: University of Wisconsin Press, 1987); and Jane Tomkins's *Sensational Designs: The Cultural Work of American Fiction, 1790–1860* (New York: Oxford University Press, 1985).

If Larry J. Reynolds's *European Revolutions and the American Literary Renaissance* (New Haven: Yale University Press, 1988) had been in print while I was writing this study, that book also would have been among the primary analogues and influences. So, too, would the book of another Reynolds (David S.): *Beneath the American Renaissance: The Subversive Imagination in the Age of Emerson and Melville* (New York: Knopf, 1988). Most of all, the book to which I must pay respect as a guiding influence is Karl Mannheim's brilliant classic, *Ideology and Utopia: An Introduction to the Sociology of Knowledge*, trans. L. Wirth and E. Shils (New York: Harcourt, Brace and Co., 1952). The book is not only a porch to the house of literature, but also it is especially appropriate for writers like Hawthorne and for eras like the end of the 1980s. No commentator on the events or the critical dogmas of that era should overlook the ethical guiding vision of the Good Polis, a utopian vision the loss of which Mannheim compellingly warns against in the moving conclusion of his fourth essay, "The Utopian Mentality."

Of the friends who read the manuscript in its various phases, my grateful thanks to Irving Cummings, Jack M. Davis, John Gatta, John Wenke, and Kenneth G. Wilson for careful, detailed comments, and especially to John F. Callahan for talking me into deleting three overgeneral chapters on science, the humanities, and critical theory that for too long were too dear to my heart. And I am happy to state my gratitude to two later readers, Dan McCall and John Seelye, for helpful, intelligent, and encouraging readings.

I derive my basic principles of openness and closure through my uncertain sense of current science. There are several scientific articles and books I would cite in outlining the speculations that led me from science to openness to Romanticism to radicalism, and from science to closure to Classicism to conservatism—and from both radicalism and conservatism to Hawthorne and his American marketplace. But my inclusion of a statement about science remains problematical: although I think that my statement of theory obligates me to a presentation of the basis for theory, an offering of the scientific material within the central context of this book would be seen (and has been seen) by many readers as a distraction and, perhaps, an intrusive one at that. Therefore, I have added a brief appendix in which I sketch very briefly the nature of what I derive from science. In the notes to the appendix I offer a few citations, placing the outline of rationale after the end of the book proper, where it can be read by those who think it either necessary or interesting, or be ignored by those who think it neither. For the former I suggest that the appendix be read between chapters one and two. For the latter, although I admit that I feel too much uncertainty to be able to deny that they are right, I remain convinced that a comprehension of an operative world picture is the beginning of the comprehension of significance in applied literary criticism.

Quotations from the works and letters of Nathaniel Hawthorne are taken from the Centenary Edition of *The Works of Nathaniel Hawthorne*, W. Charvat, R. H. Pearce, and C. M. Simpson, general editors (Columbus: Ohio State University Press, 1962–87). All references to this edition will be indicated in the text by volume number and page number in parentheses.

NOTES

1. George Panichas, ed., *The Politics of Twentieth Century Novelists* (New York: Hawthorne Books, 1971); Merle Himmelstein, *Drama Was a Weapon: The Left-Wing Theatre in New York, 1929–1941* (New Brunswick, N.J.: Rutgers University Press, 1963); Donald Gibson, *The Politics of Literary Expression: A Study of Major Black Writers* (Westport, Conn.: Greenwood Press, 1981); Daniel Aaron, *Writers on the Left: Episodes in American Literary Communism* (New York: Harcourt, Brace, 1961); Joseph Blotner, *The Modern American Political Novel, 1900–1960* (Austin: University of Texas Press, 1966); Perry Miller, *The Raven and the Whale: The War of Words and Wits in the Era of Poe and Melville* (New York: Harcourt, Brace, 1956); and Van Wyck Brooks, *The Writer in America* (New York: E. P. Dutton, 1953).

2. See Diana T. Laurenson and Alan Swingewood, *The Sociology of Literature* (New York: Schocken Books, 1972). The book contains a useful introductory bibliography and pays homage to Robert Escarpit, Leo Lowenthal, and Lucien Goldmann as forebears. Among the several other books I have found stimulating and helpful, three to which I am especially indebted are Denis Donoghue's *Ferocious Alphabets* (Boston: Little, Brown, 1981); Gerald Graff's *Literature Against Itself: Literary Ideas in Modern Society* (Chicago: University of Chicago Press, 1979); and Grant Webster's *The Republic of Letters: A History of Postwar American Literary Opinion* (Baltimore: Johns Hopkins University Press, 1980).

3. A specification of all, or even most, of the intelligent and insightful Hawthorne scholarship would require a fat book of bibliographical essay. I will indicate what I think of as exemplary by citing only two works beyond those in the acknowledgments. One is a piece of periodical literature, the other a book. No good reader will agree or disagree wholly with any one of the worthy critical and scholarly works in the Hawthorne canon, and the limitation to any two works is certain to raise protestations: that is as it should be. Nevertheless, I offer these examples as representative of the several excellent studies I do not cite; I choose them because they touch closely on the considerations I find significant. Marius Bewley, in *The Eccentric Design: Form in the Classic American Novel* (New York: Columbia University Press, 1959), wrote:

> There is evidence that throughout his life . . . [Hawthorne] suffered an incapacity to adjust himself practically to the society that, as an American, he wished to believe in. He wished to express his solidarity with it, and this became a nervous necessity in that degree in which he found it difficult to cast aside his dissatisfaction with it. To state the case succinctly: Hawthorne's compulsive affirmation of American positives, particularly in the political sense, led to a rejection of the idea of solitude; and solitude as an expression of aristocratic withdrawal seemed to side with Europe rather than with America when the two traditions stated their respective claims. But unfortunately it also seemed to side with the practice of his art. (p. 115)

In his essay, "Hawthorne's 'Familiar Kind of Preface,'" *ELH* 35 (1968): 422–39, Dan McCall wrote that the real subject of Hawthorne's prefaces

> is not aesthetic theory; rather it is Hawthorne's attempt to borrow a commonplace of literary theory in the mid-nineteenth century, the distinction between Romance and novel, in order to mitigate his sense of failing his materials and the best in his own talent. In all his work he held to the notion that isolation was a crime, yet his craft allied him against the community on the side of that crime. In his art and in his life he never was able to resolve the problem. (pp. 438–39)

Within the context of my book, the reader will see how apt is the choice of these works as representative of the many that could be cited as important studies of Hawthorne.

Hitherto, the negative side of the "unattachedness" of the intellectuals, of their social instability, and of the predominantly deliberate character of their mentality has been emphasized almost exclusively. It was especially the politically extreme groups who, demanding a definite declaration of sympathies, branded this as "characterlessness." It remains to be asked, however, whether, in the political sphere, a decision in favor of a dynamic mediation may not be just as much a decision as the ruthless espousal of yesterday's theories or the one-sided emphasis on tomorrow's.

—Karl Mannheim,
Ideology and Utopia

1

A Universal Context

The core of this book, an appraisal of Nathaniel Hawthorne via *The Marble Faun,* depends upon the historical contexts of Hawthorne's literary marketplace. Nevertheless, this study is not centrally biographical. Rather, I have attempted to organize familiar materials into what I see as a deeply political pattern. Furthermore, my approach to Hawthorne has a double purpose. The first is to suggest a mimetic connection between the literary act and what appear to be "absolute" universal principles inferred from science. The other is to present Hawthorne as a paradigmatic illustration of an ongoing literary relationship between those "absolute" principles and the millennialistic context of American culture. I use the term *millennialist* in the sense that has become a commonplace among the breed of scholars called Americanists: I do not refer to specific millenarian movements but to the phenomenon, noted by almost all commentators on American literature, that from the beginning the American self-image was that of the idea or even the type of millennium—from the "city on a hill" and the "new Jerusalem" to "God's Country, love it or leave it."[1] Therefore, especially in the critical currents of the 1980s, it seems appropriate to begin by stating my own biases in explaining the purpose of this book.

My sense of Hawthorne derives from a perspective that leads me to honor him for a difficult identity he was willing to bear in his vocational pioneering. But in one basic consideration my sense of the man runs counter to the admiration heaped upon him in his time and ours. I think that Hawthorne was not able to bear the full implications of being a writer in America in his own time; yet the writer's trade and no other was what he yearned for, even in his teens. His shortcomings were a political failure of nerve that had effects on his writing not to be explained away by irony or similar instruments of defense with which modern criticism rationalizes what I see to be serious flaws in his fiction.[2] I am interested in creating a sense of Hawthorne's voice, which ranged from quiet brooding to falsetto yips of righteousness, as his arguments with his society become arguments with himself. The sources of Hawthorne's implicit narrative persona and his politics were inextricable from each other. My insistence upon the connections between Hawthorne's voice and the cultural contexts of his literary marketplace are the connections between American literature and American history. That history and that literature are interconnected like two countries, the actual America and the America of the mind.

As the field of American Studies has demonstrated, and as "everyone knows," the actual America in our national literature is a matter of experience and cultural fact; the America of the mind amounts to a vision of millennium. The relations between countries are a matter of politics, and that applies no less to the relations between the two Americas. Those relations, in turn, were central to Hawthorne's imagination and his writing. All of his novels (especially *The Marble Faun*) and many of his short fictions are attempts to work out those relations in dramatic offerings that are moral instructions to Americans. And although Hawthorne was consistent in his priorities of moral values in the relationships between individuals, he was "ambiguous"—he waffled— when those relationships reflected the politics of *national* values.

Politics is the social dimension of relationship between a self and others. Even for Immanuel Kant, whose categorical imperative would apply to the behavior of the last person on earth, the emphasis on behavior is predicated on what it means to be a sentient human: one becomes both self and other as responsible *behavior* that defines the good self forms the basis for what is categorically human. And also for Aristotle, at the other end of the spectrum, ethics and politics are inseparable. The essence of humanistic endeavor is the creation of self-consciousness, which inevitably and inextricably is bound to an awareness of the other. That awareness is the creation of civic consciousness, which, in turn, is the creation of social conscience. The essence of ethical behavior, which in these terms is what Hawthorne felt was at the center of his literary behavior, is really quite political: the creation of the consciously responsible self in an ethical society. The moral illumination of that behavior was the political center of Hawthorne's fictions; and it was precisely that center he feared to hit dead on because of the risk of being rejected by his society as un-American.

The politics of the two Americas essentially concerns the dialectic of

Romantic and Classicist perspectives, or what I call *utopias* (after Karl Mannheim) of openness and closure.[3] By utopia Mannheim did not mean an Edenic dreamworld. Rather he meant something like essential vision, not at all necessarily chiliastic and not necessarily absolute, but necessarily ethical, moral, principled. On the other hand, Mannheim noted, ideology is the instrument of power. It is opportunistic and temporizing, utilizing the rhetoric of utopian principle, but in coercive, jingoistic, and sloganeering ways, exactly like the nationalistic rhetoric of democracy and patriotism that confronted Hawthorne in his literary marketplace.

My purpose in this book is not a choice of either ideologies or utopias. For good or for ill, militantly ideological approaches to literature seek to create a tradition and are important at least in that sense. But in looking, via Hawthorne and *The Marble Faun*, at the effects of millennialistic ideology on literature in America, I am seeking not to create a tradition but to illustrate a familiar one in action. The cultural tension between the two Americas, which I might now call the ideological America (the actual culture) and the utopian America (the country in the visions of the mind), provides my points of departure into Hawthorne's works. The context provided by Mannheim furnishes my point of departure into my terminology, which is very simple: *openness, closure, ideology, utopia, Romantic, Romanticist, Classicist, radical, and conservative.*

The context for openness and closure, like the context for any absolute universal principle, demands a world picture. The arts and humanities always have translated what we take to be the facts of nature into meaning, the raw externalities of experience into internal moral and aesthetic senses of order: chaos into polis. Regardless of how humanity's pictures of the world might change, the process of making those pictures inevitably continues. And though they sometimes seem suspensefully close to it, the scientists themselves are never—or at least never yet—at the point of certain, final fact in a unified field theory that merges particle theory and astrophysics into a coherent whole. Consequently, my awareness of my scientific ignorance is somewhat mitigated by my awareness that as far as "absolute" scientific "facts" are concerned, the scientific concepts I borrow from today might be (probably will be) scientific jokes in twenty years and antiquarian curiosities in fifty. And that will be as true for the scientists themselves as for humanists who, like me, come stumbling behind them. But the principles of openness and closure that construct my working world picture seem to apply to all scientific contexts of the past and the present—and, one has to assume, a future.

Apparently, in our universe openness and closure are a priori conditions of existence. In their inevitability and ubiquity they are the essential preconditions of IS. In fact, once perceived, they are so obvious that one wants to dismiss them as useless concepts, saying, "Well, of *course;* that's the way things *are.*" One may dismiss them as platitudes: everything begins (or there would be no being) and everything ends (or there would be no change)—all is born and all changes. But to dismiss things "as they are" would be to contemplate them too quickly, for the usable complications, at least in our universe, are in *the way* things end. Although neither a final cosmic stasis of equable dispersion (openness) nor a final condensation (closure) and new Big Bang (openness again) are humanly usable in and of themselves, their implications are considerable for concepts of life, purpose, value, and polis. What intrigues me is that *the way* much of Hawthorne's fiction ends very often has a lot in common with the complicated collision, or change, of principles of openness and closure involved in the paradoxical way a star comes to an end. And (as I hope I suggest in this book) the way Hawthorne's fiction comes to an end has something to say about the way much American fiction comes to an end. The endings generally center on the problems of openness and closure, either in a repudiation of the expectations of openness, as in "My Kinsman, Major Molineux," or in a celebration of the possible triumph of openness, as in "The Artist of the Beautiful." But the "absolute" facts of our universe suggest that for the politics of human expectation as for the laws of matter, there really can be no absolute condition of openness or closure.[4]

Whether matter and space develop according to a predictable and absolute set of mechanics, or whether new mechanics develop as space and matter change, or whether there is an interactive change of matter and mechanics, or whether such interactions are the consequence of random development to be studied in the formulas of chaos are subjects of primal investigation for the cosmologist. But they suggest an infinite dialectic for the humanist.

Openness is characterized by a bursting out, by newness in time and space, by what appears to be limitless opportunity of combination and recombination and enlargements of identity. We may say that the principle of openness is a revolutionary, future-facing, and explosive repudiation of past and present states, and is associated with newness, experiment, freedom, chance, and limitlessness. Also, when it is regnant it gives birth to its opposite. Closure is characterized by a pulling in, tight control and gravitational centralization, compacted time and space. This compaction and changelessness are associated with conservative control and limitation. They, too, produce their opposites. Perhaps one can say that existence is the enactment of a dialectical life-producing irony, in which each opposite prepares for the other in the very nature of its being. The irony could be stated as a paradox: the universe is *closed* into repetitions of *openness,* a cosmic existential play within which there are endlessly repeated opportunities for new cosmic identity. People have created emblems for the unity of openness and closure, the ongoing, interlocked pulsations of birth and death in many ways: the yin and yang of Oriental cultures; the unity of various opposed eachnesses in the Brahmanic all; Mazda and Ahuramazda; the three-in-one of Christianity; the variations on two, in fours and sixes symbolizing the directions and powers of the gods in cultures from the Chinese to the Amerindian.

In a further step of humanistic application, one might say that the extremes of openness and closure are the limits of anarchy and totalitarianism, and that they create each other. In the tension between the extremes of the polar exertions, existence repeatedly is generated though combinations of holding in and revolutionary change. The process was not unfamiliar in the American literature of Hawthorne's moment.[5]

As I hope this book suggests, the American assumption of openness as an absolute of American identity creates an ongoing dialectic of affirmation and repudiation of the proposition that as God's country America is the good polis and that dissent from its ideological assertions is wicked. That was the problem Hawthorne, like Edgar Allan Poe, confronted in his marketplace. He felt that nationalistic assumptions of absolute openness were destructive evasions of nature, of metaphysical and cosmic truth. He insisted upon the Classicist utopia from which he saw into the human psyche, and yet, as a man who wished to be a citizen among citizens, he was also uneasy about its political dimensions as literary material.

In his sense of personality as an idiom of universal laws, Hawthorne was not alien to the inferences to be drawn from science in the 1980s that openness and closure are as fundamental to the human psyche as to cosmology. For Hawthorne, the unidimensional ego, the closure of personality, whether that of the prideful monomaniac like Chillingworth or Rappaccini or that of the idealist absolutist like Aylmer, leads inexorably to death. Hawthorne sensed the rhythms of the universe as an ethical norm, and he wrestled with his uneasiness about the unidimensionalism of his country's millennialistic identification of America and the American. No matter how outmoded the world picture of Hawthorne's mid-nineteenth century might seem to us now, the current facts and theories of late twentieth-century science provide through openness and closure a human context no less applicable to the politics of Hawthorne's American fiction than to the national questionings of Saul Bellow, Norman Mailer, or Joan Didion, writers with whom I conclude this book in a brief illustration of the proposition.[6]

Somewhere at the center of world pictures and of metaphors for the human there remains a tension between self-enlargement and responsibility, a tension between a free, new, unlimited self and a self bound by the anti-absolutist rhythms of existence. This tension between the all-encompassing principles of openness and closure is what Steven E. Whicher called the "freedom and fate" at the heart of Ralph Waldo Emerson and American literature.[7] It is certainly at the heart of *The Marble Faun,* whose author countered Romantic assertions of openness with a metaphor of a fall from the Tarpeian Rock for Classicist closure: the aftermath of the Fall in all human affairs.

In the terminology I use in this book, openness and closure become organic analogues for Romanticism and Classicism.[8] Romanticism celebrates primitivism and the primacy of the naked, natural self. The savage state is extolled as the physical record of what Emerson asserted as a benevolent tendency streaming through the universe and is manifested in Henry David Thoreau's urge to eat a woodchuck raw. The intense emotional response to that tendency, like the perception of it, is Emerson's gladness "to the brink of fear," the oceanic Romantic sense of transcendent oneness with the universe. The literary analogue of that transcendence is Romanticism's penchant for abstract speculation and soaring universalization. Therein is a curious Romantic community with Sigmund Freud's late musings on the mind's own pleasure principle (quite distinct from, even opposed to, Freud's better known pleasure principle of the body), which drifts away from any contingency in space, time, and matter. Hawthorne could accommodate the absoluteness of aesthetic or intellectual transcendence, as his creation of "The Artist of the Beautiful" attests. But he was uneasy even with the Yankee haven of transcendent intellection: Owen Warland was just about Hawthorne's only triumphant absolute idealist, his one tribute to openness. But Hawthorne was also uneasy with what to him was Peter Hovenden's trap of closure, a total identification with space, time, and matter, the Yankee enterprise of getting and holding. Also, when earthliness was manifested in the activity of the body's pleasure principle, it proved too much for Hawthorne: he has to have Hester put her hair back up and don her cap and leave the woods. He was as anti-Romantic about sex as about metaphysics. For all that he recognized what went on in the depths of the psyche despite his society's Victorianism, Hawthorne was not one to reconcile openness and closure within the contexts of the primitive.[9]

It has always been Romanticism's problem to try to reconcile the polarities, seeking to justify the trap of nature (closure) as a symbol of spirit (openness) and to validate spirit in the processes of nature. As a perception of spiritual life within all physical existence, Romanticism is an assertion of consciousness as the creative source that all physical existence symbolizes. Thus Thoreau goes to the woods to find the purified self *through* the brute self.

Classicism steers a more modest course, recoiling from the primitive and tending to see organized society at large as the necessarily mediated activities of otherwise unmediated individual selves. It distrusts the open intensity of Romantic response. The Classicist seeks neither the unzipped psyche nor the unmediated state of nature, but a pragmatic society that at once caters to and controls reptilian, selfish aggrandizement. The Classicist temperament distrusts high abstraction and soaring speculation, although tending to emphasize neocortical rationality. It wishes to contain the individual aggressiveness of the self, accepting the very principle of conflicting aggrandizements as the underlying given requiring society's mediating function. As the Dionysian Romantic asserts intensity, the Apollonian Classicist asserts moderation. As the Romantic asserts individual vent, the Classicist asserts centralizing control and restraint. As the Romantic asserts openness, the Classicist asserts closure.

I do not use the terms Romanticism and Classicism necessarily as associations with the historical periods we call Classic, Neoclassic, or Romantic, for there were Romantic elements in Classical Greece and Rome and in Augustan England and America, just as there were Classicist elements in Romantic England and America. Rather, I use the terms as T. E. Hulme outlined them in defining their essential characteristics as contending directions of human perspective and historical force in any era.

The divergence of the two forces regarding primitivism is based upon their diverging concepts of the self. The Classicist sees the human self as fixed and limited, a being whose essential nature at best is mixed and at worst is totally depraved. To release the naked, natural, inner being—the essential, unartificial human—is to release selfishness and savagery. Classicism emphasizes closure: restraint, decorum, precedent, hierarchy, obligation, and tradition. The Romantic sees the self as inexhaustible in potential and possibility because, ultimately, the human identity is essentially divine. To release the naked, natural, inner being—the essential, unartificial human—is to release goodness and love. Romanticism emphasizes openness: spontaneity, liberty, egalitarianism, self-expression, feeling, newness, experiment, and change.

Consequently, Romanticism tends, like Jean-Jacques Rousseau, to see the past as a restrictive example of the misuse of human energies and the repression of aspiration. The Romantic, therefore, repudiates the past and embraces the future as a destruction of old limitations and as a realization of the cosmic stature that is the limitless potential of human energy. But Classicism embraces the past as an instructive precedent to be followed. Because of the fallen nature of humankind, the future will be a continuation of past experience, a cyclic repetition of past events. For the Romantic the present is a vast wave of upheaval moving toward the liberated realization of the human soul, a millennial consciousness in a future that lies on the other side of the ultimate, triumphant revolution in perception. Nature itself becomes an interconnected series of symbolic evolutionary expressions of the process, constantly swelling toward higher and higher consciousness, and, presumably, total consciousness in the future. Institutions, especially religious institutions, and the imposition of dogma and ritual become impertinences, impediments, and blasphemies. But for the Classicist the present is a moment in which the future is to be controlled by adjustment to the past. Nature becomes an interconnected series of examples illustrating discipline and order. Institutions, as the collective, ordered, and established wisdom of the human race, are the practiced means for necessary regulation and, therefore, for the expression of good human behavior.

It follows that Romanticism is given to lyrical outburst, to expression and realization of the self. As Emerson put it, "Expression is all we want; not knowledge but vent." Romantic expression emphasizes feeling and a sense of the cosmic. Its American manners and rhetoric, as magnificently proffered by Walt Whitman, tend to be grand effusions of emotion, especially of exaltation, love, and the millennial change arriving through the world's invincible development toward a constantly enlarging future of increasing consciousness. Classicism is given to dependable order and to expression that emphasizes rules and traditions in its recognition of a very fallen history. Its manners and rhetoric tend to be social rather than cosmic, a sharpening and polishing of established conventions, an emphasis on wit rather than emotion.

Perhaps the major difference between American and British nineteenth-century Romanticism within which Hawthorne broke into the literary market is that Americans were more concerned with paradise regained than with paradise lost. Perhaps the major difference between the American and British neoclassicism that immediately preceded Hawthorne is that the Americans were much more certain about a properly ordered society in the glowing future. Both American and English Classicists agreed that the limitations of human nature demand rules, restraints, and social conventions. (John Adams replied to what he saw as Thomas Jefferson's "preference to savage over civilized life," "I would rather be the poorest man in France or England, with sound health of Body and Mind, than the proudest King, Sachem, or Warriour of any Tribe of Savages in America.") But the paradox of the American vision was that the national assumption and rhetoric, asserting the Classicist vision of the rationally checked and balanced civilization, subsumed within themselves, in all their avowals of closure, the Romantic openness implicit in the certitude of a new history and new humankind in the triumph of the good revolution.

When we translate the universal polar tugs of openness and closure into Romanticism and Classicism and then translate those basic perceptions into political allegiances, Romanticism most organically converts into revolutionary radicalism (and often, but by no means always, historically does so), with a strong flavor of back-to-nature primitivism; and Classicism most organically converts into counterrevolutionary conservatism (and often, but by no means always, historically does so), with a strong flavor of institutional priorities to which the patriotic citizen will conform. The Romantic is self-identified as progressive and sees the Classicist as reactionary. The Classicist is self-identified as realistic and sees the Romantic as visionary. Hawthorne seized on the realistic and the visionary in his national culture for the materials of many of his fictions, exemplified by such works as *The Blithedale Romance,* "Earth's Holocaust," "The Birthmark," "Peter Goldthwaite's Treasure," the sketch of the Custom House prefatory to *The Scarlet Letter,* and, most explicitly, Holgrave's political conversion in *The House of the Seven Gables.* Coming down on all sides of the identification of "the dreamer," Hawthorne recognized the complexity of (and therefore waffled within) the conflict between closure implicit in the national approbation of a materialistic status quo and openness implicit in the rhetoric of that approbation. That is, in his own terms he was caught in a conflict not so much of ideologies, as of the distinction between utopias and their ideological expressions.

Specifically, within Romanticism (which is a notoriously slippery term no matter how defined) the principles of atavism, individualism, and organicism can be susceptible to a conservative political stance. The emphasis upon the unbridled natural self as a vehicle of universal spirit militates against an emphasis upon rationality and organization, and it repudiates restrictions upon the openness of individual choice. Translated, especially in the nineteenth and twentieth centuries, into economic laissez-faire and transmuted through social Darwinism, an essentially Romantic utopia blends into a states' rights, free marketplace, rugged individualistic reaction against radical ideologies. Emerson's Romantic conservatism, as demonstrated by his resistance to collective social movements, is a variety of American example. Conversely, within neo-Classicism, the principles of rationality, social mediation, and "the laws of Nature and of Nature's God" can be susceptible to a radical political stance. Jefferson's Declaration of Independence and the Bill of Rights are obvious American examples. The emphasis upon the rationally socialized individual as the vehicle of universal law scientifically derived militates against an emphasis upon selfish behavior and repudiates social, political, and economic inequality. Translated, especially in the nineteenth and twentieth centuries, into collective welfare and transmuted through Marxism, an essentially Classicist utopia becomes the democratic socialist reaction against conservative ideologies.

I am aware of the conflicts and contradictions within my schema and offer some modifications. One cannot discuss utopia and ideology in the American context without recognizing the complex changes and countercurrents of relationship between them, or without recognizing that any scheme of definition requires—and has produced—entire books, and very different books, devoted to specification of meaning and of historical facts.[10] Nevertheless, it remains sensible and fruitful to refer to the Romantic utopia as a sense of openness, a vision of a limitless self increasingly expressing spiritual or cosmic truth in the true and good society available on the future side of human history; and to refer to the Classicist utopia as a sense of closure, a vision of a fallen or fixed self expressing a limited condition in the repetitions of history, which demand an imposition of closure and a sense of the past. It also remains sensible and fruitful to associate (*not* to equate) the Romantic utopia with radicalism and the Classicist utopia with conservatism. And it remains sensible and fruitful to see that the essential paradox confronting Hawthorne was that the nationalistic *ideology* of his marketplace insisted that the Romantic *utopia* is realized now in America or is just about to be realized. The coercive, Romantic ideological insistence was paradoxically a conservative force of closure against open possibilities for the dissenting expression of a Classicist utopia.

The matter of terminology is a necessary complexity of the politics of rhetoric. Affairs of nomenclature are characteristics of what Mannheim means by *ideology,* surface or *tactical expression* of underlying philosophical or utopian perspectives. The conscious definitions of the human creature, of history, and of a world picture, as the philosophical bases of the Romantic or Classicist positions, are the utopias from which radical and conservative ideologies arise. Too often, as the stupidity of political campaigns illustrates, the relationship of the ideological superstructure (allegiances, movements, personalities, slogans) to the utopian foundation is not one of philosophical, utopian consciousness and becomes lost in the advantages of power that each side seeks. This was fully as true for the Whig or Loco-foco, for Young America, for the abolitionist or slavery-compromiser of Hawthorne's moment as for the bitterest conflicts of our own. The one ideological agreement that all sides shared, however, was that in the conflict of the two Americas, the ideal of openness (America *is* the open promised land in which all new identity and liberty are possible), if not already immanent within the actual, was imminent just ahead. In Hawthorne's marketplace, to deny that ideal was to deny the postulates upon which America was defined; and, as I hope to show in my examination of the narrative strategies in *The Marble Faun,* that was more than Hawthorne's courage would bear.

Ideologically, in the continua of openness → Romanticism → radicalism and of closure → Classicism → conservatism, the radical seeks to change the status quo and the conservative wishes to preserve it. Presumably, a utopia of openness would result in radical ideology and a utopia of closure would result in a conservative ideology. But clearly, in this context matters do not rest so easily, for the philosophical implications of rhetoric and nomenclature make politics a more complex matter than ideology versus ideology or utopia versus utopia. (In the rhetoric and nomenclature attendant upon the restructuring of Eastern Europe, the old apostles of the utopian radical revolution are the ideological status quo conservatives.) Politics is also a matter of the relationship between any given utopia and the ideology concomitant with it. Even more important than the distinctions between rival ideologies is the conflict that may arise between utopian foundation and ideological superstructure within a given complex of supposed allegiances. Triumphant utopias become triumphant ideologies, which then resist the very process by which the replacing utopia achieved its successes: conservative or radical, the openness principle of the triumphant revolution immediately, by virtue of its triumph, becomes the closure principle of the new status quo. At once the actor who was the radical champion of the revolution in the making becomes the conservative champion of the revolution successfully made. Ideologies may—and do—become betrayals of their utopias. By virtue of the extent to which ideological conservatism is allegiance to what is established, history offers the paradox of conservative allegiance to superstructures established on radical foundations, and neither Hawthorne's America nor ours escapes the dialectical relationship of the universal principles of openness and closure. The defender of the revolution becomes the social conservative in relation to the dissenter in the state where the revolution has triumphed into a new status quo.

Because its utopian foundation is a balancing of eighteenth-century bourgeois conservatism and eighteenth-century Deistic radicalism, America is not so clear an ideological superstructure as are totalitarian states of right or left. And obviously it is in the marginal superstructures of parties of the totalitarian right or left that ideology becomes most apparent in the United States. Nevertheless, within the mainstream of American culture, Romanticism and Classicism, radicalism and conservatism, define discernible and universal psychological poles as well as discernible and national ideologies.

One offers one of those clichés that reveal experiential truth when one suggests that Romanticism and radicalism *tend* to belong to the young, for whom the largest reality is the present and future rather than the past. In personal experience, the past, for the young, is dependent childhood, necessarily characterized by closure: limitation, restriction, and adult rule. The future is liberation into selfhood through an insurrectionist (however peaceful it might be) process of openness: taking adult power from those who had imposed the established conventions of yes and no. Conversely, Classicism and conservatism *tend* to belong to older people, for whom the largest part of reality is the present and the past. In personal experience of night and day, week and season, birth and death, and the consequent intimations of universal openness and closure, the past, for the old, is prologue to the essentially repetitious nature of human history. The future is limited, holding an imminent inevitability perceived through long experience with mortality. The fact of youth does not necessitate radicalism (although it usually betokens Romantic attitudes) and the fact of age does not necessitate conservatism (although it usually betokens Classicist sensibilities). But the perspective of youth (not all youths) is openness as that of age (not all elders) is closure. The major tendencies are so deep in collective human experience that they have remained stereotypes for as far back as literature records human attitudes. Not without exceptions, they indicate one of America's major utopian contexts: young, new America's foundation was essentially Romantic, millennial, and radical.[11] It was a context in which Nathaniel Hawthorne did not believe.

By the time of the Era of Good Feelings into which Hawthorne was born, the ideological rhetoric of American Romantic openness closed into chauvinistic self-affirmation and allegiance: if this is the Good Society created by the Good Revolution that finally has succeeded in throwing off the Bad Old World, do not dissent from it. Coercive patriotic rhetoric and values do little for the American writer who rises to consciousness, as Hawthorne did, in a culture that insists nationalistically on newness, youth, equality, and progress as the millennialist essence of the achieved and redeeming state. Such insistence does little for the writer engaged in an actual literary marketplace whose new, insecure, and consequently boastfully self-gratulatory society demands conformity to newly triumphant ideologies: express the Romantic utopia and write about America as God's New Country or be un-American. Since the early culture of the Republic there has been inherent in the very materials of American literature a conflict between the two Americas. It is a central problem of cultural criticism in the study of American literature to identify narrative effects in the intricate crossovers of the language of ideologies from their own to opposing utopias. *The Marble Faun* is a paradigm of the issues at stake for a writer who sees the nationalistic implications of the relationship between his Classicist theme of closure and his narrative statements of affirmative patriotism.

At once a representative Classicist conservative as a man and a vocational radical dissenter as a writer, Hawthorne, juggling the man and the writer, was to enter a calling and a literary marketplace whose conflicting demands were to result in thematic anomalies that make him, even now, one of the most culturally significant of America's writers. His world picture was one in which Newtonian mechanics "finally" explained the nature of matter. Except in terms of essentially Christian idealism, he could not have foreseen a world picture in which matter dissolves into unheard of complexities of energy and space. His scientists, like Rappaccini and Aylmer, who sought to control the "spiritualization" of matter, were mistaken and destructive, but he understood the philosophical centrality of the ontological implications of matter. In his sense of the presentness of the past within a new and expanding nation, he understood the relationship of openness and closure that Newtonian physics and American history revealed as inescapable conditions of existence. As a political Democrat and a private conservative, he understood the force of being part of and in conflict with one's popular culture. Within his own contexts, he understood the political relationship among literary expression, literary marketplace, and an age's world picture. His literary needs, in short, remain as culturally significant for our world picture, which he could not begin to glimpse, as for his own. He would not have heard of cosmic singularities or Mannheim, but he would have known what to make of them in writing a *utopian* conservative message that his *ideologically* conservative popular culture was disinclined to understand or accept in the America of his day.

NOTES

1. One has to be carefully explicit in using the term millennial. Theodore Bozeman has compellingly argued in *To Live Ancient Lives: The Primitivist Dimensions in Puritanism* (Chapel Hill: University of North Carolina Press, 1988) that the assumptions scholars have made about the American emphasis on futurity, especially since F. O. Matthiessen, do not necessarily accord with the facts of Puritan aims and assumptions. Many historians and students of American literature agree with his argument that the Puritans did not think of themselves as establishing a *new* society, but of returning to the classic simplicity of early biblical generations. Nevertheless, the sense of American society's relation to history remains essentially millennial. That is, whether one conceives of society as a return to a lost past or as an experimental breakthrough in the future, the dynamic remains the same: here, in this New World, the good polis *will* be established. The rest of human society has either lost or not yet found the "Good Place." America will be a beacon, a city on a hill, in which either for the first time in human history the lost goodness will be reestablished or the new goodness established. Insofar as the idea of millennium is the establishment of the perfect domain (the thousand-year type of the City of God on earth for the religious, or whatever the utopian vision is for the secular), in my use of the idea of the millennial, the specification of the good polis in the making does not change the identification of it with the New World.

2. Commentators in Hawthorne's own day questioned his commitments, and ever since D. H. Lawrence, in his *Studies in Classic American Literature* (1923), questioned Hawthorne's sincerity, modern commentators have found that the questions remain a rich source of critical inquiry.

3. Mannheim did not use the term utopia in the common sense of a perfect and usually unworldly never-never land. But he did use it to refer to moral roots, to a fundamental philosophical assessment that is an ethical guiding vision for a good polis, whether religious or secular. In that sense of the word, my terminological use of Mannheim should not prove confusing or inappropriate, even in a cultural context that evokes more commonly understood utopianism deriving from such phenomena as Brook Farm, Fruitlands, Oneida, New Harmony, or Charles Fourier's phalansteries.

4. The reader who might be interested in the basis of my assertions (and who might not have seen the invitation in the preface) is invited to read the appendix after finishing this chapter.

5. Using Pierre-Simon Laplace's nebular hypothesis, in *Eureka* Edgar Allan Poe expressed his own dissent from American assertions of the good world achieved. He repudiated all mundane actuality in a vision of a supernal, timeless, spaceless, matterless state of rest, an absolute closure in perfect Unity and, therefore, in perfect Beauty. With one vast burst, this state exploded itself outward in equable irradiation in all dimensions, thereby creating time, space, and matter. Poe envisioned the irradiation in a constant state of deceleration until, at one instant of zero velocity, openness freezes in another instant of stasis, at which moment all matter begins to fall back toward its original source.

The return is one of steadily increasing acceleration toward the common center, the Eternal Return being a mirror-reversal of the Fall. The quality of space, time, and matter, by definition of what it is (the opposite of the still, supernal state), is the opposite of perfect Unity and Beauty. Consequently, all matter, and especially the human, contains a kind of sentience that is a yearning for return to the supernal state of Perfect Oneness. The distance from Perfection is what infuses an element of the horrible and the perverse throughout physical existence. But as all matter rushes back in upon itself, it squeezes out space, it leaves time, and in an act of supreme closure, matter cancels itself out through its own density, ceasing to exist. The ecstatic exultation with which Poe imagines the total act of closure (gravitational Attraction back to the supernal point) into what twentieth-century cosmologists would call a singularity is evident in the very punctuation and capitalization of the rhetoric with which he presents his utopian vision:

> Now the very definition of Attraction implies particularity—the existence of parts, particles, or atoms. ... Of course where there are *no* parts—where there is no absolute Unity—where the tendency to oneness is satisfied—there can be no Attraction. ... When, on fulfillment of its purpose, then, Matter shall have returned into its original condition of One—a condition which presupposes the expulsion of the separative ether, whose province and whose capacity are limited to keeping the atoms apart until that great day when, this ether being no longer needed, the overwhelming pressure of the finally collective Attraction shall at length just sufficiently predominate and expel it—when, I say, Matter, finally expelling the Ether, shall have returned into absolute Unity,—it will then (to speak paradoxically for the moment) be Matter without Attraction and without Repulsion—in other words, Matter without Matter—in other words, again, *Matter no more.* In sinking into Unity, it will sink at once into that Nothingness which, to all Finite Perception, Unity must be—into that Material Nihility from which alone we can conceive it to have been evoked—to have been *created* by the Volition of God.

Yet Poe does not leave it at that. Somehow he senses that an eternal return is connected with an eternal Big Bang and concludes that existence is a continuing pulsation of outward bursting materialization and inward condensing stasis. He does not explain why a Perfect Unity that is All unto Itself should manifest Itself in the eachness of what is imperfect. But then, no theology ever has successfully explained the *why* of creation, and it is pointless to fault Poe. *Eureka* furnishes a way to see the concepts of openness and closure derived from a world picture working both ways in the interrelationship of science and literature. On the one hand, through scientific hypothesis, *Eureka* works toward an explanation of human affairs, an exploration that leads Poe to the conclusions he draws about human life and poetry in "The Poetic Principle," which is the appropriate companion to *Eureka.* On the other hand, the values implied by the excited rhetoric and punctuation of *Eureka* encourage us to surmise that Poe yearned toward an ultimate state of closure. This provides the act of literary criticism with a way toward a definition of Poe: although the materials of his imagination were those of Romanticism, especially gothic Romanticism, Poe was essentially a Classicist in temperament. That is, the tone and punctuation of the rhetoric in *Eureka* are signs of a conservative utopia as an engine of Poe's imagination. The punctuation has politics. And the politics have a relationship to Poe's literary connections, in which he stood out against the rhetoric of openness in the ideological pronouncements of his nationalistic marketplace.

6. As one reader has suggested, writers like Thomas Pyncheon and William Gaddis, who are allegorists and moralists at heart, are modernist versions of Hawthorne, and in that sense are closer to him than Saul Bellow and Norman Mailer. As another reader has suggested, there is a great disparity and unevenness of quality among the writers, from Henry James to Joan Didion, whom I choose for my brief discussion of endings in chapter five. But it is precisely because of unlikeness and unlikeliness as well as likeness and likeliness that I chose the writers, in order to indicate that Hawthorne is indeed an example of the greatest magnitude and centrality in a discussion of the cultural significance of American literary endings.

7. *Freedom and Fate: An Inner Life of Ralph Waldo Emerson* (Philadelphia: University of Pennsylvania Press, 1953).

8. Here I must restate my debt to T. E. Hulme, that crusty old conservative with whom I probably would have disagreed sharply on almost any political issue had we been alive at the same time. His classic essay, "Romanticism and Classicism," has been useful in some of my previous publications and in my thinking generally, as it has to almost three generations of commentators since its publication in *Speculations,* ed. Sir Herbert Read (London, 1924).

9. Two very useful approaches to this topic from very different points of departure are by Frederic Crews, *The Sins of the Fathers: Hawthorne's Psychological Themes* (New York: Oxford University Press, 1966), and Ellen Moers, *Literary Women* (Garden City, N.Y.: Doubleday, 1976).

10. For instance, the scope of what would be a considerable bibliography is indicated by the differences in points of departure, purpose, terminology, materials, and area of discipline between Carl Woodring's *Politics in English Romantic Poetry* (Cambridge, Mass.: Harvard University Press, 1970) and William Appleman Williams's *The Contours of American History* (Cleveland: World Publishing Co., 1961).

11. The reader will be aware of the specifics arguing for conservative or at least Classicist foundations of the Republic. Any number of historical actualities, from the significance and rhetoric of the Annapolis convention to the correspondence between John Adams and Thomas Jefferson, will offer ammunition against my assertion that the foundation of America is essentially Romantic and millennial. If I were writing a history of the facts, as they are definable, I would say things *very* differently. But as I suggest in note 1, my concern is with the *dynamic* of American expectations. Whether the utopia is or was Classicist

or Romantic, whether the ideology is or was conservative or radical, the consensus of expectation was and, partly, still is, that the good polis (however defined) has been, or is, or will be established HERE as the example to all the rest of the human race, and therein is the essentially millennial character of national assumptions. It is on that foundation of openness, or Romantic assertion, that the closure of conservative nationalism is founded, and *that* paradox generated the political relationship between Hawthorne and his literary marketplace.

2

An American Context

In America, a political impulse that has been one of the major sources of fictive characterization and event is the writer's response to the peculiarly Romantic and millennialistic tone of the materialist culture. Expressed in the idiosyncratic terms of the talents of individual writers, perennially manifest concepts of innocence, newness, and redemption in depictions of American experience become the generative center of dramas of affirmation or denial. America is "the Dream"; America is the betrayal of "the Dream"; America should be but is not; America cannot be, will be, will not be; America is the Good New World; America never existed. One way or another, the idea of life unfolding in a golden promise of unlimited openness is a recurrent subject in the American political and literary imaginations. The subject enjoys ongoing vitality because, finally, a free literature expresses types rather than stereotypes: there is no such thing as a single, monolithic entity, America, just as one cannot identify a national population by *a* category for *the* Americans. One of the triumphant virtues of the American Revolution has been a continuing leeway, despite moments of narrowness and threat, for revisionism and dissent.

But ideological injunctions of one kind or another exist in any society, and what is unmistakable and inescapable in totalitarian societies is only a raw expression of what is more subtle and hidden in other, freer cultures, including the American. America has had its own share of coercive certitudes. The assumptions of chiliastic sects would have been a version of antinomian heresy to the American Puritans; nonetheless, the Puritans carried centrally within their theology a typological sense of their "plantation religious" as the city on a hill that would be, supposedly soon, the type of the millennium. In the eighteenth century some of the New Light legatees of the Puritans were literally chiliastic. For that matter, even the rationalistic secularism of the Revolutionary and early Federal period looked toward possibilities for the polis and for the individual human creature as a perfected "republican machine" that would transcend, supposedly soon, anything ever known in all human history. Divine structure, the liberation of the mind, and the liberation of the underclass would combine in the social and political structures of the Good New World. The non-Christian religiosity of the American Transcendentalists envisioned the complete redemption of humanity's fallen state of being and the common person's resumption of a cosmic, divine self. The millennialistic typalism of the image of America generates a response that pits experience against idea, and in that tension reside the political and literary materials of conservative and radical impulses, Classicist and Romantic assumptions. Through all the permutations of form and all the cross-migrations of rhetoric, two great constellations of national identity—the millennialist Dream and historical experience—remain expressible as a tension between the two Americas. The central paradox of American ideology is that in the interrelationships of openness and closure, the nationalistic insistence on America as God's Country realized, intolerant of contradiction, is the hardening of radical expectation into conservative conformity.

July 4, 1826, the fiftieth birthday of the nation and the deathday of Thomas Jefferson and John Adams, is often marked as a significant and symbolic division between the early Republic's statesmanship during the Revolution and the Federal period (the type of the idea of America) and the modern brawling politics of privilege and party hacks (the type of the American actuality). Somewhere at the center of this division, apparent in the difference between the Jefferson-Adams correspondence, on the one hand, and Andrew Jackson's populistic spoils system, on the other, was the change from the idea of government as the enactment and representation of concepts of the state to the idea of government as the enactment and representation of constituencies. The change from utopian consciousness—the philosophical perceptions of the state—to ideological consciousness—the pragmatic perception of power—is the change from the idea of the philosopher-statesman to the idea of the pragmatic politician. Regardless of historical facts, the division exists as legend in the national mind: the difference between the Founding Fathers as statesmen and subsequent political figures as politicians. The change is one way of identifying the increasingly materialistic quality of American nationalism, in which the religious and philosophical dimensions of the type of the millennium were translated into wealth,

territory, and power. Nathaniel Hawthorne saw all around him a culture that identified material success with good citizenship. As Hawthorne
suggested in "The Gray Champion," the mythic figures of the old days
no longer characterize the quotidian experience, but return only at
those moments when the nation is in danger of losing its identity. In the
America of present-day actualities for Hawthorne, the representative
good citizens, like Peter Hovenden and Robert Danforth, are concerned
solely with material actuality. For them the good citizen inhabited the
good country. The good country provided economic, material, and
social *openness.* To speak against the values of the good citizen was to
speak against the good of the nation. To speak against the values of the
nation was to speak against the good of the good citizen. The post–Civil
War march westward in the 1870s and 1880s and the realization of
enormous expansionism, urbanization, and industrialization by 1910,
when the last continental frontier is officially pronounced closed, mark
the essence of the nineteenth-century history of the United States. But
even in Hawthorne's agrarian America, early marked by the Era of Good
Feelings, in which Hawthorne's boyhood consciousness developed, the
opening and expansion of American power were manifest in the Louisi-
ana Purchase and the Mexican War. From the Era of Good Feelings to
the muckrakers, one salient context for national literature is the openness and expansion of wealth and property. It was proclaimed gleefully
in the popular literary marketplace in works such as Russell Conwell's
Acres of Diamonds and repudiatingly in the marketplace of the serious
literati in what Robinson Jeffers was to characterize as a thickening to
empire in "Shine, Perishing Republic." And in his own time (he died,
after all, before the Civil War was over), Hawthorne was surrounded by
strong examples of literary dissent from American materialist values.

It really is quite astonishing that with the exception of Washington
Irving, every one of America's great, classic writers over the entire
course of the nineteenth century, disparate as they are not only in voice
but also in historical moments, concurs in a repudiation of what clearly
is the overwhelming and triumphant energy of their times. It is even
more astonishing that a society should honor as its greatest literary
representatives the voices that repudiate the national actuality as a
perversion of the national idea. There is James Fenimore Cooper's
continuing argument, in his novels as well as his lawsuits, with his
society's unphilosophical materialism and misuses of both property and
the idea of democracy; there is Edgar Allan Poe's antinationalistic
repudiation of the idea of American literary primacy; Ralph Waldo
Emerson said enough about accepted, conventional religiosity to drive
Andrews Norton wild and enough about economic and political values

to earn the hostile ridicule of the conventional burghers of State Street's investment-banking Boston; Henry David Thoreau's repudiation of Concord's values and of finance's acquiescence to slavery is in almost every word he wrote; Hawthorne centrally dismissed the very concept of the Good New World as history redeemed and changed; Herman Melville traced his increasingly dark denial of transcendent America or of an absolutely good human state in every one of his novels; Harriet Beecher Stowe made profoundly significant use of Christian principle as a moral test against which to measure her condemnation of the American social consequences of the open economics that demanded the buying and selling of human beings. The contrast between Walt Whitman's sense of America in the 1855 Preface to *Leaves of Grass* and his post–Civil War "Democratic Vistas" has occupied the attention of many commentators as a study in disillusion; Mark Twain, who as much as anyone was caught up in the rush to riches, nevertheless left more than an epigram or two about a "damned human race" whose behavior he saw paradigmatically in the very America in which he so actively participated; there is Henry James's appalled response to the New York to which he returned and then left forever; in the ideological context of self-aggrandizement expressed in a world of high manners, Edith Wharton chronicled the breakdown of utopian openness within the soulless closure of the society James abandoned; and by 1900 Theodore Dreiser already had found his major mode of expression in the materials of an American capitalist system whose feverishly enticing openness of alluring promise was belied by the dehumanizing closure of its actualities.

The total effect of the different literary voices is one of angry admonition. By and large, the response to the American actuality by the American writer has been one that muses on the politics of American energy: the vitality of the actual America in the destruction of the ideal. The politics of the relationship between the American writer and the American context is identified by all the implications of the writer's disapprovingly holding up a mirror to the society. The individual writer's voice in its particular time and place is the enactment of literature's synesthetic function: the mirroring device is a voice that defines the writer's relationship to the listening audience—a literary politics of which Hawthorne was acutely aware.

The voices of admonition are as various as the individual writers. In the nineteenth-century context, Cooper is aristocratic, scornful, and sharply critical, placing legal and social arguments directly in minilectures from the narrator or in the conversations of his sympathetic characters, as in *Home as Found* (1838). One glimpses the development of disillusion in that voice in the difference between Cooper's sense of

America in an early work like *The Pioneers* (1823) and in a later one like *The Littlepage Manuscripts* (1844–46). Poe's is a desperately repudiating voice, depending almost entirely upon rhetorical intensity, as in the very punctuation of *Eureka* (1848) when he reaches his climactic ecstasy over annihilation of the quotidian disunities of space and matter, or in the imperative intensity of "The Poetic Principle," wherein he rejects the actual for the supernal.

Hawthorne's genius is centered in his ability to evoke the past—one *feels* the oldness of his materials—as the rich human alembic of everything in the present. Hawthorne's is a voice that strokingly murmurs over the dark furniture in passing, so that in works like *The Marble Faun* (1860) or The Custom House introduction to *The Scarlet Letter* (1850) or *The House of the Seven Gables* (1851) the tone becomes one of musing. The tonal intention becomes neither Cooper's acerbic rebuke nor Poe's shrill repudiation, but rather sad observation in response to America's assumptions about itself.

Emerson's distinctly gnostic and gnomic voice is Yankee Vatic, an elliptical utterance of olympian rapture about consciousness. It offers nothing but calm disdain for values that give primacy to what Emerson called "commodity," a disdain perhaps most succinctly summed up in his poem "Days" and developed in the negative implications of "The American Scholar." Stowe's impassioned tones are effectually those of a Jeremiah at a meeting of intellectually serious revivalists. There is hardly a *voice* more explicit than the auctorial intonations in the "Concluding Remarks" of the last chapter of *Uncle Tom's Cabin* (1852):

> This is an age of the world when nations are trembling and convulsed. A mighty influence is abroad, surging and heaving the world, as with an earthquake. And is America safe? Every nation that carries in its bosom great and unredressed injustice has in it the elements of this last convulsion. . . . Christians! every time that you pray that the Kingdom of Christ may come, can you forget that prophecy associates, in dread fellowship, the day of vengeance with the year of His redeemed?

Thoreau's sharp, clear precision—his famous description of the battle of the ants, for instance—like Whitman's enraptured, expansive chant, indicated the ways in which the Transcendentalist voice called opening directions to literary realism and to social democracy by emphasizing the representative details of common life in which the ideal is realized. But significantly, those details were natural, not societal, even for Whitman, in those instances in which the actual American social experience was seen not as a representation of divine democracy but as an enactment of false values. And in the cosmopolitan delicacies and strengths of her own voice, Wharton dissects higher levels of that very same social experience. The social fact engages in Thoreau as in Wharton a combination of Poe's repudiation and Emerson's disdain, most assertively put in "Civil Disobedience" (1848) but as evident in almost every page of *Walden* (1854) and in the problematical undertone of despair in *The Maine Woods* (1864) as in the episodes and careers in *The Custom of the Country* (1913) or *The House of Mirth* (1905). One thinks of Whitman surpassing Emerson and Thoreau in his omnivorously loving Transcendental embrace of social and historical as well as natural fact, but even his unmistakable voice shares in the possibilities of recoil from historical actuality not only in the differences between the 1855 preface and the 1876 "Democratic Vistas," but also in the increased departure from the mundane fact and terrestrial landscape in the later poetry.

Wellingborough Redburn's tearfully joyous rapture and rhetoric on returning to America (1839 very fictively recalled in 1849) dissolve in Melville's developed skepticism about American (and all) society in *The Confidence-Man* (1857). The "nervous, lofty language" of Melville's rolling periods in *Moby-Dick* (1851) and *Pierre* (1852) gives way to hard, characterizing, allegorical dialogue and event in *The Confidence-Man* (1857), as the author expands metaphysical terror and nausea within a satirically bitter denial of Romantic litanies of openness. Melville's fiction becomes increasingly darker until his confidence man leads foolish, helpless, trusting old humanity off into a blackness as total as the improbability that the human creature ever can maintain enough goodness or define enough truth to create the good polis of its visions out of the cannibalism of its actualities. And Twain's voice mirrors a society at which one can do nothing but laugh unless one gives way, as Twain often did, to misanthropic fury. As every commentator has pointed out, his great central book, *The Adventures of Huckleberry Finn* (1885), offers at once the laugh and the substratum of hopeless outrage, which becomes more pronounced the more we float through the society to which the mirror is held. The development of darkness is at once apparent in a comparison of the jubilant sense of rough-and-ready morning adventure in an early book like *Roughing It* (1872) with later ones like *The American Claimant* (1892) and *Pudd'nhead Wilson* (1894) on the American scene, and *The Mysterious Stranger* (1916) and *What Is Man?* (1906) in a universal context.

The voice of James becomes a more intricate problem because he consciously experimented with narrative technique. Nevertheless, it is to the point to recall that his novels mirror America and Europe more complexly as James's sense of "the international theme" develops, and the later James no longer awards all the future or all the palms of consciousness and conscience to the American. James set the direction of expatriation, so tentatively attempted earlier by Hawthorne, and by the time the nineteenth century had passed through the dark looking glass of heartland natives like Dreiser and Sherwood Anderson into the twentieth century's response to World War I, the voices of dissent had synesthetically become the major literary social mirror.

One central connection between nineteenth-century "high" literature in America and the society in which it arose is that the serious literature can be said to have amplified an increasingly dissenting voice within America in direct proportion to the extent to which America became a greater and greater bourgeois world power. When we consider that Hawthorne's fiction emerged at a historical moment when nationalistic optimism, not dissent, ruled the literary marketplace, we then have a summary overview of the extent to which the antitranscendent, nonmillennialistic dissent of Hawthorne's themes gives him a lonely and uncomfortably heroic place at the head of an historical literary development in which he would have continued to feel uncomfortable.

The literary mirrors of Hawthorne's day were successful when they approved of the American social scene as desirable and good. As the popularity of the sketch in Hawthorne's marketplace indicated, the reading audience *expected* the writer to enact cultural nationalism in the literary mirror. It is not just that Hawthorne early began to publish in George P. Morris's New York *Mirror,* nor even that such publication was urged by Hawthorne's very good friend, Horatio Bridge, as a deliberate tactic for welcome within the popular literary marketplace. More than that, the marketplace itself made abundantly clear the kind of mirror it would look into approvingly. Popularly celebrated and financially rewarded literary voices, male and female, were typified by writers like Nathaniel P. Willis, whose sketches of the national scene, saccharine, sentimental, precious, pretentious, and approving, won acceptance and acclaim.[1] The literary mirror is an essentially political instrument, and Willis's voice emerges as a titillatingly snobbish assertion of the rightness of the status quo. More than once it developed nuances of what was to spawn in the twentieth century as "love it or leave it" pieties. One could say that Willis *was* the voice of the popular literary marketplace. As admiring reflector, he became a guru to the aspiring middle-class society to which he held the mirror, the society that bought and read books and magazines. He held a flattering mirror and was one with what was in the selectively arranged reflection. Willis is recorded in literary history as a writer of fluff, and it is his relationship to the mirror that explains why.

As our great major writers stood at one remove and held complex relationships of both immersion and repudiation with American society, they fashioned their mirroring voices for the purpose of indicating why they saw distortion and fog in the surface of Edenic appearances demanded by popular nationalism. But Willis (his periodical, *The Mirror*, was deliberately named as a sign of approval of the reflection), like many of his popular contemporaries, accepted the nationalistic—and class—values attached to the social scene: all is good, all is well. He reflected rather than explored surfaces. He investigated nothing beneath the surfaces, and his voice thereby developed a simper. Willis's cultural importance does not lie in his literary results, for he was but a tiny literary participant in time and scope. It lies in what one might conclude about the deep political differences between fluff and serious literature: in what one might conclude about acceptance or unpopularity during Hawthorne's emerging career in a marketplace that insisted upon the unshadowed, salubrious sunshine of the American scene.

Nathaniel Willis's dates (1806–67) were almost identical with Nathaniel Hawthorne's (1804–64). Both men reached literary celebrity in the 1830s. In 1837 *Twice-Told Tales* first began to bring reclusive Hawthorne some of the recognition for which he longed; by 1835 *Pencillings by the Way* consolidated for the socialite Willis the adulation that his effusions had claimed from an adoring, female, reading public. What one might conclude about serious literature and what one might conclude about popular acceptance offered diametrically opposed political definitions of successful literary identity as well as the diametric opposition of basking within the sunshiny circle of those who belong or mooning with the outsiders in the chilly shades. Within the writer from Salem, two Nathaniels, one who envied Willis and one who scorned him, were locked in a political struggle of adjustment to each other. Hawthorne's American context was one in which he wrestled with a double self characterized by a hunger for the populous sunshine and a certainty of the lonely shadow. It was exactly that darkening from sunshine to shadow that characterized the perspectives of America's dissenting, serious nineteenth-century writers among whom Hawthorne developed as forerunner and contemporary. The literary shadowing that deepened after Hawthorne's death was an unfolding of the contradictory tugs that Hawthorne felt so crucially in his own career.

The darkening motion that characterizes nineteenth-century American literature has been noted most specifically in the motifs of light and dark in the works of Hawthorne, Melville, and Twain. But the whole corpus of serious literary work participates in the movement toward deepening shadow. That development of "the darkness of blackness," as

Ishmael calls it, is not merely a matter for exercises in literary patterns, but is a development of national literary voices and theme, toward which Hawthorne's temperament and Classicist view nudged him from the beginning. America's great nineteenth-century authors are bound in a remarkable unity of dissent from bourgeois, commercialistic, and nationalistic assumptions about America as the realization of redeemed history and the goodness of unrestricted Romantic openness. The dissent is traceable in image clusters of light and dark that reveal a common agreement in the otherwise various and often differing metaphysical orientations of America's major writers between 1830 and the Civil War. There are essential examples in those works that are the central masterpieces of the several writers. In the first full flush of Romantic expression, light in Emerson's "Nature" is all openness. Emerson delights in images of open distances or horizon, of clear, far *seeing,* and of light as a metaphor for the transcendent state of consciousness to be achieved in the new democracy.

> If a man would be alone, let him look at the stars. . . . The stars awaken . . . reverence. . . . There is a property in the horizon which no man has but he whose eye can integrate all the parts. . . . Most persons do not see the sun. . . . The sun illuminates only the eye of the man, but shines into the eye and heart of the child. . . . I become a transparent eyeball . . . what angels invented these splendid ornaments . . . this ocean of air above . . . this zodiac of lights, this tent of dropping clouds . . . the eye is the best of artists by the mutual action of its structure and the laws of light. . . . And as the eye is the best composer, so light is the first of painters. . . . The health of the eye seems to demand a horizon. We are never tired so long as we can see far enough. . . . I see the spectacle of morning from the hilltop . . . the long slender bars of cloud float like fishes in a sea of crimson light.

These hymnic sentences celebrating Romantic openness are but a few of such tropes at the beginning of "Nature"—at the beginning of the American century's literary expression of high Romanticism. Emerson concludes his seminal and summary essay with a certainty of openness in the triumph of the Coming of the Light: "To our blindness these things seem unaffecting . . . but when the fact is *seen* under the *light* of an idea . . . as when *summer* comes from the south . . . so shall the *advancing spirit* create its ornaments along its path. . . . *The kingdom of man over nature . . .* a dominion such as now is *beyond his dream of God*—he shall enter without more wonder than the blind man feels who is gradually restored to *perfect sight*" (italics mine).

Similarly, Thoreau's *Walden* also ends with total openness in the advent of spring, sun, growth, and light. The ending heralds a beginning of total seeing: "Only that day dawns to which we are awake. There is more day to dawn. The sun is but a morning star." And Whitman concludes "Song of Myself" with the grass beneath the bootsole brought to light, being totally seen as the universal, cosmic self whose voice is the romantic openness of the poem. Like "Nature" and *Walden,* the poem creates a motion upward and outward, from earth and flesh into space and light. At least in their insistence on openness there is no conflict between American nationalism and the Romantic assertion of limitlessness democratically available in a national dawn, a symbol of cosmic fulfillment, that bursts into light even beyond the twilight:

> I sound my barbaric yawp over the roofs of the world.
> The last scud of day holds back for me . . .
> I depart as air, I shake my white locks at the runaway sun,
> I effuse my flesh in eddies and drift it in lacy jags . . .
> If you want me again, look for me under your bootsoles . . .
> I stop somewhere waiting for you.

If the high Romantics and their imagery of light, dawn, limitlessness, and airy openness may be taken as America's major literary starting point, in the nineteenth century's early literature Hawthorne may be seen as coevally signalling the beginning of the change from the Coming of the Light to the Duration of the Night. Although as a Christian Hawthorne maintained a strong sense of spirituality, as an essentially Classicist observer he did not share the metaphysics behind the Transcendentalist's avowal of absolute openness. Especially did he not share a Whitmanian sense of the fulfillment of that possibility as likely and imminent in the morning of American democracy. For Hawthorne, American life is identified with a sense of light, but rather than the bright flush of a new dawn, it is the hard, bright, noonday light of the business day, illuminating practical activity that cheerfully creates wealth and empire. When, in his famous introduction to *The Scarlet Letter,* Hawthorne called for light, it was a very different kind of light, one that is implicitly a repudiation of the possibility or even desirability of unmitigated sunshine:

> I sat in the deserted parlor, lighted only by the glimmering coal-fire and the moon, striving to picture forth imaginary scenes, which the next day might flow out on the brightening page in many-hued description. If the imaginative faculty refused to act at such an hour, it might well be deemed a hopeless case. Moonlight, in a familiar room, falling so white upon the carpet and showing all its figures so distinctly, making every object so minutely visible—all these details, so completely seen, are so spiritualized by the unusual light that they seem to lose their actual

substance, and become things of intellect . . . whatever has been used or played with during the day is now invested with a quality of strangeness and remoteness, though still almost as vividly present as by daylight. Thus, therefore, the floor of our familiar room has become a neutral territory, somewhere between the real world and fairy-land, where the Actual and the Imaginary may meet. . . . The somewhat dim coal-fire has an essential influence in producing the effect which I would describe. It throws its unobtrusive tinge throughout the room, with a faint ruddiness upon the walls and ceiling, and a reflected gleam from the polish of the furniture. This warmer light mingles with the cold spirituality of the moonbeams, and communicates, as it were, a heart and sensibilities of human tenderness to the forms which fancy summons up. . . . Glancing at the looking-glass we behold—deep within the haunted verge—the smouldering glow of a half extinguished anthracite, white moonbeams upon the floor, and a repetition of all the gleam and shadow of the picture, with one remove from the actual, and nearer to the imaginative. Then, at such an hour, and with this scene before him, if a man, sitting all alone, cannot dream strange things and make them look like the truth, he need never try to write romances.

The familiar passage indicates that, like Emerson and Thoreau, Hawthorne too believed that when "all these details" of the commonplace are "so distinctly," "so completely seen," they become "spiritualized" by light "and become things of intellect." Also like them, he would turn to "the haunted verge" of the spiritualizing "looking glass" for the significance of the "Actual." But Hawthorne's is an "unusual light" that shows forth a significance neither that of Romantic nor nationalistic openness; his light is identified as much by darkness and shadow as by limitlessly illuminated vision. For the Romantics light was the endless vista of the Ideal; for the society it was the sunlight of successful enterprise. As for the looking glass itself, the Willis-mirror of the popular marketplace reflected the best world achievable materially; the Emerson-mirror reflected the best world achievable spiritually; the Hawthorne-mirror reflected darknesses that denied the unmixed possibility of either achievement in life. Hawthorne's recoil from Romantic openness is seen on the spiritual level in his humorous rejection of the Giant Transcendentalist in "The Celestial Railroad" and in the themes of all his serious writings; on the level of the actual his recoil from Romantic openness is seen in his change from expectation to revulsion in the short period between mid-April and early June at Brook Farm (1841). Hawthorne's Classicist sense of things distrusted idealist visions— pure "moonlight." As he indicates in his preface to *The Marble Faun*, he feels that he must make a good, American statement of allegiance to the "broad and simple daylight" of hard actualities. Yet, divided in his

allegiances and repelled by the unmitigated materialism of his nationalistic society, he much prefers, as a vision of reality, the antinationalistic
idea in the mirror—the haunted and haunting vision of darkness, the
specter of closure and the Fall:

> Italy, as the site of this Romance, was chiefly valuable to...me as
> affording a sort of poetic or fairy precinct, where actualities would not be
> so terribly insisted upon as they are, and must needs be, in America. No
> author, without a trial, can conceive of the difficulty of writing a romance
> about a country where there is no shadow, no antiquity, no mystery, no
> picturesque and gloomy wrong, nor anything but a commonplace prosperity,
> in broad and simple daylight, as is happily the case with my dear native
> land.

In fact, of course, the actualities in Hawthorne's dear native land in
1860 were both more interesting and more terrible than he suggests, but
here Hawthorne, as in his entire career, wavers between his real sense of
closure and his allegiance to "actualities" rendered at least partly sunshiny
by his consciousness of his readers' nationalistic assumptions. The
intricate relationships between the literary ideas of mirrors and of
darkness in nineteenth-century American literature help place the intricate relationships between writer and marketplace, writer and writer. In
the mysterious relationship between Hawthorne and Melville, for instance,
it remained for Melville to question the reality of idea behind the actual
in the spiritualizing mirror. Perhaps in plunging beyond what the more
genteel Hawthorne was willing to face, Melville caused the rupture in
the friendship. Ahab's doubloon mirrors back merely what comes to it,
a deconstruction of all idealisms, including the spiritualizations with
which Hawthorne concurred. "Merely" what comes to the mirror includes
God and the cosmos. Melville suspects that what there is of actualities
is the semiotics of what there is of God. If there is any humanly useful
or perceivable divine purpose in the universe, it is in the actualities
before the mirror. To understand the human universals in one's historical society, therefore, is to know the possibilities of metaphysics. As
Hawthorne's light was a bridge between the light of the Transcendentalists and Melville's kind of darkness, so, centering fervently on the idea
of Idea in the universe, Melville's imagination provided the bridge
between Hawthorne's kind of light and Twain's kind of darkness. The
Hawthorne-Melville nexus paradigmatically spanned the continuum
from Romantic optimism to the naturalist-existentialist nexus in
twentieth-century American letters. Because of his unorthodox (relative
to conventional Christianity) ideas and his lively sense of the absurd,
Hawthorne was unwilling to abandon his own Idea, his Classicist

utopia, for the ease of superficial religious optimism. And because of his Classicist utopia, he was unwilling to abandon the relatively orthodox dimensions of his spirituality for the premises of Transcendentalist metaphysics. His own lights were his own lights—and his own darkness was his own darkness. But in going the step farther into the implications of closure, Melville refused to regard light as a revelation of any kind of purposive spiritual absolute, as defined by Hawthorne, the Transcendentalists, Andrews Norton, or any Idealist system of thought. For him, as for Hawthorne and the Transcendentalists, light was the medium of meaning, but for him that meaning was that there was no absolute spiritual meaning. In and of itself devoid of idea, light becomes momentary, blinding, the agent of that ultimate darkness, the terrifying revelation of zero. Melville saw through to the philosophical essence of Hawthorne's wavering allegiances: the exclusive triumph of either openness or closure is nonexistence, and the concept of idealist openness led to Melville's central conclusion and conundrum: endless openness is empty closure. The color of idealessness is white, and the whiteness of Melville's speculum takes Emersonian light into new spectra of possibility in American literature:

> Is it that by its indefiniteness whiteness shadows forth the heartless voids and immensities of the universe, and thus stabs us from behind with the thought of annihilation, when beholding the white depths of the milky way? Or is it, as in its essence whiteness is not so much a color as the visible absence of color, and at the same time the concrete of all colors, is it for these reasons that there is such a dumb blankness, full of meaning, in a wide landscape of snows—a colorless, all-color of atheism from which we shrink? . . . all deified Nature absolutely paints like the harlot, whose allurements cover nothing but the charnel-house within; and when we consider that the mystical cosmetic . . . the great principle of light, forever remains white or colorless in itself, and if operating without medium upon matter, would touch all objects, even tulips and roses, with its own blank tinge—pondering all this, the palsied universe lies before us like a leper, and, like wilful travelers in Lapland, who refuse to wear colored and coloring glasses upon their eyes, so the wretched infidel gazes himself blind at the monumental white shroud that wraps all the prospect around him.

Here light "*shadows* forth" all the prospect; seeing is lighted by a medium that is a "visible absence." The meaning of light thus mirrored is the meaning of zero, with all things, or "colors," being only themselves. Zero idea, "the visible absence of color," is "at the same time" all actualities, "the concrete of all colors." If in universal whiteness there is a "dumb blankness, full of meaning," then in the eachness of things and colors there is a dumb meaning of full blankness. All goes back to white again. The eachness of closure and the allness of openness are each other: "the visible absence of color and at the same time the concrete of all colors." The ultimate darkness of whiteness was not what either the Romantic or the nationalistic ideologies could accommodate, for in either case it radically changed the concept of light in a denial of infinite possibility through divine design. Melville's work traces in itself the change from Emersonian dawn to Twain's total night in the literary mirror's reflection of light.

Typee, Melville's first book (1846), in many ways his gayest, begins with sparkling visions of "flashing blue waters" in the morning sunshine of a youth's tropical life. The bright, apparently paradisiac setting seems to be a throwback in time to the Edenic, Romantic dawn of human promise. Openness: morning, warmth, verdant nature, sex, youth, and sunlight characterize the surface of Melville's first fiction. But when we turn to the last fiction that Melville published in his lifetime, *The Confidence-Man* (1857), and to the last chapter, titled "Increase in Seriousness," we are choked off in a claustrophobic setting. In this closure, in the bowels of a *narrenschiff,* the only light—a "solar lamp"—is extinguished by an ever-present and shape-shifting being who leads away a very *old* man into absolute darkness. At the beginning of the first book, the objects floating in the water are coconuts and young maidens; at the end of the last book, the life preserver that the old man trustingly hugs to his bosom is a toilet seat. The line from total, dazzling sunlight to total, blinding darkness is not a precisely incremental pattern from Melville book to Melville book, just as it is not from nineteenth-century American author to nineteenth-century American author, but it is steady and it is very much there.

The contrast between millennialistic American nationalism (which at first Melville jingoistically shared, in part) and spectacles such as the Mexican War and slavery (which sickened him) created in Melville an enormous sense of the possible meanings implicit in the vastness of the gulf between history and the presumed Ideal. In slavery in America he saw the type of that gulf: "The world's fairest hope linked with man's foulest crime," as he wrote in his poem, "Misgivings." Like all his contemporaries, from Emerson to Hawthorne, Melville saw in America the greatest and most intense paradigm of the march of all human society throughout all human history. Melville's consequent sense of a conscienceless universe threw him back in recoil from God to human society—where, except for a few innocents and good hearts and noble heroes (the rare Billy Budds and Charlie Millthorpes and Jack Chases), all dupes or victims lost in the past, Melville observed creatures and a history that fell far short of liberal Idealist assumptions and were very Real in their actualities. Society became for Melville the mirror reflecting its human creators, and they, in turn, reflect whatever first cause might ever have existed. Melville's mirror reflected complexities of idea that the Nathaniel named Willis could not have begun to dream of.

The trouble was that the Nathaniel named Hawthorne could. His imaginative brilliance led him into visions he did not want to abide and that his wife did not wish to entertain. He came repeatedly to the edge of that Pisgah from which Melville plunged—or soared—but could not quite take the final epistemological and ontological steps that Melville did. His work indicates profoundly that he felt his dark visions were glimpses of truth and yet that he was glad to be able to maintain acceptance within his society and marketplace, living in a secure burgher's world from which he could look pityingly down upon Melville's endless rounds of beliefs and unbeliefs. Melville must have made Hawthorne very uneasy. Whatever the actual events in the rupture between the two greatest American fiction writers in the first seven decades of the nineteenth century, their emotional and philosophical differences concerning relationships with their society, their wives, and their marketplace must have been felt early in the friendship. Melville wanted to write books that were said to have "failed," as he wrote to his father-in-law. His recognition that the literary marketplace's rhetoric of national openness was a fixed ideological closure made him spurn the idea of belonging to the America he depicted in *Pierre.* Early in his career he was already an apostle of darkness when he most rejoiced in the Hawthorne he hailed as a kindred nay-sayer in the Berkshires—even at the peak of his nationalistic jingoism in his anonymous review of Hawthorne's *Mosses from an Old Manse.* Hawthorne well might have gone beyond uneasiness into a measure of fright and even revulsion at the philosophical and literary risk Melville represented, as though Melville demanded an openness of commitment that Hawthorne's Classicist temperament could not accept. Twain could and did make Melville's leap. The prevalence and imagery of light and morning and openness in early books like *Roughing It* (1872) become the empty darkness at the end of *The Mysterious Stranger,* or, what is effectively the same, the terrifying whiteness of a glaring microscope light, within which the human world is but an infinitesimal specimen under a *looking* glass, in "The Great Dark." The span of Twain's work indicates the same kind of progression in light imagery that characterizes Melville's work. But Hawthorne, in what was his most characteristic posture, held back a little. As a young author he emerged into Transcendentalist dawnlight and went his own distance in developing the progression of darkness from Emerson to Twain. Despite his holding back a little, despite the ambivalences in his fiction, his own trailblazing was an act of courage.[2] He cut his paths through shadows at a moment when his Willisite marketplace saw, demanded, and rewarded a fullness and a constancy of sunshine.

NOTES

1. A paper delivered by Stephen Nissenbaum at the American Antiquarian Society (Worcester, Mass.) in 1988 triggered considerations that I am happy to acknowledge here as a debt. Many scholars (and once more I acknowledge Nina Baym and Ann Douglas primarily, though not alone) have indicated that several among Hawthorne's "damned mob of scribbling women" must be reevaluated, and Willis, the male, must take his place among those who sentimentalized and prettified the marketplace. Jane Tomkins's argument in *Sensational Designs: The Cultural Work of American Fiction, 1790–1860* (New York: Oxford University Press, 1985), that Hawthorne benefitted from a *male*-dominated literati, bears on the matter. Michael T. Gilmore's study of the socio-literary context, cited in the acknowledgments, is especially valuable. Baym, Douglas, Gilmore, Nissenbaum, and Tomkins are representative of some of the newer scholarship that reveals the significance of writers like N. P. Willis, so appropriate to a discussion of Hawthorne's contexts.

2. I do not mean to suggest that Hawthorne was alone at the head of a line of succession. Charles Brockden Brown, especially in *Arthur Mervyn* (1799), anticipated the problematics found in Hawthorne and revealed similar tensions between Romantic openness and Classicist closure. So, too, did John Neal, a writer Hawthorne read and admired, especially Neal's long Romance about the American Revolution, *Seventy-Six* (1823) and his Salem witchcraft fiction, *Rachel Dyer* (1828). In fact, it is the prevalence—the Americanness—of the problem that leads me to honor Hawthorne at the very moment I sense his weaknesses, for in his own internal ambivalences he fashioned expression for the genius that lifted him above Brown and Neal and made him the paradigm and leader.

3

A Marketplace Context

I

With rare exceptions, such as "The Artist of the Beautiful," Nathaniel Hawthorne's fiction indicates an essentially Classicist spirit of closure, implicit everywhere in his work and explicit in anti-Romantic cautionary tales like "Earth's Holocaust." Hawthorne's books reveal a utopian conservatism predicated upon a sense of history as repetitive and continuous, rather than progressive and perfectible or millennialistically discontinuous, even in the American Revolution. His view of human possibilities was that they are limited rather than ultimately transcendent. The illusion of perfectibility is death, says "The Birthmark." The illusion of complete power is death, says "Rappaccini's Daughter." The illusion of transcendent superiority to the ordinary human community is death, says "Ethan Brand." The illusion that human life can proceed according to an unvitiated ideal is a dying hour of gloom, says "Young Goodman Brown." Despite the exceptions, the overpowering direction of thematic energy in Hawthorne's fiction is toward the inevitability and even moral necessity of human limitation, toward the revelation of the transcendent openness of all possibility as a dangerous illusion.

But by the end of the War of 1812, Hawthorne's Young America had a very different view of things. Accelerated by the chest-thumping exuberance of America's final military declaration of independence, national energies poured into the increasingly Romantic certitudes with which the openness of land, wealth, power, and all possibility were proclaimed as the natural right to all in the new democracy. Politically and economically, at least, America was not the type but the realization of heaven. And if, in God's country, everyone has the right to everything, there is no development of which the self is not capable. To deny this is un-American, unpatriotic, and unworthy. It is a denial made by the outsider in the thin moonlight, not by one who belongs in the broad noonlight.

One of the familiar stories in the history of American literature is the ostracism of James Fenimore Cooper. He discovered very quickly that one may not raise questions about the progress of the American democracy without immediately being cast as the enemy of the people. In the fervent cultural nationalism of the early nineteenth century, there were not many choices of allegiance open to American writers. Choices of allegiance translated into choices of vocation. Those who became famous and made money in the popular literary marketplace satisfied conventional social and patriotic mass values. Nathaniel P. Willis, in his anti-egalitarian snobbish gentility and social vanity, was never attacked as an un-American enemy of the people. He told his society what it wanted to hear: that it was refined, gracious, and pretty, and that people who did not like or live up to its values were of no consequence and could become citizens of somewhere else. Real men were men of society and successfully did the work of the practical world. Real women were ladies. The lady was chaste, conventional, domestic, and social. Physically enticing, but in her physical frailty requiring gallantry, she could exercise an indomitable will in spiritual purity that uplifted and ennobled those around her. Confronted with his ideologically conservative marketplace, Hawthorne could not fully express his utopian vision of all human beings as fallen, for woman had to be lady. The conventional deification, or at least sanctification, of the female victimized women as well as men in its ahumanity of specification. In its coercive falsity it led to interesting reversals, especially in *The Scarlet Letter* and *The Marble Faun*, in what Hawthorne felt he could say to the ladies' literary market about our common humanity.[1] Not in an assessment of women, or of his nation, or of progress, or of history, could Hawthorne validate his vocation in the terms that the literary marketplace and the larger society reflected. Henry James's recognition of Hawthorne's failure of nerve was gauged by the extent to which an artist is willing to take his vocation seriously and dedicate his entire identity to it. But for Hawthorne and his time, that dedication demanded a far deeper commitment than aesthetic or vocational allegiance. It was a matter of the social and political dimensions of one's entire life. As I hope to demonstrate, various aspects of *The Marble Faun* and the endings of many of his works reveal that consciously or otherwise, Hawthorne buckled at some of the pressure points of his internal conflicts. The wonder is not that he suffered a failure of nerve, but that he persevered as well as he did, for the conditions of the marketplace did little to help him.

As literary historians often have pointed out, lack of copyright agreements and the prevalence of literary piracy made it possible for any American publisher to offer his customers the most popular, proven, and respected British authors. An American, especially an unknown American, would not easily find a native publisher willing to risk printing and distribution costs. Not only was the British name the recognized commodity, but, unlike the American, the pirated Briton did not have to be paid. With rare exceptions, such as Cooper, Americans did not begin literary careers as unknown novelists fresh from the first fruits of their inspiration. Often, both initial publication and recognition were given in England before American publishers would risk their enterprise. And, as in the case of Cooper, even established writers could be mauled financially by the absence of copyright protection. Looking at the market about them, young American literary hopefuls saw quickly that their best—perhaps only—chance for breaking into the literary establishment, such as it was, lay in the native newspapers, gift books, and magazines. For a man with the high literary ambitions of a Nathaniel Hawthorne, the prospect offered by such publications was apt to induce high literary nausea. Nevertheless, failing in his attempts to publish a book-length collection of tales (to have been called *Provincial Tales*) in the year following the appearance of his dismal failure, *Fanshawe,* Hawthorne turned to the popular periodical market.

That market was split between a few gentlemen's magazines and periodicals of wider circulation, generally by and about ladies, and certainly for them. As a rule, the gentlemen's magazines did not publish fiction, and the biographies they favored were not those of artists, tormented Puritans, or outcast sinners, but of eighteenth- and nineteenth-century men of the world. These men of actualities were august Ciceronian exemplars of statesmanship and decorum (men were dignified into the gentleman almost as remorselessly as women were etherealized into the lady). They were leaders in public patriotism, philanthropy, and accomplishment in military, commercial, ecclesiastical, financial, scientific, or political endeavors.[2] The ladies' magazines were swamps of sentimentality, purple prose, maudlin gentility, and melodrama. In *Pierre* Melville satirized the lush literary manifestations of conventional lady's sensibility as all peach juice and attar of roses, messages written on violets by the beaks of lovebirds. The ladies' darling, Nathaniel Willis, whose pleasant, chitchatty sketches of travel (*Pencillings by the Way*), fashion, and society were immensely popular, added such quivering productions as *Bianca Visconti; or, The Heart Overtasked: A Tragedy;*

and slender volumes of *Poems of Passion.* When the anonymous *Fanshawe* was reviewed in the *Critic,* it must have overtasked the severe and ambitious Hawthorne's heart—although the review inadvertently was an apt and instructive appraisal of *Fanshawe's* quality—to see the reviewer tremulously ask, "Is it not quite possible that Willis wrote this book?"[3] Referring to the nature and popularity of ladies' publications with names like *Pearls of the West, The Bower of Taste,* and *Friendship's Offering,* and of the success of bustlebound writers and editors such as Catherine Sedgwick, Maria Susanna Cummins, Sarah Josepha Hale, and Lydia Sigourney, Hawthorne wrote his famous statement to W. D. Ticknor that "America is now wholly given over to a damned mob of scribbling women, and I should have no chance of success while the public taste is occupied with their trash—and should be ashamed of myself if I did succeed."[4] Not only did those "scribbling women" deserve more respect than Hawthorne was willing to allow himself to state publicly, but, despite his haughty *diktat,* it was precisely within that very same market, in gift book annuals like *The Token,* that Hawthorne gladly began to publish his work and take his initial steps toward literary success. It would be a vast overstatement to assert that Hawthorne's awareness of the nature of the literary market led him to prostitute himself to it. But it would be foolish to pretend that he remained entirely above the influences exercised by the clearly established decalogues of the market within which he began to practice. So often has the reference to the "damned mob of scribbling women" been quoted that it is easy to forget the sentence that follows in Hawthorne's letter and its revelation of Hawthorne's lasting concern with successful sales in the damned mob's world: "What is the mystery of these innumerable editions of the Lamplighter, and other books neither better nor worse? —worse they could not be, and better they need not be, when they sell by the 100,000." (*The Lamplighter; or An Orphan Girl's Struggles and Triumphs,* by Maria Susanna Cummins, first published in Boston in 1854 by John P. Jewett and Co., sold tens of thousands of copies each year, was quickly translated into several foreign languages, triggered spinoff books—Jewett published *The Lamplighter Picture Book* for children in 1856, for instance—and new editions by various publishers were issued through the years as late as 1912.)

Although Hawthorne recoiled from the world of the literary marketplace, he did not want that world to recoil from him. The offended recoil of established society from a radical manner is clear enough: there is no mystery about the critical reception of Walt Whitman's early work. But one's manner may be impeccable; yet if the substance radically challenges the establishment's assumptions, the threat is cast out, as Ralph Waldo Emerson learned when he angered Andrews Norton. By the end of the Era of Good Feelings, the Romantic utopia of open possibility had hardened, in the nationalistic ideological uses made of it, into the closure that allowed no deviation from the proposition that the progress of America had become the actualization in history of the true, good, and divinely special fulfillment of a cosmic plan. If one chose to be a serious artist, one could be Romantically "unhandselled," like Emerson's nature, but then one could not expect approval from the marketplace. The fervent nationalism of the young nation demanded acquiescence in its self-image. Conformist approval and belonging meant patriotism in culture as well as in politics. Nationalism demands ideological conservatism.

In all his political instinct, James Fenimore Cooper was a conservative. Yet for all his fame, acceptance faded as he scolded his society. Never a radical, he was repudiated in his own lifetime because he chose publicly to challenge the assumptions of egalitarian openness that characterized the ideological status quo. Although politically and philosophically Hawthorne was more of a democrat than Cooper, he shared with Cooper an essential temperamental conservatism. But his acceptance by his society continued throughout his lifetime in part because his dissenting views were disguised in allegory, or, if they were directly authorial statements, they were cast in meditative observations tucked into the protective disclaimers of Romance (Gentle Reader, this is the world of the imagination, not the actual). Whatever a writer's utopia, dissent from the prevailing nationalism brought one's entire identity into question as a male or as a female and as a citizen. One was thrust into the identity of either a radical dissenter or a vapory luxury in the bustling young practical Republic. Disconnected from the work of the world, like Owen Warland, Hawthorne's Artist of the Beautiful, the male writer was too easily disowned as "unmanly"—a person of vaguely epicene uselessness or detriment to the mainstream of Americans fulfilling God's plan among the important actualities of life. (Not insignificantly, Margaret Fuller's "womanly"—read "ladylike"—instincts were brought into question by hostile critics.)

No one felt the implications of isolation more than Hawthorne. He was aware that isolation and what amounted to vocational radicalism were concomitants of each other. Of course, one might be a fiery crusader who could face conflict, like Fuller, or who generated his own warmth and did not need society, like Henry David Thoreau, or who created his own society, like Emerson. But temperamentally, those were never options open to Hawthorne. One could be the ghostlike, detached observer, shuddering in the cold, or one could take one's place by one's cozy and secure fireside as a comfortable member of society who made enough money to own an enviable hearth. Hawthorne feared the destructive isolation of the artist in burgeoning young America. He observed American artists drifting abroad together for society in precincts less inhospitable to art than his own "dear native land," as he called it in his preface to *The Marble Faun*. But he felt that cut adrift in foreign places, these American artists lost the creative originality that their nativeness had given them. Anticipating Henry James, Hawthorne saw that the artist needed both Europe and America, and that if the two worlds offered him different sources of strength, they also offered him different kinds of annihilation. *The Marble Faun* presents a gathering of American expatriated artists in Italy, "this Land of Art," where "they are free citizens," as a herding together in which "artists are conscious of a social warmth from each other's presence and contiguity. They shiver at the remembrance of their lonely studios in the unsympathizing cities of their native land. For the sake of such brotherhood as they can find, more than from any good that they get from galleries, they linger year after year in Italy; while their originality dies out of them, or is polished away as a barbarism" (132). Hawthorne had hot literary ambitions, which made him shiver all the more feverishly in what he felt was the bleakness of his vocational isolation, and as much as he desired the independent, speculative privacy of a serious artist, he wanted desperately to come in from the cold. He trod the same circle all his life. In America he wanted to be a triumphantly successful writer and respected member of society. But in Salem society he opted to be "a citizen of somewhere else." That somewhere else was independent separation into the autonomous imagination. In order to reach that somewhere else, he wanted the accepted independence of the private artist. In order to have that acceptance and independence, he wanted to be a triumphantly successful writer and respected member of society. In Europe the artist's function was respected. But in Europe he wanted to go home.

Within his own opposing temperament and desires, as well as within his opposing social and vocational identities, Hawthorne was both realist and dreamer, representative burgher and outcast. Paradoxically, his utopian conservatism, which denied the Romantically optimistic rhetoric of nationalism, kept him from finding a comfortable home in ideological conservatism. His personality prevented his finding a home in the extroversion that is a part of acquiescent belonging. He was at home in neither the values nor the mores of the Custom House.

The manifestations of Hawthorne's conservatism are complex. Anything but an extrovert, Hawthorne nevertheless felt an impulse toward the conventional and gregarious. His avid desire "to open an intercourse with the world" was at least in part the desire for acquiescent belonging in an amiable and respected place in established society. It was an impulse toward ideological conservatism and cannot be judged entirely fairly within the context of social inequities in post–Civil War American society. In the early nineteenth century, the general social experience in America (always excluding blacks and Irish immigrants) was that of the cottager, farmer, and artisan—the respectable, even poor worker—rather than that of the debased peasant or urban *lumpenproletariat.* On a personal level, Hawthorne's experiences, unlike Melville's, were never those of men engaged together in the underdog life of bestial labor that one found even on American ships on the high seas. Hawthorne's view of the ongoing community, together with his utopian conservatism, made him certain that there was a rich, shared wisdom in the high priority given by common folk to the status quo of the humble daily meal and yearly income rather than to the theories of change that were to revolutionize and improve them. It was best to rest content with the bird in the hand. This part of Hawthorne anticipated Gustave Flaubert's observing the bourgeois Sunday promenaders and saying, "Ils sont dans le vrai." This conservatism is expressed on the utopian level as the constant insistence in Hawthorne's fiction that we limited human beings inevitably must settle for an imperfect and incomplete world because of our common and equal condition of inescapable sin. This sense of sadly and meditatively wise pronouncement, which one receives from all Hawthorne's fiction is, finally, not only a tonal signature. It is the thematic and political characteristic that unites the significantly revelatory "Wakefield" (one should never abandon one's accepted and established place in the heart or in the community) with the brilliantly representative "My Kinsman, Major Molineux" (all humans inevitably are initiated into the pain of sin and limitation).

From this conservatism arose Hawthorne's sympathetic sense of human oneness and his sad but wistful willingness to accept defective human society as it is, for to recognize the truth of one's own limited nature is to recognize the mutual identity shared with everyone in all times and in all nations. Thus, the call for an honest self-assessment in *The Scarlet Letter,* "Be true! Be true!," an injunction that, if literally followed, would seem to separate one from society either in shame or defiance, is actually a call that arises from the same source as the desire to open an intercourse with the world. When tone, theme, and ideology successfully unite, as they usually do in Hawthorne's work, that coherence is the result of the moments of congruence among his psychology, metaphysics, and politics. Hawthorne's temperamental impulse toward introversion was intensified by the cultural effects of materialistic nationalism, which forced the paradoxical merger of his utopian conservatism with the vocational radicalism implicit in his choice to be a writer of Romance. The sense of isolation created by that merger accentuated his extroverting desire to belong. Introversion and extroversion converged thematically in Hawthorne's central idea: one must never commit the unforgivable sin of breaking the sympathetic "magnetic chain of humanity."

Yet the matter will not rest so simply, for there are many stressed moments of functional disunity in Hawthorne's work. Many of Hawthorne's statements, The Custom House preface to *The Scarlet Letter* most prominent among them, vigorously resist the impulse toward acquiescence and membership in his actual society.[5] "Wakefield" and "My Kinsman, Major Molineux," two anchors between which ride all the implications of almost all of Hawthorne's short fiction, reveal the counterthrusts within the thematic current. In "Wakefield," the moral is explicit: "Amid the seeming confusion of our mysterious world, individuals are so nicely adjusted to a system, and systems to one another and to a whole, that, by stepping aside for a moment, a man exposes himself to a fearful risk of losing his place forever. Like Wakefield, he may become, as it were, the Outcast of the Universe" (IX, 140).

But as clear as the moral is, there is an equally clear emphasis on Wakefield's mysteriousness of purpose, a quality that Wakefield's wife calls "a little strangeness." Wakefield's creator adds, "This quality is indefinable, and perhaps non-existent." But he cannily presents it at the end of the paragraph that enumerates Wakefield's qualities, thereby italicizing it in the reader's memory, emphasizing the strangeness at the very moment that the narrator speculates that it might not exist (IX, 132). However inscrutable and irrational Wakefield's purposes forever remain, we do know that whatever reasons we might assign to Wakefield's joke on his wife, we are witnessing a moment of openness, of bursting out.

But Hawthorne does not know what to do with the devilish Romantic impulse. He seems not to be able to conjure up the imaginative interior of a radical career, and, indeed, "Imagination, in the proper meaning of the term, made no part of Wakefield's gifts" (IX, 131). Wakefield must, and does, remain inexplicable—and hardly radical beyond the open moment of radical departure. Having given Wakefield a strangely Romantic act, Hawthorne can do nothing with that act but assign Wakefield to *another* "nicely adjusted" and "unexposed" system. The only difference is that this one is without a wife. Is Hawthorne fictively sublimating the Romantic within himself? Is he fictively sublimating the urge to break out and see the death of the Sophia-world of "Phoebe" and

"Dove"? In almost every way Sophia Peabody was paradigmatic of the strain of ideological conservatism within Hawthorne, despite her flirtation with Transcendentalism. His pet names for Sophia, "Phoebe," and, especially, "Dove," personified in *The House of the Seven Gables* and *The Marble Faun,* have unmistakably one-dimensional functions of allegiance to established, conventional manners and mores, and in both cases the characters provide redemption for a male artist who otherwise could remain isolated in the world of his art. Doves and Phoebes will not be Outcasts of the Universe. In marrying Sophia Peabody, Hawthorne completed his intercourse with the world. He accepted the lady; he married the values of his literary marketplace; he wed the conventions and shibboleths of his society. It is not insignificant that this female incarnation of his tendency toward ideological conservatism liked *The House of the Seven Gables* the best of all his books because it was the most overtly socially conservative and, in the sunniness of its happy ending, the most unambiguous.

Yet, despite the joy he clearly took in his marriage, that combination of utopian conservatism and vocational radicalism deep within him must have resulted, at least on the subconscious level, in a restless sensation of stifling. "Wakefield" is a stifling story. It is entirely one of almost claustrophobically cozy immurement, threats to snug safety arising only out in the streets. When we "follow close at . . . [Wakefield's] heels" in his nervous flight through the thoroughfares, "after several superfluous turns and doublings, we find him comfortably established by the fireside of a small apartment . . . in the next street to his own, and at his journey's end" (IX, 133). It is as though Hawthorne, having dramatized the moment that bursts the stifling, feels the pull of established systems so strongly that he finds no area for action but another system. The wife *almost* dies. Finally, there is no difference between Wakefield's alternative system and his original domestication. He has gained no new world and is simply better off with his wife. So, after dwelling within his own claustral snuggery "upwards of twenty years," he returned home and "entered the door one evening, quietly," to stay (IX, 130). We are left with antagonistic coequals: on the one hand, an explicit moral about a fixed place for everything and everything in its place; on the other hand, our sense of stifling and the mystery of the act of breaking out. The power of the mystery creates the tale's tone. Tonally, the tale sets up a countercurrent as strong as the overt and undeniable thematic celebration of a place in a system.

Finally, it is not the theme of closure, the explicit moralizing about one's obligations and relations in the world, or the changes within Wakefield—all of which undeniably occupy a continuing frontal place in the tale—but the "little strangeness" of the tale that continues to itch in the reader's mind. The tonal hesitancy, the very mysteriousness, is what gives the tale its purpose in the telling and is what Hawthorne claims as the subject in the two opening paragraphs. In a tropistic attraction to the mystery of Wakefield's act rather than to the act itself, Hawthorne leads himself to his incapacity to resolve the inexplicability of breaking out. It is an act "without the shadow of a reason" (IX, 130). Paragraphs three ("What sort of a man was Wakefield?") and four (Wakefield's crafty smile) set the itch in place, and Hawthorne gave them a narrative power that makes the mystery lastingly coexistent with the "pervading spirit and . . . moral . . . done up neatly and condensed into the final sentences" concerning adjusted systems and Outcasts of the Universe (IX, 131). The wry, self-mocking consciousness with which Hawthorne alludes to neatly condensed morals indicates his uneasy self-awareness as a narrator and his (subconscious?) sense that what he really is saying might not be so easily packaged and so acceptably in accord with his public function as a writer. He disguises what he can: Wakefield, in all his personal characteristics, is anything but a Romantic. But then—but then . . . *why?* Hawthorne centers and centers on that nagging why. As he does in many of his fictions, in "Wakefield" Hawthorne scratches his hidden itch, touching what he wishes to deny, revealing what he fears might be a malady, acknowledging the power of the Romantic utopia, the force of openness, and the attractiveness of breaking out. They last.

"My Kinsman, Major Molineux" is about the act of breaking in. Robin breaks into the adult world and is broken-in to the world of mortal limitation. As in "Wakefield," the thematic force is one of closure. Young Robin exists at a moment just prior to recognition of the fact that one can't go home again. Consequently, he maintains the childhood illusion of a world in which the father's protection assures open possibility in the future. Despite what the Charon-like ferry crossing suggests about a change of worlds, clothed and armed with equipment from his childhood, from his father's house, Robin seeks to extend that childhood indefinitely in finding his surrogate father, Major Molineux. He does not understand the thematic nature of his mission, and he innocently takes success for granted. But in all the emblemology of initiation into the actuality of the City of Dis, emblemology that unbrokenly carries forward the action of initiation and the thematic assertion that no one is immune as we are all led by the devil in one vast communal parade, Robin's expectations are denied.

Artistically, the tale is Hawthorne's most perfectly embellished short statement of utopian conservatism. Yet even here, as in "Wakefield," there is a curious tonal countercurrent created by the complexity of emblemology. What amounts to the denial of the Romantically perceived father accords with the tale's thematic force. Neither Robin's father nor Major Molineux can provide exemption for themselves or others from the satanic touch of human limitation. Within the tale's political dimensions, even the bigger father, the King, is not immune, for the masquerading cavorters in the devil's party are none other than revolutionaries setting out on an equivalent of the Boston Tea Party. But within the tale's theological dimensions, in the curiously inserted denial of the Biggest Father, Hawthorne allows the introduction of implications he does not or will not confront. Robin's glimpse of the shivery "awful radiance" on the Great Bible in the church is both explicitly and implicitly a suggestion that the realm of God is too pure and cold for human use and is aloofly, totally removed from the hot needs and messy actualities of Satan-flawed humankind.

The devil is here in the city, and he is but our own leading energy. We are given the clinically observant, auctorial kindly gentleman, but this type of Hawthorne himself is as close as we come in the tale to the possibility of guidance and support for the innocent in need. The most that the type of the author-gentleman offers is kindly spectatorship. Very limited human succor is all that fallen mankind may expect in this fiction. Like the motif of laughter, which swells into the world's amusement at the moment Robin laughs loudest at himself in his initiation from his "shrewd" childhood into an adult recognition that his own future is as mortally contracted as that of any low-born fellow citizen who has no kinsman, the motif of light also illuminates the difference between childhood and adulthood. As the trembling moonlight in the church suggests, the night world of moonlight and torchlight is the mortally "earthly and impure" world of nature. It is anything but the world of bright openness that Robin associates with the Major.

It is "nine o'clock of a moonlight evening" when the boy enters the actual world. The ferryman examines him by the firelight of a lantern and the light of "the newly risen moon" (XI, 209). Robin denies that his father's realm lies in a world where "the moonlight enters at the broken casement" (XI, 210). "The light of the moon, and the lamps from numerous shop windows" (XI, 215), moonshine and firelight, are the constant lights for Robin's vision, either in the open air or in the interiors of this surreal-seeming Boston. The watchman, who watches not at all over Robin, proceeds sleepily by the light of a dim lantern; the "hem-hem"ing man of civil authority, who offers Robin the protection of neither civility nor authority, confronts the youth by the outstreaming lantern light "from the open door and windows of a barber's shop";

Robin first meets "the devil" in the smoky firelight of a tavern. Innocent Robin's first introduction to a whore is enacted when he is unprotected by any father, in a street where the "moonlight fell on no [other] passenger" (XI, 216). The prostitute's very voice is moonlight, "the airy counterpart of a stream of melted silver" (XI, 217). Consistently, Hawthorne provides fire and moon as the uncertain and only sources of light in a world of insurrection, sin, and the devil—a contracted world fundamental to the Classicist utopia and the opposite of Robin's Romantic expectations of openness.

The sunlight of home turns out to be childhood's dream of "shrewd" youth, a dream of love, not limitation. The dream family sits in a communion of love, concern, and prayer beneath the leafy, great dooryard tree, in "the going down of the summer sun," in whose beams the father holds "the Scriptures in the golden light" (XI, 222, 223). Although the sun is going down, presaging the end of the dream and the darker world into which Robin will fall, the light is warm and golden, distinctly different from the redlight-moonlight of the hellfire scene at the climax of the story.

As golden sunlight represents the lost dreamworld of unlimited youth and promise and security and love, everything Robin expects when he finds his kinsman, Major Molineux, and as indistinct, mysterious moonlight and firelight represent the actual world of humanity's fallen condition (how reminiscent of and yet how different from Hawthorne's famous use of those lights in "The Custom House"), the light of divinity is different from both. Moonlight scarcely "dares" to mix with it, betokening divinity's transcendence above human actions. When Robin peers into the church, "the moonbeams came trembling in" and a "fainter, yet more awful radiance was hovering round the pulpit, and one solitary ray had dared to rest upon the opened page of the great Bible. Had nature, in that deep hour, become a worshipper in the house which man had builded? Or was that heavenly light the visible sanctity of the place, visible because no earthly and impure feet were within the walls? The scene made Robin's heart shiver with a sensation of loneliness, stronger than he had ever felt in the remotest depths of his native woods; so he turned away" (XI, 222). It is interesting that in his evocation of lights, Hawthorne confuses the lights of the sky and the lights of heaven. The passage distinguishes between natural moonlight and an "awful radiance" that hovers around, apparently emanating from, the Bible itself. The light of nature tremblingly *approaches* the Bible and has to "dare" to rest on a page. As moonlight, *nature* has become a worshipper; but then, in a momentary confusion of sky light and heaven light, Hawthorne makes it impossible to continue the distinction, for, although the distinction leads one to expect that the "awful radiance" is the "heavenly light" of "visible sanctity," the construction of the sentence suggests that the moonlight is the heavenly light. But the confusion, though there, is unimportant, for it is clear that what Hawthorne is doing is separating the world of human-kind from the world of the Biggest Father, and in that cold separation Robin can find neither help nor comfort.

In his generally masterful control of his materials, Hawthorne adjusts the relationship of the actual (the contracted state of existence) to the imaginary (an expected openness of possibility) with brilliant success. Except for the confusion of lights in the church and, much more significant, the intrusion of the Man in the Moon, in every case the surreal and fantastic are related to the historical and can be explained realistically as a phenomenon of the actual: the devil's face as paint and an unusually pronounced physiognomy; the strange creatures in the street as masquerading revolutionaries using code language; the dream sequences as hallucinations caused by youthful Robin's extreme fatigue, high state of anxiety, and acute hunger. That is why the one major flaw in the tale—the moment when the Man in the Moon, hearing the terrestrial uproar, gives a jolly laugh and says, "Old earth is frolicsome tonight" (XI, 230)—is so intrusively noticeable. The Man in the Moon is not introduced through Robin's experience and, unlike every other event in the motifs of lights and laughter, is not explicable in a context of the actual. The Man in the Moon belongs not to Robin but to the author; it is the narrator's departure from investment in a serious and motif-ordered explanation of events. It is a moment that Henry James might have used to take Hawthorne to task for not taking his fiction seriously enough, just as James chided the older writer for his passage on Judge Pyncheon's smile. For Hawthorne creates an essentially existen-tial context for human action in "Molineux," and cannot or will not confront its implications. His intentions are very different, after all.

He does not intend to be an author who says, in effect, that there is no God. Yet, even given his tendencies, his time, and his place, the very intensity of the church scene indicates that there were profound noncon-formist and iconoclastic energies in the tale and its author. The hysterical, communal laughter of ironic self-recognition, led loudest by Robin at the moment of his newly initiated perception of things, should not have had *any* kind of personified response among "cloud spirits" who "peeped from their silvery islands" (XI, 230) or from the Man in the Moon, for the integrity of the motifs and techniques of the tale had established the moon either as "visible sanctity" divorced from the human or, more truly, as the actual light of fallen nature itself. As that deafening laughter swells up to the sky, through the farthest verge of space there should have been the silence that betokens that in all of the natural universe the only *humanly* identifiable sound is that of fallen humanity's own ironic making.

Furthermore, the introduction of the Man in the Moon reduces the emblemology to child's play. One is willing to suspend disbelief concerning all the other semisurrealistic settings and events because of the serious reverberations of metaphysical, political, and psychological freight carried in the dreamlike vehicle of the tale's method. The Man in the Moon is Hawthorne's (again: subconscious?) way of squaring himself with his practical, pragmatic society, nudging his readers, winking, and saying, "But we all know that story-telling is for children, and I'm a real, belonging, respectable grown-up, just like you."

At one and the same moment, Hawthorne displays his artistry, his courage, and his failure of nerve. It was not to Hawthorne's marketplace advantage to cast a hellfire light on colonial American rebellion against the crown. Indeed, when he treated the subject as the center of a fiction, as in "The Gray Champion," he wrote directly to his community's patriotic sense of what was appropriate:

> And who was the Gray Champion? Perhaps his name might be found in the records of that stern Court of Justice, which passed a sentence, too mighty for the age, but glorious in all after times, for its humbling lesson to the monarch and its high example to the subject. I have heard, that, whenever the descendants of the Puritans are to show the spirit of their sires, the old man appears again. When eighty years had passed, he walked once more in King Street. Five years later, in the twilight of an April morning, he stood on the green, beside the meeting-house, at Lexington, where now the obelisk of granite, with a slab of slate inlaid, commemorates the first fallen of the Revolution. And when our fathers were toiling at the breast-work on Bunker's Hill, all through that night, the old warrior walked his rounds. Long, long may it be, ere he comes again! His hour is one of darkness, and adversity, and peril. But should domestic tyranny oppress us, or the invader's step pollute our soil, still may the Gray Champion come; for he is the type of New-England's hereditary spirit; and his shadowy march, on the eve of danger, must ever be the pledge, that New-England's sons will vindicate their ancestry. (IX, 17–18)

Yet, in "My Kinsman, Major Molineux," Hawthorne's motifs work against the revolutionary rebellion inherent within the Romantic utopia. What makes the tale one of the very best of all Hawthorne's fictions is its author's courageous integrity, with which he stuck to the demands of his art rather than to the ideological demands of his marketplace. In the tale, leaving the home of the father (in the expanded historical dimension of the tale, leaving the home of the King) results in the nighttime discovery of the devil's mark of limitation inescapably upon us all, not in the dawn's early light discovery of that Great Getting-Up Morning anticipated in the open setting out, with which the youth expectantly begins his future and America sets its identity.

Implicitly, the tale's anti-Romantic theme is counterrevolutionary, and instead of being pictured as heroic Gray Champions, the rebel population, in all the insinuations of the rhetoric, is pictured as a despicable mob led by the devil. The King's agent, Major Molineux, is "an elderly man, of large and majestic person, and strong, square features, betokening a steady soul." He has a "broad forehead" and "his eyebrows formed one grizzled line" in "a head that had grown gray in honor" (XI, 228,229). But the American rebels heap "foul disgrace" upon that head, and there, where "the torches blazed the brightest . . . [and where] the moon shone out like day," they befouled the old man in "circumstances of overwhelming humiliation" (XI, 228, 229). Their exultant "trumpets vomited a horrid breath" (XI, 228), and on "they went, like fiends that throng in mockery round some dead potentate, mighty no more, but majestic still in his agony. On they went, in counterfeited pomp, in senseless uproar, in frenzied merriment, trampling all on an old man's heart" (XI, 230).

Yet, at the very moment of climax, at the very height of the instant in which he brought together all the thematic values of Classicist closure demanded by the tale, and in effect thereby defied the ideological openness demanded by his audience, Hawthorne ducked out from under the identity of the Author by momentarily disengaging, with the Man in the Moon, from fully serious commitment to art—thereby taking his place among the citizens of actuality who condescend to storytellers. When this symptomatic failure of nerve reveals itself in his fiction, it invariably does so at a moment either when Hawthorne feels that his society's values are being threatened too closely or when he feels his own orientation is in danger. The moment of the Man in the Moon is an example of both. Hawthorne indicates that his society's nationalistically exclusivist assumptions of special destiny are laughed into annihilation at the moment of the devil's triumphant initiation of Robin. In the same vein, the totality of the existential absence of divine essence allows us all indeed to make our own way as we will. "Perhaps," the Hawthorne-like omniscient gentleman tells Robin, "as you are a shrewd youth, you may rise in the world, without the help of your kinsman, Major Molineux" (XI, 231). In this superb fictionalized instance of his own sense of social dissent and existential possibility, Hawthorne, in a moony gesture of an instant, backs away from full commitment to his act of fiction in what becomes one of the most revelatory moments in all of his writings of the narrative effects of the politics of openness and closure. Within the tale's combined theological and historical suggestions of utopian closure, Hawthorne removed himself from himself before his marketplace audience.

The strong element of utopian conservatism in the existential glimpse of history (once we have imposed our identities, the viscous universe flows amorphously on, and the next Robin must learn his own initiation) leaves us with the Sisyphean task of experience to be done all over again, each time anew. But, on the other hand, the very emptiness of the universe, our very fatherlessness, allows that exercise of will that opens all possible identities. Granted, "Molineux," like "Wakefield," is unmistakably a tale of closure and expresses Hawthorne's utopian conservatism. But like "Wakefield," it leaves a tonal sense of something more going on, for what we are left with in "Molineux" is a sense of human crowding and cosmic emptiness—when the crowd goes by there is nothing but silence—in a world led by the devil. But he is a devil who is the embodiment of our own ubiquitous human frailties. It would be either critical supercleverness or superobtuseness to invert these tales into stories of openness. They are denials of openness. Hawthorne, consequently and rightly, does nothing with the possibilities of openness because they should not be there—but they are. It is the significant subliminal presence of counterforce against the victoriously prevailing thematic energy that provides the materials for a definition of Hawthorne's famous ambiguity. In almost every instance those ambiguities are the conflict of political opposites, usually, as in the case of these two tales, a conservative repression of a radical tendency. The counterforce exists in moments, in implications. One can see the ambiguity in momentary operation even when the political theme is reversed.

That reversal, the best, and perhaps the only pure example of the exception to Hawthorne's prevailing expression of Classicist closure, is "The Artist of the Beautiful." In this tale, precedent, history, community, limitation, and the diurnal concerns of human beings are repudiated as inimical to the artist's creative search for the ideal. This rare example of a triumphant Romantic utopia in Hawthorne's fiction is a reversal of what the rest of his fictions say: only in maverick isolation from a community one repudiates is one able to attain the utopia that is true. Redemption comes in breaking the magnetic chain of humanity: in fact, at the end of the tale Owen Warland attains a detached and invulnerable superiority to people and events. What in other Hawthorne fictions would implicitly or explicitly be condemned as an unforgivable sin in this tale is implicitly and explicitly a sympathetic nobility and goodness. Owen Warland, the artist, another type of a Hawthorne-self, is approved. Owen goes through phases of isolation in which he almost succeeds, and phases of isolation in which he is no more than a lethargic chump. But his final metamorphosis from his various sluglike larval and pupal states is one in which he becomes within himself the essence of the perfect butterfly, the successful artist's final attainment of the pure ideal. At that moment, the ordinary world and visible signs of attainment no longer matter:

> And as for Owen Warland, he looked placidly at what seemed the ruin of his life's labor, and which was yet no ruin. He had caught a far other butterfly than this. When the artist rose high enough to achieve the Beautiful, the symbol by which he made it perceptible to mortal senses became of little value in his eyes, while his spirit possessed itself in the enjoyment of the Reality. (X, 475)

Conversely, the human world of the plain folk majority that in Hawthorne's other fictions cannot and must not be denied is successfully denied as inadequate, undesirable, and paltry. The types of what Hawthorne saw in his surrounding society are all repudiated: the conventional, affectionate, and unimaginative domesticity of Annie Hovenden (for once the Sophia-world is transcended), the coldly optimistic certainty of Peter Hovenden that profitable and pragmatic business service will keep society running well, and the good naturedly optimistic certainty of Robert Danforth that force and power are what make the world go round. In this reversal of "Wakefield," breaking out wins over comfortable belonging. In this reversal of "My Kinsman, Major Molineux," an ideal condition of immunity to history is achieved. Openness wins out over closure, the Romantic over the Classicist, the radical over the conservative. Transcendence is possible and the ideal can be attained. The perfect companion to "The Artist of the Beautiful," of course, is "The Birthmark," which is entirely more representative of Hawthorne's major theme. Yet, even in "The Artist of the Beautiful," the one fiction in which he gives himself over completely to what otherwise remains a repressed or subconscious or controlled countercurrent, Hawthorne cannot avoid the flawed moment of reversal that is a sign of the internalized political conflict.

Given the values set forth in "The Artist of the Beautiful," the butterfly is infinitely more precious than any of the world's values. Everything that Annie, Peter, and Robert are and represent and treasure is dross by contrast. They are all one: fittingly Peter and Robert become father and son as Annie and Robert become wife and husband. Their baby is the distillation of that oneness, and, especially at the moment that he contemplates the butterfly on his hand, his shrewd, wizened little face exhibits the essence of his lineage and identity. The baby is a monster, and Hawthorne comes close to allowing himself that characterization. But he does not. When the baby's parents murmur to each other, "How wise the little monkey looks," the absence of any kind of authorial or symbolic qualification leaves Robert's and Annie's approbation to stand as the tale's momentary criterion. And then the author offers what for this context is a very strange thing.

> "I never saw such a look on a child's face," answered Annie, admiring her own infant, *and with good reason,* far more than the artistic butterfly. "The darling knows more of the mystery than we do." (X,474; italics mine)

Annie's evaluation of the baby, at a moment when the entire tale points in exactly the opposite direction, is, at that very moment, approved by the authorial voice. But because the tale itself offers not one jot for that approval, the immediate salient question is, where, then, does the approval come from? From the same source from which we accept the qualifications that allow us to acquiesce in the qualitative difference between Annie and the others, between the baby and the others. That is, women—or ladies—are of finer clay and more spiritual development than men. That is, babies are gifts from God and come trailing clouds of purity from their spiritual home. That is, all along the tale has been operating in small part according to the clichés and conventions that exist in the ideological conservatism of the literary marketplace, and they, in turn, reflect the conventional and conservative pieties of the society at large. That is, Hawthorne's abasement as Romancer in a practical society once again gives priority to the actuality of real babies over artistic butterflies. That is, finally, "The Artist of the Beautiful" is pulled in opposing directions by the presence of the very society that the tale's prevailing energy repudiates. It does not matter that Annie is found wanting. It does not matter that this baby is monstrous and is the genetic summation of everything stupid, conventional, grasping, cold, brutish, mindlessly unimaginative, calculating, and destructive that the tale has provided. Given the abstract category, baby, and the abstract category, butterfly (babies *are* more precious than butterflies, mothers *should* love their babies more than any objects around them), the reader has little choice but to submit to conventional pieties when conventional abstractions take momentary precedence over the otherwise unmistakably opposing specifics of the tale. In this case, "the darling" knows nothing of the mystery of the butterfly except his impulse to grab and crush it. But Hawthorne allows Annie's loving statement about baby to stand unchallenged and undiminished. In this moment of recoil from the entire force of all the details of his fiction, Hawthorne abruptly but briefly curtails his own artistic nobility, paying a rather mechanical obeisance to the ideological forces outside himself and revealing the conflict among ideology, utopia, and vocation within himself.

In the tale, commitment to the idea of the Ideal makes the visible symbol by which it is attained, the work of art, of secondary importance. Ironically, in the teller, commitment to the marketplace does the same thing. Hawthorne was not about to question the holy validity and unassailable rightness of mother love in any tale that bore his signature. Consequently, sanctity becomes sanctimoniousness. Questions about the nature and validity of parental evaluations do not properly belong in the tale, but neither do the anti-Romantic assumptions implicit in Annie's "rightness." Quite properly, Hawthorne does not take them up. But they are there, and he has put them there, and has done so, revealingly, at the very moment of the climax of the tale, where they cannot but intrude into the reader's sensibilities. Wakefield's moment of choice and Robin's glimpse of the church's interior are momentary stirrings of the radical counterforce; the author's approval of Annie and her baby are momentary stirrings of the conservative counterforce: they are mirror-image reversals of each other. They are the sources of ambiguity in a set of tensions in which the conservative tendency toward closure counterattacks against or, almost without exception, overwhelms the tendency toward openness. Classicism almost extinguishes the flicker of Romanticism; the continuation of that flicker is the paradox of the necessary temperamental radicalism of vocational choice made by a man of temperamental conservatism within the marketplace.

Hawthorne's divided self complicates his conservatism. How is one to "be true"? Is the truth that one should take up membership in society, knowing that all societies are flawed, or is the truth that one should renounce it for its falseness? Hawthorne was aware of the chorus on all sides proclaiming in self-satisfaction that American progress was the triumph over all the history of the past, and he recoiled from the noise. A radical like Thoreau listened to the same chorus and recoiled in contempt because the revolutionary-radical insistence on America as a total change from all the history of the past had settled into a conservatively nationalistic celebration of space, material, and status quo. For Hawthorne, the new American society was self-deceived because there was no such thing as a revolutionary change of the human spirit in the first place. For Thoreau the new American society was self-deceived because it had failed to become a true fulfillment of the coming revolution of the spirit. Hawthorne was the lonely outsider in his viewing of his nation's Revolution. Nevertheless, although he created subliminal questionings of the Revolution, as in "Molineux," his desire to belong led to overt praise of it, as in "The Gray Champion." Thoreau became the maverick outsider criticizing post-Revolutionary America because it had forgotten the true revolution; he refused acquiescence and membership in his society of progress because it was not nearly progressive enough. Although Hawthorne also stood aloof from the hosannahs to progress, he could neither temperamentally nor tactically confront his hoped-for market with open repudiation. In this matter, Thoreau is representative of all of Hawthorne's Romantic contemporaries: the difference in overt response between Hawthorne and Thoreau indicates why Hawthorne could find no community with the radical Romantics who felt the same recoil from society that he felt in his conservative classicism. They had a clear sense of their revolutionary relationship to society that in Hawthorne was an opposing set of tensions resulting in ambiguity. He hung back shyly from a society whose assumptions he could not accept, yet he desired very much to be an accepted part of that same society. The political question of identity was deep in the center of Hawthorne's personality, his vocational choices, his themes and failure of theme, his artistic pioneering and his failure of nerve, and in the form, and even the syntactical structure, of his fiction, as I shall try to demonstrate with *The Marble Faun*. His writing was to become an organically political act of autobiography in the attempt to discover, through avatars of aspects of himself and his utopian convictions, how his own identities as a male, an American, a citizen, and an artist could be reconciled and unified.

The task was to prove too much for him, for the complexities of identity did not arise only from antagonistic oppositions between his utopian conservatism (his Classicist sense of closure, the sameness of all history, and the limitations of the human heart) and his ideological conservatism (his enormous desire to *belong*, despite his society's jingoistic vocabulary of Romantic openness and despite the contradiction of his other desire: to withdraw reclusively). But there was also a tension between his ideological conservatism and his vocation: Hawthorne's appeals for the freedom of the Romance always were associated with his right to be free from the belonger's actualities on which his society "so terribly insisted," as he observed in the preface to *The Marble Faun*. His appeal for the freedom of the Romance was an appeal for his utopian expression of closure and conservatism, a function of his disagreement with his society's assumptions about infinite progress. This "nay-saying," which Melville so delighted to celebrate in his review of Hawthorne's *Mosses from an Old Manse,* was exactly what Hawthorne claimed the right to and feared at the same time. He feared it, for by its nature the Romance he vocationally championed was radical in its insistence upon the openness of the transcendent imagination. It pulled away from the past and precedent by asserting that there are modes of truth not bound by actualities. But Hawthorne saw all around him the ideologically conservative assessment of the true, the good, and the beautiful in terms of the actual, the profitable, and the useful, as "The Artist of the Beautiful" makes clear. And the implications of the Romance's epistemological assumptions (transcendence is available) did not accord with the Classicism of Hawthorne's utopian conservatism (historical realism and mortal limitation). Moreover, the very act of Romance writing had no clearly functional identity in a culture that had not yet established the legitimacy of the fictionist. The overt dissent of the major Romantics demanded an essay or revolutionary lyric poetry of fervent and intense statement. The Transcendentalists did not write novels or tales. (Whitman's one uncharacteristic gesture of acquiescence to the popular marketplace, *Franklin Evans,* was a novel. In its uncharacteristic nature it was a dismal failure that Whitman disowned and tried to expunge from the record.) And behind the American culture's reservations about fiction loomed two centuries in which, for different reasons, neither the Puritan nor the rationalist Deist sanctioned fiction. What fiction there was belonged to a popular marketplace inhabited mostly by the lady. Therefore, if one were to be merely a popular Romancer, one slid into sentimentality, melodrama, and gothic mysticism. But if one were to be a serious Romancer rather than a Willis or a lady, one would stand in opposition to his time and place both in vocation and ideas. Hawthorne's struggle to create a fiction free from actualities in order to examine seriously his society's assumptions was a radical challenge to the perceptions and values of the status quo. This man who both did and did not want to be an ideological conservative, who was very much a utopian conservative, who temperamentally could not and did not want to be a radical, dedicated himself, in his desire to belong, to the isolation of the vocational radical. If ever there was an ambiguity of identity, it was that of Hawthorne, for whom the central paradox was that his philosophical conservatism reinforced his vocational radicalism and conflicted with his ideological conservatism. Only in the Romance could he speak his utopian truth.

Thus, even Hawthorne's theme and his sense of vocation were at odds with each other. The vocational radicalism of Romance writing was an ally of his temperament and his utopian conservatism in Hawthorne's characteristic desire to withdraw from the manly tumult of official optimism. Yet the logical conclusion of his dominating utopia was that the dim outlines of truth are not discovered beyond history and experience, but within the illumination that the undeniable past sheds upon human limitation in the present course of society. Consequently, the major thematic force of Hawthorne's fiction, evoking the presentness of the past, drives toward homilies of intercourse with and integration into society. With few exceptions, on the homiletic level Hawthorne's fictions express his utopia. But the essence of the Romance is its freedom to move beyond the actualities. It is just that movement that is reinforced by the need for a disguising allegory, a need for masks fostered by his temperamental recoil from the rebel's open confrontation with his society.

The Scarlet Letter, for instance, is a tale of the relation of the private individual to the communal state; it is also a tale of the relation of the private individual to the soul. As homily, explicitly in its closing authorial observations, the book is a prescription for the integration of soul and society. But soul is approached only through an honest self-appraisal that results in the painful recognition that one participates without exception in the universal fallen condition of the entire race. The state, however, is characterized as inimical to soul from the beginning, when the beadle with great relish summons Mistress Prynne to her public shame, setting *her* forth as the type of everything the society claims that it is not: "A blessing on the righteous of the Massachusetts," proclaims the beadle loudly and smugly. *There* is the type of the literary marketplace and of the society within which it exists, with their loud optimism and coercive nationalism. Because those forces are inimical to the utopian conservative truths derived from the secret history of private individuals, one's true, inner humanity either must openly confront the society as an enemy, as, at the very first, Hester does, or must shrink from it as too overwhelming a force to be faced openly with the inner truth, as Dimmesdale does. In his hunger for the Romance, Hawthorne stood in the same relation to his own injunction, "Be true! Be true!," as Dimmesdale did to his own homiletics in his own sermons. The creation of Dimmesdale, a compelling voice enchanting a compelled audience, is at once an act of confession and self-discovery for Hawthorne, an identification of the politics of his vocation. He could not have chosen a finer irony than exists in the historical setting of *The Scarlet Letter*, for the Puritan community, founded upon the most conservative utopia as far as its view of human nature and human history is concerned, made it ideologically impossible to exercise as public policy the compassionate brotherhood of *The Scarlet Letter's* homiletic prescription: the good Puritan could never sympathize with sin. And because his own Classicist philosophy was a descendant from the Puritan utopia and in its insistence on the Fall somewhat reflected the lineaments of the ancestor, Hawthorne must have felt with intense keenness the improbability of his theme's message. The politics of his conflicts led to a wearying conviction that increasingly enclosed him toward the end of his life: an ever more encompassing sense of pointless reiteration of the same insistent state of closure, a sense of the futility of writing.

The rhetoric of Hawthorne's marketplace helps us reconnoiter the neighborhood in which, through Hawthorne's haunted characters, the politics of his self met the politics of his literary milieu. The fleeting tactical maneuverings and rising and falling of reputation among editors and literary stars and coteries are not primary here, for Hawthorne was neither a man of the salons nor an importunate hanger-on at publishers' offices. But a deeper sense of the politics of literature lies in the interaction between the power of established social values—ideologies—and literary practices that permeated the marketplace so thoroughly that they were an exposition of the relationship between the literary act and national attitudes. The marketplace rhetoric surrounding the literary act comprised for Hawthorne both the key terms of his prefaces and the critical vocabulary of approbation and rejection. The terms—"actualities," "manly," "patriotic," "American," "chiaroscuro," "sunshine," "shadow," "gloomy," "moral," "morbid," "subjective," "true," "verity," and "verisimilitude"—were not exclusively or even primarily expressions of purely literary fashion.[6] They were ideological materials for a definition of the point of conjunction between Hawthorne's temperament and his literary times.

II

"a Conservative after Heaven's own fashion"

Some reviews of his work showed explicit ideological approval of Hawthorne articulated by strangers who vibrated in immediate sympathy with the chord of conservatism he struck in his fiction. These responses displayed his way to belong. Without exception they reflected stereotypes such as "solid citizen" and "useless dreamer" and reinforced the ideological conservatism that made Hawthorne partly ashamed and defensive about his radical vocational identity at the same time that he took pride in his rather heroic attempts to forge it. He was never able to shake the feeling that there was justice in the distrust that sensible and solid men of affairs showed toward the visionary and, by vocational extension, the writer of Romance. That the solid citizen did distrust the cloudlands of "somewhere else" was made amply clear, both in censure and in praise, in the response of the marketplace to Hawthorne's publications,

"It happens," said one sturdy Whig, "that we have not only found Conservatism, but a good many other things we have asked for, in our national literature, expressed through the pages of Nathaniel Hawthorne." What that "Conservatism" means is contentment with actualities, for when the palpable world, which is taken without question to be the real world, is scrutinized, one finds that the ongoing reality in America is very lovely indeed in every way, surpassing all the plans and reforms of dreamy-eyed idealists. What the reviewer, Charles Webber, offers becomes significant when we recognize that his praise of Hawthorne is very like Peter Hovenden's approval of Warland when Owen toes the mark:

> It is a favorite expression with regard to Hawthorne, that he *"Idealizes"* everything. Now what does this Idealization mean? Is it that he *improves* upon Nature? Pshaw! This is a Literary cant. . . . Talk to me of *Idealizing* the violet, and you talk nonsense. . . . Hawthorne does not endeavor to improve upon the Actual, but with a wise emulation attempts—first to reach it, and then to modify it suitably . . . he is led by his fine taste to . . . make you see it in precisely that light in which . . . its highest beauty is revealed. . . . We can't get away from the physical, and just as our material vision informs the inner life will that inner life know Wisdom. When some of our crude Theorists have learnt to realize this truth . . . they will have come to the knowledge that one Fact of the external life is worth a thousand Dreams, and that they need not waste their lives in seeing sights that have no substance, and dreaming Dreams that have no reality; for if they will only wake up, and look at the real World as it absolutely is, they will find that they have a Paradise made to their hand.

One cannot dismiss this as merely the smugness of a man whose satisfaction with the "Fact" is that in his world facts are apparently quite comfortable, for at the heart of this shallow ideological conservatism is a view of history that is a working reduction of Hawthorne's own utopian conservatism:

> But there is a still more interesting and even wiser exhibition of the Ethical Conservatism of his mind, given in that fine allegory, "Earth's Holocaust." Here he represents a saturnalia of the Reformers, men like Emerson and that whole brawling tribe of Innovators—each of whom imagines he has certainly found the Archimedean lever, and is heaving at it in the effort to turn the world topsy-turvy.[7]

A clergyman reviewing *Mosses from an Old Manse* was quite clear about the political sense one was to take from the storyteller.

Hawthorne's residence at Concord was, perhaps, either cause or effect of his sympathy with the amiable and highly cultivated, but misty and groping, philanthropists of the "Concord sect" and the "Roxbury phalanx" Brook Farm. This sympathy, we regret to see and say, appears here and there, in his last volumes. It seems, however, to be more a sympathy of heart and sentiment, than of intellect and conviction. For his native good sense evidently distrusts, and declines to adopt, their loose doctrines, and their unsubstantial plans and theories.[8]

Throughout his literary life, Hawthorne evoked and was immersed in similar critical receptions. *The Blithedale Romance,* ready-made for political response by those so inclined, was praised because "Mr. Hawthorne is not a disciple of that school of human perfectibility which has given rise to plans of pantisocracy and similar Arcadias."[9] As one of the close followers of Hawthorne's writing, Henry Chorley, astutely said,

This "Blithedale Romance" is eminently an American book. . . . Mr. Hawthorne's America is a vast new country, the inhabitants of which have neither materially nor intellectually as yet found their boundaries,—a land heaving with restless impatience . . . to exemplify new ideas in new forms of civilized life. But Mr. Hawthorne knows that in America, as well as in worlds worn more threadbare, philosophers and philanthropists however vehemently seized on by such fever of vain-longing, are forced to break themselves against the barriers of Mortality and Time . . . in short, to recommence their dream and their work with each fresh generation, in a manner tantalizing to enthusiasts who would grasp perfection for themselves and mankind, and that instantaneously.[10]

It is interesting that when a reviewer to the left of Webber, Dutton, and Chorley attacked *The Blithedale Romance,* he did so because Hawthorne failed in his presentation of socialism—Hawthorne's error as seen in this case was not the presence of radical thought, but the neglect of it. But even at that, the radical British reviewer joins his conservative American opponents in a demand for the kind of novelistic realism in the use of materials that results not in Romance but in didactic usefulness:

"Blithedale," then, as a socialistic community, is merely used here as a scaffolding—a very huge one—in the construction of an edifice considerably smaller than itself! And then, the artist leaves the scaffolding standing! Socialism, in this romance, is prominent enough to fill the book, but it has so little business in it, that it does not even grow into an organic part

of the story, and contributes nothing whatever toward the final catastrophe.
. . . Having occupied the ground, Hawthorne owed it to truth, and to a fit
opportunity, so to dramatize his experience and observation of Commu-
nistic life, as to make them of practical value for the world at large.[11]

The point of view expressed here does not reveal any particular
difference between British and American reviewers: there were American responses that voiced socialist disappointment with Hawthorne's
uses of the Brook Farm experiment. Nor is this review unique in
demanding a focus other than the one Hawthorne gave to his book. But
the review does highlight the extent to which Hawthorne's work is
affected by a division of focus within himself. His conservative sense of
history constantly made him reach toward the past as a means of
discussing human behavior. The historical past as setting or active force
leads toward an attempt at verisimilitude in reconstructing materials.
So much more is this true in the use of the publicly historical present,
where public materials demand verisimilitude and historical actualities.
If for nothing more than setting, history demands a certain amount of
realism in treatment. Hawthorne turned toward public materials for the
verisimilitude, the "actualities," that the marketplace demanded. But
the social and historical materials—whether Rome and art in *The
Marble Faun*, or the Puritan community in *The Scarlet Letter*, or the
bourgeois New England world in *The House of the Seven Gables*, or the
socialist community in *The Blithedale Romance*—are never what
Hawthorne's books are centrally about. They are about the progress of
the individual into an enactment and realization of Hawthorne's utopian conservative certainty that the individual's inescapable human
limitations, and especially one's recognition of their meanings, define
the relationship of the private self to the public community. The materials of the public world, therefore, are either emblems of the utopian
perceptions, as particular works of art and the city of Rome are in *The
Marble Faun*, or they become superfluous. The individual in Hawthorne's
fiction is not representative of the effects of particular social or historical forces at work. Rather, the historical forces merely form a setting in
which their particularities become allegorically ancillary to the individual being educated into a human history that is one and unchanged in
all particular periods and circumstances.

For Hawthorne to focus on his individuals as representatives of particular social forces and their effects—socialism, Puritanism, capitalism—he
would have had to do the one thing from which he shrank. He either
would have had to sacrifice his utopia completely to the ideologies of his
world and show the actualities of history as a verification of America's

special common prettiness and goodness—and he tended to do this precisely in those sketches that his marketplace applauded and he came to disdain—or he would have had to sacrifice completely to his utopian conservatism his ideological possibilities of belonging and to dramatize in open confrontation his dissent from his society's ideology. He would have had to renounce the one vehicle he cherished for his purposes, the Romance, in favor of the terrible actualities. The division of focus within Hawthorne between his ideological conservatism and his vocational radicalism manifests itself methodologically in his relation to realism. He needed both the appearances of verisimilitude and the vehicle of the Romance. His materials and his plots come from two different kinds of worlds, related to different realities. When they are integrated in the fiction, as they are most completely in *The Scarlet Letter,* Hawthorne's art succeeds. When the background materials begin to repeat their function too often, they become obtrusive. That is what accounts, in part, for the general agreement that *The Scarlet Letter* and *The House of the Seven Gables* are the most fully realized of Hawthorne's Romances and that *The Marble Faun* and *The Blithedale Romance* have an aura of the traveler's guidebook about them. In insisting that Hawthorne should have written another book than the one he did, the English socialist reviewer was critically inappropriate in his comments; nevertheless, he indirectly indicates why Hawthorne's true metier was in the fantasy materials of the tale and the Romance, which were the foregrounds of his fiction, rather than those of the sketch and the novel, which were their backgrounds.

But by no means was it necessarily a socialist ideology that missed the focus of *The Blithedale Romance.* From his olympian ultra-Catholicism, Orestes Brownson turned savagely upon his communitarian and radical former friends, among whom he had once occupied so fiery a place. He opined that "*The Blithedale Romance* may be read by our Protestant community with great advantage, and perhaps nothing has been written among us better calculated to bring modern philanthropists into deserved disrepute, and to cure the young and enthusiastic of their socialistic tendencies and dreams of world reform. . . . In this point of view, we can recommend *The Blithedale Romance,* not as unobjectionable, indeed, but as little so as we can expect any popular work to be that emanates from an uncatholic source."[12] It is noteworthy that although both radical and conservative reviewers came at the book with the same ideological misapprehensions about what properly was background and what was foreground, it was the conservative reader who was ideologically pleased.

The identification of Hawthorne as a conservative continued through his life. An example of his reception among the people of actualities was provided by an influential member of the New York literati, Evert Duyckinck. In 1852 he greeted Hawthorne's campaign biography of Franklin Pierce by welcoming the author "down from the subtle metaphysical analysis . . . to a healthy encounter with living interests."[13] Three years later, an influential review in Britain discussed *The House of the Seven Gables* by concluding that "surely this pretty creation [Phoebe] of Mr. Hawthorne's must stand for the Middle Classes of Society, to whom has been committed by Providence the mission of social reconciliation which, once completed, the disunited are joined, the unblest, blessed, and the 'wild reformer' becomes a Conservative after Heaven's own fashion."[14] Four years before the end of Hawthorne's life, E. P. Whipple, the American critic who was considered by Hawthorne himself to be the most instructive and perceptive of all his reviewers, wrote a retrospective essay in which he found in Hawthorne an attitude that is at the center of the Romancer's utopian conservatism. He attributes to Hawthorne "a misanthropy which remorselessly looks through cursing misanthropes and chirping men of the world with the same sure, detecting glance of reason . . . a misanthropy which has no respect for impulses, but has a terrible perception of spiritual laws."[15] And in a memorial tribute that aimed directly at Hawthorne's art within the context of the vast political tides of the Civil War, the conservative George William Curtis also noted the essential center when he wrote that Hawthorne "does not chide you if you so end effort and life itself in the ardent van of progress, but he asks simply, 'Is six so much better than half a dozen?' He will not quarrel with you if you expect the millennium tomorrow. He only says, with that glimmering smile, 'So soon?' "[16] Yet, when he considered the upheavals of the war and the detached serenity of Hawthorne's fiction, even Curtis could not help but speculate about the withdrawal in Hawthorne that kept his fiction in the realm of fantasy and never really reflected the enormous and passionate historical turmoil of which the external world was made. Hawthorne's background materials never became his true foreground materials. His neglect of the Civil War in his writings is less the mystery it appears than it is one more expression of the political internalizations through which his temperament chose the tale and the Romance over the sketch and the novel.

Like the English socialist who had commented on Hawthorne's earlier career, Curtis failed to see that Hawthorne had made a strength out of his weakness by spending his life in a struggle with the politics of his self. The thematic polarities of his fiction—"The Artist of the Beautiful," as contrasted with "The Birthmark"—are a dialogue of oppositions. Just as the prefaces are Hawthorne speaking to his society, the fictions are Hawthorne talking to himself, as though in anticipation of W. B. Yeats's famous dictum about poetry and rhetoric. But in Hawthorne's case, it is necessary to insert a middle area, in which his conflicts connected art and politics: the rhetoric of our arguments with others makes politics; our politics make our arguments with ourselves; out of our arguments with ourselves comes art. Hawthorne's prefaces are duplicitous in the root sense of the word: they are an expression of his double sense that his art is a commodity for the literary marketplace in which he was a vendor and his art is also the production of a utopia unfit for that market. They are statements about the politics of relationship, the connective arguments between the American romancer and his mid–nineteenth-century society.

III

"the obscurest man of letters"

In the frequently quoted preface to the 1851 edition of the *Twice-Told Tales,* Hawthorne staked his famous "claim to one distinction, which as none of his literary brethren will care about disputing it with him, he need not be afraid to mention. He was, for a good many years, the obscurest man of letters in America." But the retrospective statement following his claim to obscurity is not often repeated by posterity, and yet it tells us more about that obscurity than the claim itself. For Hawthorne then suggests that he was acutely aware of what his relative successes were and where the road to popular notice began: "These stories were published in magazines and annuals, extending over a period of ten or twelve years, and comprising the whole of the writer's young manhood, without making (so far as he has ever been aware) the slightest impression on the public. One or two among them, the 'Rill from the Town Pump' in perhaps a greater degree than any other, had a pretty wide newspaper circulation; as for the rest, he had no grounds for supposing that, on their first appearance, they met with the good or evil fortune to be read by anybody" (IX, 3).

Yet contemporary reviews prove that if Hawthorne really meant what he said, and sought acclamation not from the tastes of a wide populace but primarily from that discriminatingly all-congenial "Gentle, Kind, Benevolent, Indulgent, and most Beloved and Honored Reader" he was to invoke in the preface to *The Marble Faun,* he already had it during his years of obscurity. At least two reviews, one in *The Token* for 1836 and one for 1837, hailed his work and called him "the most pleasing writer of fanciful prose," and "second to no man in the country" always "except Washington Irving."[17] Lewis Gaylord Clark, in the November 1837 issue of the *Knickerbocker Magazine*, asserted that the author of "Peter Goldthwaite's Treasure and the *Twice-Told Tales* is a man whose writings are *well* known in every sense to our readers."[18] This is not to say that Hawthorne met with widespread early accolades, but he did attain special recognition during those years when, with his eyes on the best sellerdom that was accorded to others, he sighed about his unique obscurity.

Edgar Allan Poe described the mingling of discriminating approval and minor popularity that characterized the reception of Hawthorne. Quoting himself from the preface to his sketches of the "New York Literati," Poe asserted that in his own mode Hawthorne "evinces extraordinary genius, having no rival either in America or elsewhere; and this opinion I have never heard gainsaid by any one literary person in the country . . . this opinion, however, is a spoken and not a written one." And then Poe added, "The reputation of the author of 'Twice-Told Tales' has been confined, indeed, until very lately, to literary society; and I have not been wrong, perhaps, in citing him as *the* example, *par excellence*, in this country, of the privately-admired and publicly-unappreciated man of genius."[19] What Hawthorne remembered in 1851 when he wrote about his obscurity in the 1830s was not that he had had no serious literary recognition but that he had had relatively little *popular* success and fame in the mass media of his day. We must see Hawthorne in a slightly different light from that of his own arranging when we consider that at least one part of this avowedly hermitic man, who asserted a deliberate cultivation of anonymity and expressed a desire for only those readers who could meet him on high Parnassian slopes, actively sought and sorely missed popular success and public recognition on the broad literary plain.

Fourteen years after the *Twice-Told Tales* were first collected (1837), and after Hawthorne had published *Grandfather's Chair* (1841), the second edition of *Twice-Told Tales* (1842), *Mosses from an Old Manse* (1846), *The Scarlet Letter* (1850), had seen *The House of the Seven Gables* (1851) through the press, and had become widely hailed as a literary genius, he still so smarted from his earlier public anonymity that he had to say out loud that he did not smart, that he was, after all, only quietly amused. Every line of the preface to the 1851 edition of the *Tales* is aimed at creating the impression that, although as a young writer he had been saddened and mildly hurt, he had always been above it all. Consequently, the preface carefully suggests the picture of the author as a meditatively and cozily sequestered observer, a quietly wry

man who is self-critically concerned with excellence and not popular
acclaim, the thought of which brings a faint, self-mocking smile fleetingly
to his lips. "I always really knew better," he is saying to the public. "You
didn't really touch me."

To this day, despite mid–twentieth-century biographical attempts to
the contrary, we tend to perpetuate the image Hawthorne himself helped
most to create: the reserved and gentle man who shrank from public
light and attention, the shy man of patient literary integrity who would
not prostitute his gifts and visions by writing merely popular pieces, the
despairingly amused and benevolently sad man of quiet manner and
thoughtful habits who brooded alone and who would give the world
only his truest and best regardless of whether that truest and best failed
to become novas of success in the popular literary firmament. Disdain-
ful of ephemera, here was the last man in the world who would ever live
on Grub Street.

From all accounts by those who knew him, Hawthorne was that man.
But by no means was he only that man. His prefaces, read together as
one continuous piece, protest a bit too much. Too consistently he depre-
cates what he offers the public, so that a later age is entitled to a few
suspicions. One sees the modesty and the sharp self-criticism, certainly,
but one also detects a shuffling of feet, an embarrassment that he might
receive the praise with which nonetheless he is strongly concerned. If
the pieces are that bad, why expect praise? If the pieces do not warrant
praise, why publish them? The almost obsessively repetitive self-
deprecation goes beyond literary convention and should not be dismissed
as merely an auctorial pose. For someone who was aloofly amused by
and finally indifferent to popular success, Hawthorne recurred too
constantly to the matter, like an animal licking a wound. He kept
bringing the subject up only to set it aside with one quiet sigh too many.
The cumulative effect of all that soft suspiration across these many
years is the echo of a crescendo.

Wryly offering *Grandfather's Chair* in 1841 as a "ponderous tome,"
for instance, Hawthorne asserts that "the author's great doubt is, whether
he has succeeded in writing a book which will be readable by the class
[children] for whom he intends it." In 1846 the *Mosses from an Old
Manse* are merely

> idle weeds and withering blossoms I have intermixed with some that were
> produced long ago—old, faded things, reminding me of flowers pressed
> between the leaves of a book—and now offer the bouquet, such as it is, to
> any whom it may please. These fitful sketches, with so little of external
> life about them, yet claiming no profundity of purpose,—so reserved,
> even while they sometimes seem so frank,—often but half in earnest, and

never, even when most so, expressing satisfactorily the thoughts which they profess to image,—such trifles, I truly feel, afford no solid basis for a literary reputation. Nevertheless, the public—if my limited number of readers, whom I venture to regard rather as a circle of friends, may be termed a public—will receive them the more kindly, as the last offering, the last collection, of this nature which it is ever my purpose to put forth. Unless I could do better, I have done enough in this kind. (X, 34)

Nevertheless, five years later when his increased fame had made the market appropriate for it, he put out a new edition of *Twice-Told Tales,* for which he wrote the famous preface. And nine months thereafter he published yet more "in this kind," *The Snow Image and Other Twice-Told Tales.* And in 1854 he even published a second edition of the *Mosses.*

The "Custom House" preface to *The Scarlet Letter* is replete with ironic self-deprecation (how defensive his society made him feel about the vocation he championed!) and the usual insistent presentation of his own obscurity. This preface, more than any other, reveals Hawthorne's sense of the social context of the Romance and the actual, the politics of his vocation within his American civilization. Especially, therefore, the statements about obscurity strike a false note; they contain an element of coy self-congratulation coming as they do at least four years after the time that Hawthorne's emergence into the public eye was noted by no less shrewd and professional an observer of the literary scene than Poe. Side by side with Hawthorne's serious discussion of his spiritual expatriation and his declaration of vocational independence, there is still the same old need for a demurrer to any claim to worth or fame. If my "faculties" are "found so pointless and inefficacious," he murmurs, "the fault was mine. The page of life that was spread out before me seemed dull and commonplace only because I had not fathomed its deeper import." And a year later, in the letter to Horatio Bridge that serves as his preface to *The Snow Image,* he drags forth the same old plaint, by now so threadbare as to have hardly any substance within the context of the actuality of his reputation: "I have been addressing a very limited circle of friendly readers, without much danger of being overheard by the public at large ... the habits thus acquired might pardonably continue, although strangers may have begun to mingle with my audience" (XI, 3). Characteristically, he passes himself off as a "fiction-monger" and at the same time asks, "But was there ever such a weary delay in obtaining the slightest recognition from the public as in my case?" (XI, 5). And he must add yet once more that "the public need not dread my again trespassing on its kindness, with any more of these musty and mouse-nibbled leaves of old periodicals, transformed, by the magic arts of my friendly publishers, into a new book" (XI, 6). And even two years after that he must insist that the reworking of ancient myths in the *Tanglewood Tales* is not a matter of the author's own talents, for "the stories (not by any strained effort of the narrator's, but in harmony with their inherent germ) transform themselves." As late as 1859, when he published *The Marble Faun*, it would have been altogether too blatant to claim a failure to attract a public. But—he claimed he had *lost* his public.

It had been five years since Hawthorne had appeared in print with the second edition of *Mosses from an Old Manse*, but he counted "seven or eight years (so many, at all events, that I cannot precisely remember the epoch) since the Author of this Romance last appeared before the Public." The *epoch?* Enough time out of the literary marketplace, at least, to be able to assert a loss of the attention that he had hitherto claimed he never had. With genial modesty he evoked the memory of that hypothetical "all sympathizing critic" for whom he had written his works. "I had always a sturdy faith in his actual existence, and wrote for him, year after year, during which the great Eye of the Public (as well it might) almost utterly overlooked my small productions." And surely, even if once won, that "Gentle Reader, in the case of any individual author, is apt to be extremely short lived; he seldom outlasts a literary fashion. . . . Therefore, I have little heart or confidence (especially, writing, as I do, in a foreign land, and after a long, long absence from my own) to presume upon the existence of that friend of friends" (IV, 1, 2). And so back to neglect and obscurity. The compulsive continuation of Hawthorne's concern with public attention is a proof of his awareness not only of a popular literary market but of his tactical vocational relationship to it. Despite the image of Hawthorne, one can never safely assume that he wrote without at least part of his brain fashioning his productions according to the demands of the literary market and popular success. His sense of failure therein, though not consonant with the facts of his reputation within his own lifetime, never left him. He never boomed along at the flurrying center of slick and sentimental financial success as the "damned mob of scribbling women" and Nathaniel Willis did. He knew their stuff was cheap and his was serious, and he hurt to see them sell their productions with constant financial and popular triumph to that same stupid public for whose acclaim he longed and from which he sought enormous fame. Even as late as the penultimate year of his life, in the dedicatory epistle to Franklin Pierce, with which he introduced *Our Old Home* (1863), Hawthorne quietly discounts "these poor sketches" because they merely "in their humble way ... *belong entirely to aesthetic literature* [italics mine], and can achieve no higher success than to represent to the American reader a few of the external aspects of English scenery and life" (V, 3). He could never quite shed his vocational defensiveness, and what was initially a partly true statement about obscurity becomes, first, coy, then, an unattractive tic. Finally, it becomes quite sad and revelatory in the overall perspective gained from the extremely instructive exercise of reading all of Hawthorne's prefaces chronologically at one sitting, within the context of the reviewers' actual responses from the beginning of his career. Only in the prefaces to *The House of the Seven Gables* (1851) and *A Wonder-Book for Girls and Boys* (1851), and, later, at the peak of whatever literary security and confidence he ever had, in the preface to *The Blithedale Romance* (1852), did Hawthorne display little or none of the self-deprecation and veiled resentment of the popular literary marketplace that form one of the central concerns of all his other prefaces. He might feel ashamed that his ancestors would be filled with contemptuous exasperation because their worthless descendant, a mere storyteller, "might as well be a fiddler." But even classic authors have standard ambitions.

IV

"How proud you would feel to see my works praised"

When he was seventeen and was considering vocations, Hawthorne wrote to his mother that he would not consider the ministry ("I was not born to vegetate forever in one place, and to live and die as calm and tranquil as—a puddle of water"), the law, or medicine. But, "what do you think of my becoming an author and relying for support upon my pen? Indeed, I think the illegibility of my handwriting is very author-like. How proud you would feel to see my works praised by the reviewers, as equal to the proudest productions of the scribbling sons of John Bull."[20] Not only were the reviewers and literary fame in his mind from the very beginning, but he devoted, as he said more seriously, "the whole of the writer's young manhood" to his calling. Any man who from his youth onward sacrificially makes such a heavy investment in an attempt to open an intercourse with the world most assuredly has an eye on the world's response. He even paid to have his first book, *Fanshawe* (1828), published anonymously. Although he was ever afterward ashamed of that book and shortly following its publication never thereafter acknowledged it, he nonetheless had in mind at least two other books, volumes of tales, that he hoped would be considerable bids for popular

literary eminence. Hawthorne was hardly unique in this. Alfred, Lord
Tennyson, Percy Bysshe Shelley—dozens of writers—have subsidized
their own early work. Probably all writers have some fervid motivating
ambition for fame. It is not that Hawthorne must be singled out to be
accused of desire for popular success, but the fact must be kept in mind
simply because he tried so hard to deny it.

In the general context of his personality and history, the lasting
image Hawthorne created of a man reluctantly breaking his privacy is
the truth, but it is far from the whole truth. It fails to communicate the
young man's desire for recognition and preeminence, a preeminence he
eventually attained. Between 1837, the publication of his first acknowledged book, and 1850, the critical reception was very favorable indeed;
and from 1850 on it was enormously favorable. Scrutiny of the critical
response following *The Scarlet Letter* reveals that Hawthorne increasingly was hailed—and very publicly—as the foremost living writer in
American literature, and during the last dozen or so years of his life he
was named more than any other as America's greatest author.

The contemporary reviews make it clear that except for a few attacks—
ranging from general disapprobation to vitriolic condemnation, mostly
from churchmen outraged by *The Scarlet Letter* —Hawthorne really had
no need to complain about his reception as a serious author. His
dissatisfaction cannot be said to derive legitimately from his treatment
as a literary monument but rather from his treatment as a professional
ambitiously competing for sales in the popular market. It seems too
manifest to state and restate the simple observation that Hawthorne was
a practicing professional in the popular market, but given the tradi-
tional image of Hawthorne—and it is within those outlines that we
tend to think of him—it is precisely the fact of the competing professional that most needs restatement. Comprehension of Hawthorne's
concern with his own vocational identity, and by extension comprehension of the identity of the artist in mid–nineteenth-century America,
involves the recognition that Hawthorne created his enduring works in
a context that included, among nobler artistic and moral motivations, a
lifelong attempt to capture the popular market.

Even at the very beginning, in contrast to the general quality of the
market, Hawthorne's work was so noticeable that he became an instant
success with the editors, who clamored to have his work not only for the
annuals but also for newspaper and magazine publication. S. G. Goodrich,
who published the highly successful *Token* in Boston, constantly put
Hawthorne into print. The 1837 volume, for instance, was practically a
Hawthorne issue, containing eight of his pieces. In the 1830s, when, as
"the obscurest man of letters in America," he was learning and breaking

into his trade, Hawthorne enjoyed newspaper, magazine, and giftbook publication at the average rate of one piece approximately every two weeks. He knew his literary world.

In writing for that world, Hawthorne almost never wrote about the political conflict between his vocation and his marketplace without creating the familiar clusters of opposing images that denote the imaginative world and the actual world as signs of the conflict within him: moonlight versus noonlight, secluded nook versus public square, clouds versus machinery, flowers versus law books, brooding versus action, ghosts versus beef-and-ale citizens, isolation versus sociability, past versus present, Romance versus novel, tale versus sketch, cloudland versus current events, dreams versus actualities, "somewhere else" versus "Salem," and, perhaps most important, artistic integrity versus the demands of society. What the imagery says about the distinct nationalities of Hawthorne's multiple citizenship is corroborated by the lessons Hawthorne learned from his marketplace.

V

"a refined taste cultivated among us"

Even in the act of recommending *Fanshawe* to her readers, Sarah Josepha Hale made depressingly clear which set of images had priority in the thriving young nation. If "the time has arrived when our American authors should have something besides empty praise from their countrymen," she asserts in a significantly left-handed way, nevertheless, "our institutions and character demand activity in business; the useful should be preferred before the ornamental; practical industry before speculative philosophy; reality before romance. But still the emanations of genius may be appreciated, and a refined taste cultivated among us."[21] There were few disagreements in the ideologies of taste and virtue among ladies and gentlemen. A leading male member of the literary scene, Charles Fenno Hoffman, offers the same ambiguous compliment to Hawthorne in an 1838 review of the *Twice-Told Tales*. Specifying the "types of the soul of Nathaniel Hawthorne" as a "rose bathed and baptized in dew—a star in its first gentle emergence above the horizon," he then put matters in their proper perspective:

Minds, like Hawthorne's, seem to be the only ones suited to an American literary climate. Quiet and gentle intellect gives itself, in our country, oftener to literature, than intellect of a hardier and more robust kind. Men endowed with vigorous and sturdy faculties are, sooner or later, enticed to try their strength in the boisterous current of politics or the Pactolian stream of merchandize.... Thus far American authors, who have been most triumphant in winning a name, have been of the gentler order. We can point to many Apollos, but Jove has not yet assumed his thunder, nor hung his blazing shield in the sky.... Yet men like Hawthorne are not without their use; nay, they are the writers to smooth and prepare the path for nobler (but not better) variants, by softening and ameliorating the public spirit.

That spirit implicitly is one of resistance to a "refined taste." And despite the disclaimer of "(but not better)," Hoffman turned into explicit statement the ideological overtones inherent in the nationalistic public utility of literature. Hoffman reserves his highest praise for Hawthorne's evocation of *native actualities:* "His pathos we would call New England pathos ... it is the pathos of an American, a New Englander. It is redolent of the images, objects, thoughts, and feelings that spring up in that soil, and nowhere else. The author of *Twice-Told Tales* is an honor to New England and to the country."[22] The implications have clear pertinence to a man of Hawthorne's hungry and divided ambitions. To be an American is to deal in actualities. To be an American writer is to evoke American actualities. To be a successful American writer is to seek appropriate verisimilitude—a nationalistically pleasing "reality" —for "Jove's" *foreground* purpose of literature; it is to write the novel and the sketch rather than the Romance and the tale. To be a successful, manly American writer, a "Jove" rather than an "Apollo," is to embrace the genres of ideological conservatism dictated by nationalistic optimism.

The functions of romance, tale, novel, and sketch were defined implicitly and explicitly in terms of Americanness and manliness. The reviews of the early nineteenth century make it apparent that these generic terms were freighted with ideological meaning. There was not a precise or reliably constant systematic definition of the terms; nevertheless, there was a generally consistent usage. The largely settled implications generated by these terms allow us to see the major tendencies of meaning in Hawthorne's day despite an occasionally confusing interchangability of vocabulary.

The Romance, like its shorter counterpart, the tale, was ostensibly a matter for feminine sensibility: it was ethereal, imaginary, and—the hint suggested—perhaps luxurious. It was a poetry to be indulged as a privilege of those who, uncommitted to the actualities of the real world, have time for "a refined taste cultivated among us." In the culture's Puritan-Yankee heritage, fiction itself was often suspected as at best merely pleasantly entertaining and at worst as morbidly misleading; but still, there was fiction and there was fiction. Fiction was acceptable and perhaps even useful when it performed an ideologically pleasing, didactic function. The novel, like its shorter counterpart, the sketch, was ostensibly more suited to the manly taste (and therefore was also better for ladies): it reported actualities, as did Anthony Trollope's books, or Cooper's. In the day before transportation and communication could make other social strata and other societies an available part of the average citizen's daily life, the novel could usefully broaden readers' knowledge by educating them into news of the world. Verisimilitude takes the highest priority. Unlike the Romance, the novel was verifiable insofar as its characters and actions supposedly could be validated as products of a time and a place and a way of life, and their psychology and values could be explained by reference to a history and environment. The sketch might or might not be fiction, but in either case it served the same didactic purpose as the novel, and both existed in the metonymic context of realism.

Of course, a tale might be a morally and aesthetically muscular piece, profoundly touching on human realities, as in the case of Hawthorne's and Melville's tales; and a sketch might be fashionable froth or idle reportage or shallow sentiment; but the general supposition was that the Romance was moonlight and dreams whereas the novel was sunlight and beef-and-ale. Although at its best all literature was to be acceptably instructive, at their worst the Romance and tale were "morbid" and "diseased" when foreground allegory or gothic sensation pushed the proper ideological homiletics and literary functions into "shadow" or "gloom." What this judgment amounted to in marketplace evaluation was that literature was "morbid," "diseased," and "subjective" when it deviated from conventional ("objective") models of gender roles (the chaste lady, the gentleman of actualities) for national stereotypes (cheerful moral and material progress). To be "morbid" was to be un-American, un-Christian, and unhealthy.

Woe, Hawthorne learned, unto the writer who took "morbid" liberties with American actualities. Clerical reviewers took Hawthorne to task for his sins. One representative and anonymous cleric charged that *The Scarlet Letter* "involves the gross and slanderous imputation that the colleague pastor of the First Church in Boston, who preached the Election Sermon the year after the death of Governor Winthrop, was a mean and hypocritical adulterer. . . . How would this outrageous fiction, which is utterly without foundation, deceive a reader who had no exact knowledge of our history!" The reviewer's outrage is motivated by the need to vindicate one's own, but there is more to it than that. The grounds upon which the critic bases his attack is one of actualities, a didactically as well as ecclesiastically utilitarian view of literature as national(istic) history: "Seeing that many readers obtain all their knowledge of historical facts from the incidental implications of history which are involved in a well-drawn *romance,* we maintain that a *novelist* has no right to tamper with actual verities. His obligation to adhere strictly to historical truth is . . . to be exacted . . . and we venture to question his right to misrepresent the facts and characters of assured history" [italics mine; the terms are indiscriminately used here, as was often the case]. And noting the insistently public and contemporary nature of the setting of *The Blithedale Romance,* the reviewer remarks that if Hawthorne "shaded and clouded his incidents somewhat more obscurely, if he moved them farther back or farther off from the region of our *actual* sight and knowledge, he would be safer in using the *privileges of the romancer.* But he gives us such distinct and sharp boundary lines and deals so boldly with matters and persons, *the truth of whose prose life repels the poetry of his fiction,* that we are induced *to confide in him as a chronicler,* rather than *indulge him as a romancer.* "23

The assumptions here are entirely representative of the marketplace: good prose chronicling serves an educational and national function; romancing is permissible, but its poetic quality is a privilege to be indulged and is dangerous in its power when it is "well drawn." Reducing the imagined creature, Dimmesdale, to a literal fact, the critic gives a double force to his opprobrium. Apparently he would not object to a "well drawn" (read: realistic) complimentary portrait of the historical minister, for such a portrait presumably would not be a misrepresentation of fact. On the other hand, a complimentary portrait in a fiction with "the privileges of the romancer" to depart entirely from actualities would be something merely to be "indulged." But an uncomplimentary portrait, "well drawn" or otherwise, was to be condemned as contrary to national fact. Like the socialist reviewer and Orestes Brownson in their opposition to each other, this intolerant reviewer is also drawn toward the conflict between foreground and background that society's urge toward verisimilitude imposed upon the Romance. The serious literary market didactically demanded useful instruction through the presentation of actualities: verisimilitude. A male could seriously undertake *that* literary function. But the nationalistic aspect of the literary marketplace demanded that the perceived American actualities be complimentary. Consequently, although the marketplace thought that it was demanding instructive novelistic realism when it demanded verisimilitude, paradoxically it really was demanding a sentimental and propagandistic use of the essence of Romance (the idealizing imagination). Thus, actualities, verisimilitude, and acquiescence in the ideological conservatism of nationalistic optimism were intimately allied. When

Hawthorne made his now celebrated plaint in the preface to *The Marble Faun* that "actualities" are "so terribly insisted upon, as they . . . must needs be in America," he was making a cry de profundis in his conflict with vocation, utopia, and ideology. The inescapable lesson Hawthorne took from being a writer in America was that he could not escape the trap of verisimilitude and still be seriously considered as an important American male writer. He struggled with that trap all his professional life.

The paradox at the heart of the distinction between Romance and the novel is that although the marketplace demanded the novelistically "real" report of social scenes as the literary commodity most serviceable to the nation, the Romance was the real vehicle of American literary genius in the first half of the nineteenth century, just as the novel was that of the English. An important difference between the two nations was revealed in the paradox within the history of the genres.

As F. O. Matthiessen pointed out long ago in *American Renaissance*, in monarchical, undemocratic, and aristocratically class-defined England, where the shape of civilization was well established and the firmly defined society, in its long evolution, could be taken for granted, the status quo could afford to tolerate criticism. Society had room for the eccentric, and the literary marketplace left the writer relatively free to probe and question his early nineteenth-century, confident world. In democratic and egalitarian America, where the shape of the civilization was in a state of flux and the insecure society, in its new emergence, was extremely sensitive and self-conscious, the status quo could tolerate very little criticism. There simply was not enough cultural identity to allow anything to be given away. England, the envied object of resentment, the admired archenemy and archmodel of all American cultural pretensions, was the summation of all the repressive social crime and error in the human past. Her actualities were those of history, and they were bad. Closure. America, on the other hand, was the hope of paradise to be regained, the revolutionary dream of freedom and democracy that kindled the light of redemption for the world. American actualities, that is, were those of the future, and they were good. Openness. "The American Dream," the very millennialism of the American utopian imagination that hardened into the ideological conformity of Hawthorne's marketplace, intensified an impulse toward dream, toward transcendent actions and characters in fiction, larger than the metonymic actual, encompassing all human history as open metaphor, mythic, allegorical, symbolic, metaphysical—in sum, an impulse toward the Romance. The English and the Americans both recognized an element of national identity in the literary generic differences.

Materials familiar to all students of literature indicate the way those differences were perceived. When the Englishman Trollope mused on a Hawthorne letter, that quintessential practitioner of the novelistic was well aware of national as well as temperamental differences between his art and Hawthorne's. He quoted the remark Hawthorne made in a letter to his publisher, James T. Fields:

> It is odd enough that my own individual taste is for quite another class of novels than those which I myself am able to write. If I were to meet with such books as mine by another writer, I don't believe I should be able to get through them. Have you ever read the novels of Anthony Trollope? They precisely suit my taste; solid and substantial, written on strength of beef and through the inspiration of ale, and just as real as if some giant had hewn a great lump out of the earth, and put it under a glass case, with all its inhabitants going about their daily business, and not suspecting that they were made a show of.[24]

Trollope then said, "That is what he could read himself, but could not possibly have produced, — any more than I could have produced that 'Marble Faun' which has been quite as much to my taste as was to his the fragment of common life which he has supposed me to put under a glass case. . . . The creations of American literature generally are no doubt more given to the speculative, — less given to the realistic, — than are those of English literature. On our side of the water we deal more with beef and ale, and less with dreams. . . . But in no American writer is to be found the same predominance of weird imagination as in Hawthorne."[25]

The relation of nationality to literary genre was not the product of a moment of mutual admiration between two authors. Hostile reviewers made capital of the same sense of relation. Sir Leslie Stephen, for instance, nettled even after Hawthorne's death by the American's observations in *Our Old Home*, wrote a long retrospective review, in which he accused Hawthorne of having been too much concerned with "pure mind."

> This turn of thought explains the real meaning of Hawthorne's antipathy to poor John Bull. That worthy gentleman, we will admit, is in a sense more gross and beefy than his American cousin. His nerves are stronger, for we need not decide whether they should be called coarser or less morbid. He is not, in any proper sense of the word, less imaginative, for a vigorous grasp of realities is rather proof of a powerful than a defective imagination. But he is less accessible to those delicate impulses. . . . His imagination is more intense and less mobile. . . . The products of the two races partake of the national characteristics. . . . The intangible . . . not the

vivid reality . . . is the special aptitude of mind . . . probably easier to the American than the English imagination. The craving for something substantial, whether in cookery or in poetry, was that which induced Hawthorne to keep John Bull at arm's length.

Asserting that "Poe is a kind of Hawthorne and *delirium tremens,"* Sir Leslie concluded that Hawthorne is the type of "what is exquisitely fanciful and airy in the gentle artist."[26]

As Stephen's review indicates, the difference between British and American marketplaces did not depend upon insistence on actualities. Rather everything depended upon what kind of actualities and how they could be presented. Bumptious and defensive young America found it difficult to realize, let alone acknowledge, that though she derided British social conformities she practiced her own, that though she repudiated British imperialist expansionism, she was beginning her own, and that though she disclaimed old Europe's history and identities, she was very much part of them. The national portrait was to emphasize the difference between the actualities of the parent and those of the child. The distinction between the "sunny" and the "morbid" in the first half of the nineteenth century in America reflected the nationalistic issues at the heart of the preference for actualities in the distinction between the Romantic and the novelistic. The distinction between America and England soon became internalized as a paradigm of division within America itself. There was America, the dream—the land of "somewhere else"; and there was England, the burgeoning growth of American political and economic hegemony—"Salem." The conflict between the two, in which American writers like Cooper and Hawthorne began to feel that the ideology was swallowing the utopia, that the actualities of America as historical fact were beginning to betray America as dream, helped to turn the American literary imagination away from the ideological conservatism of acquiescence in those actualities and toward Romantic dissent. Up until the Civil War, the realistic literature of actualities celebrated the assumptions of nationalism, and the Romance was the radical vehicle of dissent. The distinction between acquiescent celebration and radical dissent lay also in the derivations of the genres. In its function as vehicle of actualities, the novel descended from the instructional literary devices of a long past. The medieval romance, the morality play, the passion play, or the vision poem, like the secularized babee's book or mirror for magistrates in the Renaissance, served to explain and reinforce regnant ideologies and powers, whether those of the church or the nobility. Instructions in proper beliefs and successful conduct, these works dealt with the actualities of the prevailing world.

Even when going behind appearances, as did Machiavelli, in the implicit understanding of "this is how things are" there is an acceptance of the status quo. In essence, these instructions are works of closure. The nineteenth-century Romance, however, with its roots in the gothic, is quite something else. The gothic itself arose in that transitional moment when the Western imagination was developing from rational, Deistic admiration of the noble savage to the more unbuttoned primitivism of Romanticism. The development reflected a sense that the world picture had changed and that, consequently, established attitudes and values were in flux. The concept was itself new as thinkers shifted from Newtonian mechanism and fixity to Romantic organicism and development. The idea of the cosmos as Being in process necessarily accentuated the idea of transmutation and, therefore, of death, which gave rise to the gothic. The origins of the nineteenth-century Romance are matters of radical openness as evolutionist concepts began to replace what for centuries had been Ptolemaic and, most latterly, Newtonian stasis. The medieval and Renaissance concepts of the wheel of fortune were not concepts of development and change in the very identity of existence; they were concepts of divine order and repetition, change within the precedents and laws of history as reflections of divine appraisal of human frailty.

The Romantic imagination deified the commonplace, a tendency intensified in America by the ideologies of egalitarianism and democracy. The focus upon the commonplace tended to encourage realism. When the Civil War finally and traumatically forced a reappraisal of American actualities, the vehicle of realism, the novel, became the major literary instrument of dissent, and became so with a vengeance. But generally until the Civil War, the Romance and the tale in America tended to be the mode of the radical, which is another way of restating the conflict of vocation and marketplace, utopia and ideology, that bedevilled Hawthorne, who produced ideologically patriotic sketches— especially for children—at the same time that he wrote Romances and tales of partial alienation. Hawthorne's problem with actualities was shrewdly caught by a British reader of *The Marble Faun*, who, with the distance of the outsider, saw what Hawthorne's prefaces were really all about.

> There is a peculiar type of the American mind which is strongly in revolt against American utilities, and which is predisposed by the very monotony of its surroundings to hues of contrast and attitudes of antagonism. We have seen the manifestation of this revolt in American literature in Edgar Poe and even in Longfellow and Washington Irving. It is emphatically the desire of idealists like these and of Mr. Hawthorne to

escape from the "iron rule" of their country and the "social despotism" of their generation. They disdain to be parts of a complicated scheme of progress, which can only result in their arrival at a colder and drearier region than that they were born in, and they refuse to add to an accumulated pile of usefulness, of which the only use will be, to burden their posterity with even heavier thoughts and more inordinate labor than their own. This impulse induces them to become vagrants in imagination and reality, tourists in the old world of Europe, dreamers and artificers in the older world of poetry and romance.[27]

The reviewer goes on to note that in its presentation the American experience of Europe is characteristically more romantic and less matter-of-fact than the English.

What the reviews reveal is that the terrible insistence on actualities marked conservative reviewers on both sides of the Atlantic. But if American writers did not see native actualities the way their marketplace thought they should, they had "to become vagrants in imagination" and take out citizenship in the vocational "somewhere else" of the Romance, or "become vagrants in . . . reality" and go to Europe. Or both.

Clearly, like all nationalism in newly emerging nations, American cultural nationalism did not want objective truth. When the reviewers called for verisimilitude, they thought they meant verity or realism. But they did not seek photographic national self-portraits, warts and all. The nature of the sketches of actuality that editors bought and the injunctions of critical commentators make it clear that what was wanted was the prearranged and retouched photograph. The homely quotidian world was to be fabulized to the extent that foibles become a matter of quaintness and good humor; the real picture was to emerge as a group portrait of a lovely land in which the common folk are cheerful, bright, decent, good, respectable, solid, inventive, and energetic. The detailed sketch of common life preferably was to be realistic in technique, but the actualities so presented should conform to the society's optimistic assumption. If sketches were productive of melancholy or pathos (the ladies' market loved this), the result must be a pleasantly sentimental exercise in nationalistically acceptable heuristics. Paradoxically, the manly laborer in the young vineyards of American verisimilitude etherealized and idealized the violet in his sketches of actualities far more than did Hawthorne in any of his romances or tales of his utopian vision. The vehicle of verisimilitude enabled the writer to "Be true! Be true!" and the reader to say, "How real! How real!" and then to savor the self-gratifying aftertaste of the morals to be obtained from the apparently true portrait of himself. The "true" picture is a weapon in the struggle to create a national identity for a new country. The picture becomes a presentation to the foreigner, especially the judgmentally condescending British, but, more important, it becomes homefront proof that the nation is *in fact* fulfilling its millennialistic special destiny.

The idealizing verisimilitude of the Hudson River school of painting, coincident with the beginnings of Hawthorne's literary career in the 1830s, was an example of the vocabulary of a Romantic utopia ideologically conventionalized into national assumptions. The paintings are grand statements of the national sublime, their lines of perspective leading through vast sweeps of *openness* to the glowing source of light, where even yet more sublime landscape looms. They are stirring paintings of flowing light and space and, usually, a watercourse in motion, paintings, that is, of progress. So strong is the progress, so beautiful the landscape between the observer's viewpoint and the ultimate sublime, a sublime domesticated, as it were, that the paintings become warranties of the present as the actualized process in which the sublime is being attained. The idealizing verisimilitude functions in much the same ideological way as the collective farmscapes of socialist realism in the new Soviet nation of the 1930s. The difference is that in the Hudson River school the paintings sprang from a Romanticism to which individual artists, caught up in the exciting formulation of new conventions, gave their free, enthusiastic consent. Consciously or otherwise, they nationalistically selected and intensified the millennial beauty before them. Any given painting of socialist realism might very well have been the product of individual nationalist enthusiasm, but in any case the school was the result of state edict, in which the painters often had to falsify or literally invent the paintings' actualities, which were not the scenes of mass starvation historically experienced. The American mode was also coercive in that constraints were imposed, but not officially by the state. They were closure imposed by what amounts to officials of the marketplace: dealers, patrons, and galleries, aware of the commerce of their vocation and the tastes and needs of the buying public.

In Hawthorne's marketplace the coercions were active. For instance, the critic E. P. Whipple found *The House of the Seven Gables* "untrue" to "real" New England life until Phoebe was introduced:

> The whole representation, masterly as it is, considered as an effort of intellectual and imaginative power, would still be morally bleak, were it not for the sunshine and warmth radiated from the character of Phoebe. In this delightful creation Hawthorne for once gives himself up to homely human nature, and has succeeded in delineating a New-England girl, cheerful, blooming, practical, affectionate, efficient, full of innocence

and happiness, with all the "handiness" and native sagacity of her class, and so true and close to Nature that the process by which she is slightly idealized is completely hidden.[28]

If one were to italicize the vocabulary in the second sentence of the quotation to emphasize the representative rhetoric and values of the literary marketplace, almost every word would have to be underscored. In fact, perhaps even Whipple did not go quite far enough. Evert Duyckinck, in another friendly review, found that he had to reject even Phoebe, asserting that the sunlight of Phoebe was not a strong enough representation of daily American life, "hardly crystallizing the vapory atmosphere of the romance into the palpable concretions of actual life."[29] It is interesting that despite a lack of definitional precision in nomenclature, when the reviewers objected either to the absence or the morbid use of actualities, they categorized the work almost unfailingly as a Romance. When they praised a work for what William Dean Howells later called "the more smiling aspects of life, which are the more American," they called it a sketch or a representation. Henry Tuckerman, for instance, praised *The Scarlet Letter* in these terms: "The scenery, tone, and personages of the story are imbued with a local authenticity which is not, for an instant, *impaired* by the *imaginative* charm of the *romance* . . . so *life-like* in the *minutiae* and so *picturesque* in general effect are these *sketches* of still life [italics mine]." Fidelity to actualities in historical setting earned acclaim from Tuckerman for its *nationally useful* rendition of the past. Hawthorne, said Tuckerman, "has performed for New England life and manners the same high and sweet service which Wilson has for Scotland—caught and permanently embodied their 'lights and shadows.' Thus, with all the care in point of style and *authenticity* which mark his lighter *sketches* . . . *The Scarlet Letter* may be considered as an artistic exposition of Puritanism as modified by New England Colonial life. In *truth to costume, local manners and scenic features*, 'The Scarlet Letter' is as reliable as the best of Scott's *novels* [italics mine]."[30]

Conversely, when reviewers panned the book, they presented an opposing evaluation of exactly the same criteria: "We shall be disappointed if we look into *The Scarlet Letter* for any . . . portraiture of historical manners. There is a certain ghastliness about the people and life of the book, which comes from its exclusively subjective character. . . . The world it describes is untrue to actual existence."[31] Arthur Cleveland Coxe summed up the matter in a review that found *The Scarlet Letter* un-Christian and wished that Hawthorne had been reliable enough in his use of historical materials to show that the truth about churchmen in America's past was really both respectable and highly moral. *The Scarlet Letter*

> is an attempt to rise from the composition of petty *tales*, to the historical *novel. . . . It may properly be called a novel, because it has all the ground-work, and, might have been very easily elaborated into the details, usu-ally included in the term;* and we call it *historical*, because its scene-painting is in a great degree true to a period of our Colonial history, which ought to be more fully delineated. We wish Mr. Hawthorne would devote the powers which he only partly discloses in this book, to a large and truthful portraiture of that period, with the patriotic purpose of making us better acquainted with the stern old worthies, and all the *dramatis personae* of those times.[32]

Even Orestes Brownson, who ordinarily would find no sorrow in the discomfiture of Protestants, was incensed at what in his Catholic conservatism he saw as the un-American and un-Christian uses of *The Scarlet Letter's* historical details. He felt that he had to defend the Puritans and attack a work that had "merits" only if seen "from the position of a moderate transcendentalist and liberal of the modern school . . . but as little as we sympathize with those stern old Popery-haters, we do not regard the picture as at all just. We should commend where the author condemns and condemn where he commends. Their treatment of the adulteress was far more Christian than his ridicule of it."[33]

Like several others, Amory Dwight Mayo, Coxe, and Brownson reveal another dimension of the ideologically conservative uses of the sketch. *All* American time, not only the great national present, is patriotically sacrosanct and should disclose idealized actualities. The past should exemplify the very virtues demanded by currently established assumptions. Although the past thereby became the authoritative precedent, it still conflicted with utopian conservatism because it imposed popular nationalistic assumptions upon that precedent. With the popular ideology of the present becoming the authority of the past, the past is reduced from history to nostalgia: the literary sketch in the first half of nineteenth-century American popular culture was a conservative genre in essentially the same way that Norman Rockwell's *Saturday Evening Post* covers were in the first half of the twentieth.[34]

Consider, for instance, the white wooden church gleaming in the moonlit vale beneath the bright star on Christmas Eve. The orange lamplight glowing from the warm windows of old New England houses clustered about the snow-covered town green in the frosty twilight, the dark, surrounding hills silhouetted against the purpling horizon, the white fields and roads over which people are walking or sleighing to church, all create an appetizing picture of small town life. Lovely and typical. This is where the plain folks are, which is to say, the *real* folks. Rockwell's great talent is expressed in merging subjects so homely and uniquely recognizable that they become representative and typical, with a technique so fascinatingly realistic that anyone who has seen the winter panorama of a New England town cannot deny the actuality and therefore the "truth" of Rockwell's rendition of it. But the painting is an exquisitely careful selection and arrangement of details. Its technique advertises it to be the unretouched photograph that it is not. It is an ideological use of verisimilitude.

Because what we see is not what we necessarily are but what we would like to think we are, Rockwell's pictures are at once realistic, nostalgic, sentimental, and ideologically gratifying. In their intentions, effects, and audience, they are absolutely perfect products for the popular marketplace. They brilliantly exclude any examination of or question about the official ideologies upon which the American society is supposed to be based. They exclude serious explorations of that supposition's relationship to historical actualities. Rather, they are an affirmation of that supposition, and that is their superbly executed intent: love, neighborliness, simple humanity, simple religiosity, democracy, toleration, liberty, and the pursuit of happiness—often comic—are the homely actualities of everyday American life. Even though Rockwell's techniques of verisimilitude are more sophisticated than those of the earlier and more garish literary sketch, they are as culturally obvious in their nostalgia. Hawthorne's contemporaries, and Hawthorne himself, did exactly what Rockwell later did. In our time we assume a safe, familial, cozy, rich human warmth when we refer to old-fashioned folks and "the good old days and ways." We do not think of Hawthorne by electric light at a typewriter or a word processor. We think of him in a snug and shadowy old manse, musing by the fire, with the moonlight or candlelight or oil-lamplight imparting richness to the cozily shivery shadows. The quaint old good old times. But in fact, Hawthorne's own fiction, like that of his popular marketplace, is full of quietly yearning reference to quaint old, good old gentlemen and ladies and houses and ways and times. The surprising frequency of nostalgic imputation of value to *their* antecedent times (surprising only because the nation was relatively new and young) by Hawthorne and his contemporaries reflects, in part, the enormous popularity of writers like Washington Irving in Hawthorne's youth, just as our own nostalgia accounts for the popularity of artifacts of nostalgia in our resort shops and Christmas shops—and Norman Rockwell paintings.

Artifacts of nostalgia can function to fix historical differences, as when *1984* or *Brave New World* fix the implicit difference between a past society and the horrible inhumanity of the fiction's present moment. The good old human times are gone. But that use of nostalgia necessarily is confined either to types of science fiction and fantasy or to acutely ideological treatments of dramatic discontinuities in history, as in *Doctor Zhivago* or any presentations of Gulag or Holocaust or traumatically dramatic event. The American artifacts of nostalgia have just the opposite intention and effect: Rockwell shows us that we are *still* the good old folk. In effect, the good old days and ways are still here and discontinuities become *un*fixed. The Rockwellian artifact of nostalgia in the popular marketplace performs the complex function of covering the disjunction between the Romantic utopia and the conservative ideology: the progress that is the realization of a special national identity has not disappeared.

What gratifies the requirements of nationalism is welcome to the vulnerable individual self. Most particularly, those occupying uncertain social and economic identities are vulnerable to the lure of—and fear of failure of—nationalistic promises. In Hawthorne's as in Rockwell's America, perceived access to universally available upward mobility meant that those with doubtfully fixed identities (almost the entire population in almost every stratum of society) can become "real." For Hawthorne's as for Rockwell's populace, nationalistic promises already had been transmuted from the religious purposes of the seventeenth century, the Deistic hopes of the eighteenth, and the Romantic attitudes of the nineteenth into material success. Yet those visions continued to provide a rhetoric of ideology that never seems to become exhausted. The artifacts of American nostalgia continue to hold overtones of good Christianity as well as comfortable perfectibility—paradoxically, a stability of progress—associated with the plain old folks. (The Christmas shoppe's stocks of down-home, olde-tyme colonial and Victorian country-cute artifacts are neither commercially nor psychologically accidental.) Verisimilitude authenticates the belief that the common folk are the *real* folk and makes the belief mollifyingly visible. Verisimilitude provides the huge psychological service of identifying the yearning and yeasty mass as the satisfied and stabilized nation. Verisimilitude provides what might be called the realism of belief. For Hawthorne's marketplace the belief was bolstered by both radical ideology (it is the hitherto unfulfilled and exploited plain folk by and for whom the Revolution has been concluded successfully and its aims are put *in the process of realization,* as in a Hudson River painting) and conservative ideology (it is the plain folk who keep the world in its reliably stable place and protect it from dangerous innovation). The twentieth-century

Norman Rockwell, painter of town scenes, is the culmination of the nineteenth-century Hudson River School, itself a dramatization of the sketch and the openness therein celebrated in Hawthorne's marketplace. The political resonances of the sketch in the popular marketplace offer an illuminating clue to the apparently mysterious mingling of radicalism and ultraconservatism in American populism.

The nexus of individual and nationalistic needs, as expressed in art, is restated in the ideologically radical terms of openness that we see in the verisimilitude of differently selected actualities, such as one finds in radical art. In the 1930s, WPA paintings, for instance, provided the radical counterpart of Rockwell's conservative function for verisimilitude. The radical realism, more adventurously stylized than Rockwell's (openness shows), aimed at effects other than soothing. It made people nervous, for its depiction of the worker, the hungry good plain folk, intimated revolutionary change. The true and the good were not the process of realization of an already accomplished revolution, but the suggestion of a coming shift in status and power that is exactly the most basic threat to an identity-seeking bourgeois American society. The conservative uses of verisimilitude, however, provide the individual's identification with the huge power and goodness and beauty and rightness of the nation by offering what purports to be a mirror, precisely as Nathaniel Willis had done, thus appeasing the enormous and endless appetite of a population always close to the margins of identity. By articulating a sense of worth despite economic meagerness, the sketch pleases the lower and middle-middle classes; by providing a sense of tradition and continuity, the sketch provides the one thing that the placelessly arriviste upper-middle classes most need—a sense of settled identity and established culture. Nostalgia is neither incidental nor accidental. The conservative functions of verisimilitude explain why in Hawthorne's literary market and in Rockwell's graphics market the sketch of recognizable actualities is perceived as the art of the real people, and why criticism of it in the ideologies of democratic America is likely to be thought of as elitist, artificial, snobbish, effete, and unpatriotic—significantly, the very fears of which Hawthorne was so conscious in his vocational choices.[35]

Every emerging nation needs to create an advantageous history and lays claim to a significant past culture and a distinguished future in the same breath. And in the young America of the 1830s, the writer who helped create the required history was welcomed warmly. The praise that Henry Wadsworth Longfellow lavished on the *Twice-Told Tales*, for instance, endorsed for the tale the function of the sketch in slaking the huge nationalistic thirst:

One of the most prominent characteristics of these tales is, that they are national in their character. The author has wisely chosen his themes among the traditions of New England; the dusty legends of "the good Old Colony times, when we lived under a king." This is the right material for story. It seems as natural to make tales out of old tumble-down traditions, as canes and snuff-boxes out of old steeples, or trees planted by great men. The puritanical times begin to look romantic in the distance. . . . Truly, many quaint and quiet customs, many comic scenes and strange adventures, many wild and wondrous things, fit for humorous tale, and soft, pathetic story, lie all about us here in New England. There is no tradition of the Rhine nor of the Black Forest, which can compare in beauty with that of the Phantom Ship. The Flying Dutchman of the Cape, and the Klaboter-mann of the Baltic, are nowise superior. The story of Peter Rugg, the man who could not find Boston, is as good as that told by Gervase of Tilbury, of a man who gave himself to the devils by an unfortunate imprecation, and was used by them as a wheelbarrow; and the Great Carbuncle of the White Mountains shines with no less splendor, than that which illuminated the subterranean place in Rome, as related by William of Malmsebury.[36]

The repressive power of demands for nationalistically servile art in a totalitarian state is depressingly familiar in the twentieth century. But there can be an equally strong power in the organic, shared nationalism of a new nation in which artists and artisans, politicians and professionals, shoemakers and shopkeepers, farmers and foundrymen all feel them-selves mutually carried along in a common purpose and destiny. The kind of coercive patriotism that characterized the literary scene between the War of 1812 and the Civil War reveals the strength of organic cultural nationalism. Even Melville, who so despised the fulminations of the popular magazines, was swept up in the flood of manly literary nationalism. The same Melville who was to satirize nationalistic assump-tions as early as his third book, in the Vivenza sections of *Mardi*, the same Melville whose writings insist on an antixenophobic and anti-nationalistic universal common history and destiny of the human race, could sound like the veriest demagogue. In his famous review of "Hawthorne and His Mosses," Melville could at once make the ringing statement that "genius, all over the world, stands hand in hand, and one shock of recognition runs the whole circle round," and also write

let America first praise mediocrity even, in her own children, before she praises . . . the best excellence in the children of any other land. . . . If there were no other American to stand by, in literature, why, then, I would stand by Pop Emmons and his "Fredoniad," and till a better epic came along, swear it was not very far behind the Iliad. . . . And we want no American Goldsmiths; nay, we want no American Miltons. It were the vilest thing you could say of a true American author, that he were an American Tomkins. Call him an American and have done, for you cannot say a nobler thing of him. But it is not meant that all American writers should studiously cleave to nationality in their writings; only this, no American writer should write like an Englishman or a Frenchman; let him write like a man, for then he will be sure to write like an American.[37]

One might argue that the maverick Melville, wanting to perform a strong service for Hawthorne, deliberately played to the tastes of the marketplace. But even if the paean were privately and subtly satiric—which it probably was not—that the play was made is revealing. For the maverick or the independent, secure, educated and intelligent man of the establishment, like James Russell Lowell, the criteria were the same. Lowell greeted Hawthorne's tales for children, *Grandfather's Chair,* with a consciousness of New England history: "Mr. Hawthorne is making our New England history as delightful to the children as he already has to the parents. . . . He has painted the old New England character in true, but soft and harmonious, colors, and illustrated the gentle and more graceful elements of it by the retired simplicity of his life."[38] So also, Longfellow could exult that a "characteristic merit of . . . Hawthorne's writings is, that he seeks and finds his subjects at home, among his own people, in the characters, the events, and the traditions of his own country. His writings retain the racy flavor of the soil. They have the healthy vigor and free grace of indigenous plants."[39] Even though accounts of Old England were snapped up eagerly by a reading public that had few visual sources available to it and even slimmer personal hopes of European travel, readers and reviewers seemed agreed in their love of the celebration of New England. Even Brownson, who in 1842 was just about to turn against all his Romantic associations and associates, regarded "Mr. Hawthorne as fitted to stand at the head of American literature" because of "his sympathy with all that is young, fresh, childlike, and above all in his originality, and pure, deep feeling of nationality."[40]

If the artist were to be seen as a hero within the popular nationalistic context, that definition could not be made except within the context of the coercive ideologies of patriotism. As Richard Hofstader demonstrated in his study of antiintellectualism in American life,[41] the tradition within which the artist is defined goes back to the center of the definition of the plain, real man as the real American. Frontier practicality and hard pragmatism, combined with an exclusionary patriotic sense of special national destiny, in large part characterized the development of the American identity. The combination was virulently present in the very beginnings, in the Puritans' religiously intolerant and totally utilitarian theory of the nature and uses of art.

Hawthorne was fully aware of the cultural contexts. He employed an evidently conscious strategy in referring his own vocation back to his Puritan ancestors, as he did in the frequently cited passage in "The Custom House":

> "What is he?" murmurs one gray shadow of my forefathers to the other. "A writer of story books! What kind of business in life,—what mode of glorifying God, or being serviceable to mankind in his day and generation, —may that be? Why, the degenerate fellow might as well have been a fiddler!" Such are the compliments bandied between my great-grandsires and myself, across the gulf of time!

The evocation of his ancestors, in association with the central evocation of his Salem Americanness in "The Custom House," becomes not so much an imaginary bandying of compliments between himself and the past as it is one between Hawthorne and his contemporary society.

Poor Hawthorne! Caught in a heroic struggle with a very real loneliness, where was he to turn for his community? There was as yet no national sense of art as a profession. There were scattered groups of like-minded artists in New York and Boston, but there were no established, inclusive artists' centers such as New York, Boston, or San Francisco were to become. And there was no transregional vocational identity in which Hawthorne could establish a self in mutual support, competition, and excitement with fellow communicants. Retrospectively, Henry James was aware of what this meant to Hawthorne and of what Hawthorne meant in his lonely plaint that he always wrote with a chill in his spirit because he felt that he was writing in a vacuum. There were a few scattered precedents, such as Brockden Brown, Washington Irving, and James Fenimore Cooper; but Hawthorne also had the example of what happened to Cooper, both in the reviews and in his personal life, when the un-Americanism of Cooper's attitudes was defined. Upon Hawthorne, as the first male American writer of recognized greatness to devote his life professionally to Romance writing, fell the burden of creating the role and identity of the fiction writer as an acceptable and respectable member of the national community. There were gigantic and heroic allies (always excepting Melville because of his problematical relationship with Hawthorne) engaged in the lists of the imagination as vocation, most notably Poe, Emerson, Thoreau, and Whitman; but as the practitioner of the Romance, Hawthorne stood alone in his stature in the literary marketplace. And as a Classicist conservative, separated from Emerson, Thoreau, and Whitman, he keenly felt the paradox of his isolation. His most powerful and meaningful allies were utopian Romantics, writers with whom he could find little comfortable or lasting community. There was no place for him to go. No wonder he opted for "somewhere else." And because the only alternative domain was his own mind, no wonder he became weary of finding himself repeatedly involved in essentially the same tales of alienation, isolation, and integration. No wonder he felt himself turning into a ghost, for whose fleshly hand could he grasp?

Reification, corporealization, verisimilitude, all emanated as problems from an inescapable center: for Hawthorne the world of utopian conservatism in his mind was more of a reality than the world of progress that his contemporaries claimed lay all about in American actuality. The fictive representations of his inner world were the messengers of truth, or reality, which he sent out to the deluded, chimerical outer world. As such, they were "subjective" representatives of Romance writing as a vocation and of Hawthorne as a self. They were, in short, elements of autobiography.[42] But the autobiography toward which Hawthorne was groping was one of discovery rather than memory; his necessity was not to define himself according to all the accumulated details of actuality, but according to a definition of himself as a prophet to be honored in his own land. Paradox within paradox: what he had to do was to create himself in his vocation, within his time and place, according to the principles of Classicist closure in a world closed to any values but openness. And given the obdurate power of organic cultural nationalism and the terrible insistence upon actualities, his only autobiographical and self-creating recourse was to substitute the inner world for the outer. Perhaps it is not unfair to say that the larger, national values implicit in the strictures of the literary marketplace denied Hawthorne a fully embodied life.

His dilemma was that his hunger for popularity and esteem was one aspect of his need to discover and announce himself as both man and writer. This need brought him to a declaration of his utopian conservative vision. That proclamation brought him to the creation of the messengers from his mind. The primacy of that vision and the creation of those messengers brought him to a recognition of the opposition between his internal and external worlds. And recognition of that opposition only exacerbated his need to discover and announce himself. The circle of self-creation was endlessly self-generating. The politics of adjusting his opposing worlds and selves to each other became the repetitive round of a fictive autobiography of discovery with which Hawthorne finally became bored and sickened unto death. The significance of his eerie feeling that he himself had become an imaginary

being—a ghost—in terms of national culture is the same as the significance of his continual moan about lack of literary popularity.

Again it was an Englishman, with the perspectives of distance, who
was able to recognize the significance of Hawthorne's ghostliness. The
writer of the most observant and sensitive contemporary commentaries
on Hawthorne was, in my opinion, Richard Holt Hutton,[43] whose views
of Hawthorne's continuing disembodiment are worth quoting at length.
In a summary statement published two months after Hawthorne's death,
Hutton wrote:

> The ghostly genius of Hawthorne is a great loss to the American people. . . .
> He was really the ghost of New England,—we do not mean the "spirit,"
> nor the "phantom," but the ghost in the older sense in which that term is
> used as the thin, rarefied essence which is to be found somewhere behind
> the physical organization,—embodied, indeed, and not by any means in a
> shadowy or diminutive earthly tabernacle, but yet only half embodied in
> it, endowed with a painful sense of the gulf between his nature and its
> organization, always recognizing the gulf, always trying to bridge it over,
> and always more or less unsuccessful in the attempt. His writings are not
> exactly spiritual writings; for there is no dominating spirit in them. They
> are ghostly writings. He was, to our minds, a sort of sign to New England
> of the divorce that has been going on there . . . between its people's spirit-
> ual and earthly nature, and of the impotence which they will soon feel, if
> they are to be absorbed more and more in that shrewd, hard, earthly sense
> which is one of their most striking characteristics, in *communicating*
> even with the ghost of their former self.[44] Hawthorne, with all his
> shyness and tenderness and literary reticence, shows very distinct traces
> also of understanding well the cold, curious, and shrewd spirit which
> besets the Yankees even more than other commercial peoples. . . . Indeed,
> there are few of the tales without a character of this type. But though
> Hawthorne had a deep sympathy with the practical as well as the literary
> genius of New England, it is always in a far-removed and ghostly kind of
> way, as though he were stricken by some spell which half-paralyzed him
> from communicating with the life around him, as though he saw it only
> by a reflected light. His spirit haunted rather than ruled his body; his
> body hampered his spirit. Yet his external career was not only not romantic,
> but identified with all the dullest routine of commercial duties. That a
> man who consciously *telegraphed*, as it were, with the world, transmit-
> ting meagre messages through his material organization, should have
> been first a custom-house officer in Massachusetts, and then the consul in
> Liverpool, brings out into the strongest possible relief the curiously repre-
> sentative character in which he stood to New England as its literary or
> intellectual ghost. There is nothing more ghostly in his writings than his
> account, in his recent book, *Our Old Home,* of the consulship in Liverpool—
> how he began by trying to communicate frankly with his fellow country-

men, how he found the task more and more difficult, and gradually drew back into the twilight of his reserve, how he shrewdly and somewhat coldly watched "the dim shadows as they go and come," speculated idly on their fate, and all the time discharged the regular routine of consular business, witnessing the usual depositions, giving captains to captainless crews, affording costive advice or assistance to Yankees when in need of a friend, listening to them when they were only anxious to offer, not ask, assistance, and generally observing them from that distant and speculative outpost whence all common things looked strange. . . . The difficulty lay . . . in the greater feat of escaping from himself; and could he have done so, of course he would as much have lost his imaginative spell as a ghost would do who really returned into the body. That pallid, tender, solitary, imaginative treatment of characteristics and problems which have lain, and still lie, very close to the heart of New England,—that power of exhibiting them lit up by the moonlight of a melancholy imagination,—that ghostly half appeal for sympathy, half offer of counsel on the diseases latent in the New England nature,—were no eccentricity, but of the essence of his literary power. What gave him that pure style, that fine taste, that delicate humor, that touching pathos, in a great degree even that radiant imagination and consummate ingenuity, was the consciously separate and aloof life which he lived. Without it he might have been merely a shrewd, hard, sensible, conservative, success-worshipping, business-loving Yankee democrat, like the intimate college friend, Ex-President Pierce, whom he helped to raise to a somewhat ignominious term of power, and who was one of the mourners beside his death-bed. Hawthorne had power to *haunt* such men as these because he had nursed many of their qualities, thoughts, and difficulties, in a ghostly solitude, and could so make them feel, as the poor folks said figuratively of themselves after communing with the veiled minister, that "they had been with him behind the veil."

The only moment in which Hutton was not quite on target was when he asserted that "Hawthorne, who was a delicate critic of himself, was well aware of the shadowy character of his own genius, *though not aware that precisely here lay its curious and thrilling power* [italics mine]."[45]

More than a decade earlier, E. P. Whipple, to whom Hawthorne always listened closely, had argued himself into recognizing that Hawthorne's fictive strength as well as the source of his destruction lay in this ghostland he inhabited. Whipple had begun by admonishing Hawthorne about the lack of merger in his fiction between the public settings in the world of actualities and the functions and nature of the characters themselves. Shrewdly noting that Hawthorne's imagination is so bent upon the laws and ideas of that "somewhere else" from which he was sending messengers that the messengers tend to become disembodied ideas, Whipple commented as follows on *The House of the Seven Gables:*

> We do not know but that his eye is more certain in detecting remote spiritual laws and their relations, than in the sure grasp of individual character; and if he ever loses his hold upon persons it is owing to that intensely meditative cast of his mind by which he views persons in their relations to the general laws whose actions they illustrate. There is some discord in the present work in the development of character and sequence of events; the dramatic unity is therefore not perfectly preserved; but this cannot be affirmed of the unity of law. That is always sustained, and if it had been thoroughly embodied, identified, and harmonized with the concrete events and characters, we have little hesitation in asserting that the present volume would be the deepest work of imagination ever produced on the American continent.[46]

A year later, referring to *The Scarlet Letter* in a review of *The Blithedale Romance,* Whipple not only emphasized the point, but also came to see that it was from the imaginative realm of his utopian conservative vision that Hawthorne derived the unity of his art as well as the darkness that he held up to fascinated Salem's "light."

> In Hawthorne . . . persons are commonly conceived in their relations to laws, and hold a second place in his mind. In "The Scarlet Letter," which made a deeper impression on the public than any romance ever published in the United States, there is little true characterization, in the ordinary meaning of the term. The characters are not really valuable for what they are, but for what they illustrate. Imagination is predominant throughout the work, but it is imagination in its highest analytic rather than dramatic action. And this is the secret of the strange fascination which fastens attention to its horrors. It is not Hester or Dimmesdale that really interest us, but the spectacle of the human mind open to the retribution of the violated law, and quivering in the agonies of shame and remorse. It is the law and not the person that is vitally conceived, and accordingly the author traces its sure operation with an unshrinking intellect that, for the time, is remorseless to persons.[47]

The dilemma was indeed insoluble for Hawthorne. His intercourse with the world communicated something that was unreal and unacceptable to that world. He was not only the ghost haunting his own autobiographical mind but, as Hutton said, the ghost haunting his own society. *Nowhere* was there surcease from the terrible actualities of society and vocation. Even Edgar Allan Poe, the most slashing and disenchanted professional magazinist of the times, was not immune to the nationalistic insistence on actualities. Poe, of all people; Poe, who responded to nationalistic assertions like Melville's acceptance of Pop Emmons by insisting that a stupid book was not the better because its stupidity was American; Poe, who campaigned frantically for literature as the province of the imagination, not actualities, of "the trembling surrender of the soul to Beauty," not of intellectual or moral instruction; Poe, who detested both the ladies' magazines and the ironic and abhorrent fate that reduced him to writing for one of those very magazines (and a leading one at that) *sketches* of the New York literati, many of whom were prime examples of the kind of writer he loathed; Poe, the champion of fantasy, madness, and aesthetic principle against verisimilitude, the novelistic, and the gentilities of the marketplace—this Poe, in his parting admonition to Hawthorne, warned against too much continued "mysticism" in the tales and suggested a turn to actualities! Hawthorne, Poe said,

> has the purest style, the finest taste, the most available scholarship, the most delicate humor, the most touching pathos, the most radiant imagination, the most consummate ingenuity; and with these varied good qualities he has done *well* as a mystic. But is there any one of these qualities which should prevent his doing doubly well in a career of honest, upright, sensible, prehensible, and comprehensible things? Let him mend his pen, get a bottle of visible ink, come out from the Old Manse, cut Mr. Alcott, hang (if possible) the editor of "The Dial," and throw out of the window to the pigs all his old numbers of "The North American Review."[48]

Given Melville's earthy aspect, it is not surprising that the seafarer's Rabelaisian prescription for Hawthorne was "plenty of roast beef, done rare." And given Poe's total warfare against the New England Brahmins and the Transcendentalists, with whom Poe partly associated Hawthorne, it is not surprising that he should accuse Hawthorne of "a spirit of 'metaphor run mad' . . . clearly imbibed from the phalanx and phalanstery atmosphere in which he has so long been struggling for breath." Nevertheless, conventional marketplace wisdom from writers as supernal as Poe and as metaphysical as Melville indicates how alone Hawthorne must have felt.

A final lesson born in on Hawthorne by his milieu went under the rubric of what the reviewers loved to call "chiaroscuro." All genres and genders of literature were supposed to "make one think"—within the limits of respectability. Acceptable literature, as Melville and Whitman were to discover, avoided rugged originality, radical dissent, ugly experience and its frightening implications, and the highly eccentric. To be made to think in the literary marketplace was to be brought to a pleasantly melancholy state of mind in a musing consideration of experience that neither stretched nor basically challenged the polite limits of conventional Christianity or social and sexual respectability. To be merely entertained or brought to an aesthetic *frisson* was pleasant enough, of course, but it was not profound. But an excess of profundity— anything truly or acutely uncomfortable—was morbidity, and anything fanciful enough to be separated from the actualities was subjective. A writer who was consistently subjective or consistently morbid was accused of being monotonous. The term most commonly assigned to the thoughtful or profound aspects of literature was "shadow." Although a writer ran the risk of monotony if his work were all light or sunshine (he would be less substantial than the native genius demanded), just as he did if his works were all shadow (he would be morbid, and because gloom is not characteristic of the actualities of American life, he would also be subjective), clearly the market supported more happily those who were monotonously light than those who were monotonously umbrageous. As J. Donald Crowley pointed out, the influential editor and publisher, Samuel G. Goodrich, "put his finger on the public's preference for the simple and happy when he compared Hawthorne with Nathaniel P. Willis." Willis was all "sunshine and summer, the other chill, dark, and wintry; the one was full of love and hope, the other of doubt and distrust . . . it is, perhaps, neither a subject of surprise or regret, that the larger portion of the world is so happily constituted as to have been more ready to flirt with the gay muse of the one, than to descend into the spiritual charnel house, and assist at the psychological dissection of the other."[49] The best writers mingled light and shadow to create the highly desirable chiaroscuro. The sunshine of the sketch was there to shed light entertainingly on nationalistic assumptions; the shadow of the tale was there to offer a pensive tear to the lady and, if it were of too stern a stuff for the merely feminine sensibility, to offer thought-provoking truth to the manly.

The reviewers taught Hawthorne that he could expect charges of monotony, subjectivity, and morbidity when his works of fancy offered strong presentations of his utopian conservatism, but that he could expect a hosanna of chiaroscuros for his touches of humor, his pathos, his orthodoxy, his respectability, and his nationalistic services. Predictably, the works singled out as sketches were unexceptionably praised; the works singled out as tales or Romances received mixed response (praise was lavish, disapproval was harsh) depending upon whether they leaned toward sunshine or shadow. " 'The Birth-Mark,' 'Rappaccini's Daughter,' and 'Roger Malvin's Burial,' are the nettles and mushrooms of Mr. Hawthorne's mind," wrote Amory Dwight Mayo, reviewing the 1851 edition of *Twice-Told Tales*, "and certainly should not be tied up with a bouquet of flowers for the public. Perhaps we hate these tales the more, that they are bound in the same covers with 'The Celestial Railroad,' and 'Drowne's Wooden Image,' the happiest efforts of the author in sketch writing."[50]

When Hawthorne published the first edition of *Twice-Told Tales*, the response had been similarly instructive. Except for Longfellow, who liked everything in the book, light and dark, and for Poe, who admired the dark tales and detested the sketches, by far the great majority of readers and reviewers agreed in pointing at sunny sketches like "A Rill from the Town Pump" and "Little Annie's Rambles" as examples of the chiaroscuro they admired. Therein they found everyday American life "profoundly" presented with both humor *and* pathos. Hawthorne was not to forget that fourteen years later in his 1851 preface, nor was he to be unaware that only Poe and Melville were the consistent champions of the darkness in his work as the true and lasting greatness of his fiction. It is not accidental that when Melville began his essay on Hawthorne's *Mosses,* he felt it necessary to repudiate the prevailing opinion that Hawthorne was a writer of sunshine. More than personal taste was involved when Longfellow recommended Hawthorne to the ladies; Longfellow emphasized Hawthorne's moral instruction and variety. "Every woman," he wrote, "owes Hawthorne a debt of gratitude for those lovely visions of womanly faith, tenderness, and truth, which glide so gracefully through his pages. . . . His tragedy is tempered with a certain smoothness; it solemnizes and impresses us, but it does not freeze the blood, still less offend the most fastidious taste. . . . Indeed, over all he has written, there hangs, like an atmosphere, a certain soft and calm melancholy, which has nothing diseased or mawkish in it, but is of that kind which seems to flow naturally from delicacy of organization and a meditative spirit."[51]

Hawthorne's letters make it clear that, like the reviewers, what he most feared was monotony in his writings. Whipple had cautioned him against "excessive" gloom, and even when responses were friendly they were disturbed about what seemed to them a morbidity and subjectivity too unremitting for easy acceptance in the public market. In a review of *Twice-Told Tales* Poe speculated that "there is, perhaps, a somewhat too general or prevalent *tone* — a tone of melancholy and mysticism. The subjects are insufficiently varied. There is not so much of *versatility* evinced as we might well be warranted in expecting from the high powers of Mr. Hawthorne."[52] Henry F. Chorley, a friendly and acute English reviewer, reflected the message of many reviews when he said, "We have already so often expressed our pleasure in Hawthorne's . . . gem-like tales . . . that none, we apprehend, will mistake for covert censure

the recommendation we must now give him on the appearance of this
second volume the 1845 edition of *Twice-Told Tales* —to beware of
monotony. We do not say this because he chiefly loves the by-gone times
of New England,—nor, because of his manifest propensity towards the
spiritual and supernatural.... But we conceive our author to be a
retired and timid man, who only plays on his two strings because he
lacks courage or energy to master a third."[53] There was no doubt left to
Hawthorne about what the call for chiaroscuro meant in terms of the
political shadows within which his vision was cast.

In the need to temper radical art and utopian conservatism with the
ideological conservatism of acceptable views, Hawthorne learned from
chiaroscuro that all the lessons of the marketplace—actualities, manliness,
feminine sensibility, and the entire complex of significances implicit in
the sketch—were politically one. The purposes of literature were defined
by the boundaries of acceptability. "The worthy characteristics of a
truly National Literature," wrote Charles Wilkins Webber,

> certainly are those of a polished and elegant cultivation. . . . All we think,
> write, and say, must be tempered and modified by the *Real* —both moral
> and physical—around us. . . . Ours must be an honestly American—if it
> be not too much to say—an Aboriginal Literature! as distinct from all
> others as the plucked crown and scalplock of the red Indian—as vast, as
> rude, as wildly magnificent as our Mississippi, our mountains, or our
> Niagara—as still as our star-mirroring lakes at the North. . . . Hawthorne
> is national—national in subject, in treatment and in manner. We could
> hardly say anything higher of him. . . . [The moral reality to be found in
> the national actualities is that] . . . all that is wanted for the "Perfectibility"
> of the Race, is the requisite . . . conditions [*sic*] which will furnish . . . the
> capabilities for enjoying this Paradisiacal state a benevolent Providence
> has offered. . . . As an artist, in this respect, Hawthorne possesses the most
> consummate skill.[54]

In praise or condemnation, the criteria were the same. If, like unrelieved
shadow, the subjective was unmanly, a combination of the two was
downright unholy and un-American. As Twain was later to say in a
different but related context, it was French: attacking *The Scarlet Letter*
in a religious periodical, one righteous bishop was revolted equally
by the presentation of "the nauseous amour of a Puritan pastor"
and by Hawthorne's distortions of actualities in libelling a minister
historically innocent of the deed. "Is the French era actually begun in
our literature?" he roared. Hawthorne's conclusion, "Be true—be true,"
he asserts, should have been "Be clean—be clean."[55] As though in
rebuttal, Whipple praised *The Scarlet Letter* because "as an illustration
of the Divine order on which our conventional order rests, it is the

most moral book of the age; and is especially valuable as demonstrating the superficiality of that code of ethics, predominant in the French school of romance, which teaches obedience to individual instinct and impulse, regardless of all moral truths which contain the generalized experience of the race."[56] The dangers to one's identity were clear and present; one could lose one's Christian Americanness and, indeed, one's reality in one critical blow. Charles Hale complained that "no Yankee or Englishman could ever invest with so complete a fog of mystery the commonest object of our daily experience."[57] For an even worse condemnation than being French lay in store for the man whose Romances lose a sense of actualities: "There is something unearthly about all his characters as if he had been groping for them in the land of his dreams," Hale continued. "Mr. Hawthorne must be a German."

If the marketplace left no question about the relationship between one's national and artistic identities, it was particularly insistent on the subject in terms of the moral functions of literature. Because of the nature of his work, the moral criterion was applied especially and constantly to Hawthorne, and this was so from the beginning of his career. Appearing in his hometown newspaper, one of the earliest reviews of the first edition of *Twice-Told Tales* rhapsodized about the "delicate taste and quick perception," the "beautiful simplicity and elegance of style" that marked the volume. The value of the "finest touches of feeling and fancy" became clear in the comfortable judgment that "Mr. Hawthorne's quiet and cheerful humor brightens every view of human nature, while a tone of pensive feeling breathes out even from the lightest sports of his fancy. . . . *A fine moral tone pervades all the creations of his fancy.*"[58] And sixteen years later, after Hawthorne had become well established, even a British reviewer charged him with a "far graver" fault than his "supernaturalism" and his bent for the "metaphysical" and the "incredible": "that of making the moral subserve the art, instead of the art the moral; and furthermore, of even distorting moral truth, in order to obtain artistic effect . . . which, as it is formed at the expense of Christian reality, we do not hesitate to condemn."[59]

Orestes Brownson epitomized the extent to which an insistence upon acceptable and official morality blocked a critical penetration of fiction. When Hawthorne ventured upon an extended voyage into forbidden grounds with the plot of his masterpiece, *The Scarlet Letter*, Brownson responded bluntly. He warned his readers that "to the great body of our countrymen who have no well defined religious belief, and no fixed principle of virtue" the book "will be deeply interesting and highly pleasing." But as a moral commentator, Brownson announced himself uninclined toward "fashionable criticism."

> Mere literature for its own sake we do not prize. Men . . . are moral and accountable beings, and we look only to the moral and religious effect of their works. Measured by the paltry popular standard of morals in this age and community, Hawthorne can hardly be said to pervert God's gifts, or to exert an immoral influence. Yet his work is far from being unobjectionable. . . . It is a story of crime, of an adulteress and her accomplice. . . . Crimes like the one imagined . . . are not fit subjects for popular literature, and moral health is not promoted by leading the imagination to dwell on them. There is an unsound state of public morals when the novelist is permitted, without a scorching rebuke, to select such crimes, and invest them with all the fascinations of genius, and all the charms of a highly polished style. . . . No man has the right to love another man's wife, and no married woman has the right to love any man but her husband.

Having delivered universal truth, Brownson then opened a discussion of pride, which must have been of great interest to Hawthorne, for he proceeded to accuse Hawthorne of not doing exactly what he *did* do and of doing exactly what he did *not* do. Brownson complained about people who are "proud of their supposed virtue, free from all self reproach," and wished to say to them, "Would that you might commit some overt act, that should startle you from your sleep." Without ever recognizing that Hawthorne was preaching precisely the same text, Brownson concluded that *The Scarlet Letter* demonstrates that "Mr. Hawthorne seems never to have learned that pride is not only sin, but the root of all sin, and that humility is not only a virtue, but the root of all virtue." Having thus missed the point by concentrating upon the permissibility of Hawthorne's *materials,* Brownson was able to pronounce his moral verdict: "The work before us is full of mistakes . . . in those portions where the author really means to speak like a Christian, and therefore we are obliged to condemn it, where we acquit him of all unchristian intention."[60]

Despite the many ways in which it was contemporaneously unorthodox and carries germs of un-Christian existentialism, *The Scarlet Letter* is nevertheless a work shaped by Christian imagination, especially as manifested in Hester's career and the values that formed it. However, there can be little doubt that Hawthorne was made sharply aware of morality in the literary marketplace as Christian in explicitly conventional and respectable attitudes, even if the consequent shallowness militated against the deepest Christian strains that an author wished to embody in his work. The extent to which *The Marble Faun's* Hilda presents shallow, orthodox rigidity *triumphant*, almost a decade after the reception of *The Scarlet Letter*, is an indication of the extent to which the marketplace had its effect on Hawthorne. Even though most of the reviews were strongly favorable, Christian acceptability was a large topic in the critical reception. Although Brownson's review was extreme in its obtuseness and harshness, and although it was the voice of an ultramontane Catholic convert, it did not reflect an extreme or unusual point of critical departure in the largely Protestant marketplace. Hilda speaks also in the voice of the Episcopal bishop, Arthur Cleveland Coxe, thundering against *The Scarlet Letter*. Writing out of "the pure motive of building up a sound and healthful literature for our country," this avowedly conservative man made clear that

> the voice of the Church must be made more audible to the American public in general, and thus may exercise, for the benefit of popular authors, some salutary influence upon public taste. Our mission . . . is . . . rather religious than literary . . . in an age when literature makes very free with religion. [In this context, Coxe is] astonished at the kind of incident which [Hawthorne] has selected for romance . . . it seems to us that good taste might be pardoned for not giving [such incidents] prominence in fiction [especially at a moment when] a running undertide of filth has become . . . requisite to a romance. [Therefore, the bishop concludes,] "The Scarlet Letter" has already done not a little to degrade our literature, and to encourage social licentiousness: it has started other pens on like enterprises, and has loosed the restraint on many tongues, that have made it an apology for "the evil communications which corrupt good manners." We are painfully tempted to believe that it is a book made for the market, and that the market has made it merchantable, as they do game, by letting everybody understand that the commodity is in high condition and smells strongly of incipient putrefaction.[61]

Some commentators recognized that the book was the high point of Hawthorne's production and that it announced a new leader of genius in the advancement of American literature. But when reviewers became uneasy, they became uneasy about the subject matter of the book, about the gloom, and about the relationship between Christian pieties and the uses of a national literature. If there was any one point on which reviewers agreed in criticizing Hawthorne, it was the immorality and un-American quality of his morbidity and subjectivity. The reviewers left Hawthorne no doubt about what is properly American or about the appropriate vocational function of a writer who wished to take his place within his established society. The same Whig periodical, for instance, that delighted in Hawthorne's conservatism could also despair of the questionable Christian morality in his choice of ideas as a consequence of his morbid insistence upon metaphysical romancing: "He has no genius for realities. . . . Between his characters and the reader falls a gauze-like veil of imagination, on which their shadows flit and move, and play strange dramas replete with second-hand life. An air of unreality enshrouds all his creation." The events of *The Scarlet Letter* have

> little more than a reminiscent interest; when characters and customs were so different to all circumstance that jostles us in the rude, quick life of today, [and are merely] pale shadowy ancestry . . . with whom we have no common sympathies. [Although] Mr. Hawthorne deals artistically with shadows . . . we question much . . . whether the path he has chosen is a healthy one. . . . When an author sits down to make a book, he should not alone consult the inclinations of his own genius regarding its purpose or its construction. If he should happen to be imbued with strange, saturnine doctrines, or be haunted by a morbid suspicion of human nature, in God's name let him not write one word. Better that all the beautiful, wild thoughts with which his brain is teeming should moulder forever in neglect and darkness, than that one soul was overshadowed by stern, uncongenial dogmas. . . . It is not alone necessary to produce a work of art. The soul of beauty is Truth, and Truth is ever progressive. The true artist therefore endeavors to make the world better. He does not look behind him, and dig out of the graves of past centuries skeletons to serve as models for his pictures; but looks onward for more perfect shapes, and though sometimes obliged to design from the defective forms around him, he infuses, as it were, some of the divine spirit of the future into them, and lo! we love them with all their faults. . . . [But Hawthorne's] books have no sunny side to them.[62]

Utopian conservatism, as a dissenting departure from the national culture's cheerfully smug respectabilities, was as difficult to maintain in the competitive literary market as outright radical dissent. American literature most clearly was not yet out from under the didactic utilitarian functions assigned it by the seventeenth and eighteenth centuries. It was subject to a coercive authority in which Hawthorne partly concurred, or at least to which he partly capitulated. The combination of his own conservatism and the demands for nationalistic sunshine go far toward explaining the astounding reversal of thematic intent and structural integrity that is an important index to the political nature of structure and form in much of Hawthorne's fiction. It is especially central in Hawthorne's most richly interesting book, *The Marble Faun.*

NOTES

1. These reversals will be discussed below. An illuminating study of Hawthorne's submission to the conservative nature of the marketplace, at least

in relation to conventionally established roles of gender, is Alice Letteny's unpublished doctoral dissertation, "Hawthorne's Heroines and Popular Magazine Fiction" (University of Connecticut, 1980). In her repudiation of the critical readings that explain Hawthorne's conventionality as ironic, Letteny suggests the extent to which, at least in the treatment of gender, Hawthorne was an acquiescent ideological conservative, who today would be labelled sexist.

2. See Theodore Greene, *America's Heroes: The Changing Models of Success in America's Magazines* (New York: Oxford University Press, 1970), pp. 35–56.

3. Unsigned review by William Leggett, The *Critic* 1 (Nov. 22, 1828): 53–55, quoted in J. Donald Crowley, ed., *Hawthorne: The Critical Heritage* (New York: Barnes and Noble, 1970), p. 46 (hereafter Crowley). I am indebted to Professor Crowley for his edition of selections from contemporary reviews of Hawthorne. His book is an invaluable work of high critical intelligence, releasing future scholars from the task of digging through contemporary sources to find an overview of contemporary opinion. I have checked through most of the original reviews, and in all but one or two cases I have found no need to complete or correct Professor Crowley's quotations from the originals. As testimony to my own debt to his labors and as an aid for the reader, I offer in each citation the page numbers of the full article in its original publication and the page numbers where the snippets quoted may also be found more fully in Crowley's edition. The reader who is interested in the reviews will find this method helpful, for with Crowley's excellent book one has many archival sources available in one convenient volume.

4. Quoted in Crowley, p. 6, from Julian Hawthorne, "A Group of Hawthorne Letters," *Harper's Monthly Magazine* 108 (Mar. 1904): 606–7. However, Julian Hawthorne's article is not to be trusted. He attributes the letter to Oct. 12, 1854; not only is the date wrong, but also Julian merged letters without indicating that he was taking liberties. Nathaniel Hawthorne as quoted in Julian Hawthorne's *Harper's* article:

October 12, '54.—You speak of another piece from me. There is no prospect of that, so long as I continue in office. Thank you for the two volumes of the *Mosses.* My books will now almost fill a shelf, and I hope to lengthen the list a little yet. There is the germ of a new romance in my mind, which will be all the better for ripening slowly. Besides, America is now wholly given over to a damned mob of scribbling women, and I should have no chance of success while the public is occupied with their trash—and should be ashamed of myself if I did succeed. What is the mystery of these innumerable editions of The *Lamplighter,* and other books neither better nor worse?—worse they could not be, and better they need not be, when they sell by the hundred thousand. I wish I could make a book calculated for schools. Can't you think of any?

However, *The Letters of Hawthorne to William D. Ticknor, 1851–1864* (Newark, N.J.: Carteret Book Club, 1910), 1:66 (hereafter Carteret Club *Letters*), offers this as the last two paragraphs of the letter of Oct. 12, 1854:

You speak of another book from me. There is no prospect of that, so long as I continue in office; but if the consular bill should pass at the next session, I shall soon be an author again. It proposes to allow no more than 7500 for the salary and all expenses of the office. No consul can live as a gentleman in English society, and carry on the official business, on those terms. But it would not cost me many pangs to resign. I hardly think, however, that the bill can pass during the short session.

Thank you for the two volumes of the Mosses. My books will now almost fill a shelf; and I hope to lengthen the list a little, yet. [The letter ends here with no mention of books for schools.]

In a letter to Ticknor dated "Liverpool, Jany 19th, '55," Hawthorne writes,

But I had rather hold this office two years longer; for I have not seen half enough of England, and there is the germ of a new Romance in my mind, which will be all the better for ripening slowly. Besides, America is now wholly given over to a d——d mob of scribbling women, and I should have no chance of success while the public taste is occupied with their trash—and should be ashamed of myself if I did succeed. What is the mystery of these innumerable editions of the Lamplighter, and other books neither better nor worse?—worse they could not be, and better they need not be, when they sell by the 100,000. (Carteret Club *Letters*, 1:75)

And in a letter to Ticknor dated "Liverpool, Febry 2d, 1855," Hawthorne writes, "I hardly venture to hope that I shall do so well, this present year; but anyhow, with the assistance of my pen, I shall manage to live, even if my office should cease to be worth holding. I wish I could make a book calculated for schools. Can't you think of any?" Carteret Club *Letters*, 1:77. See Centenary *Letters*, XVII: 264–65, 304, 307.

That Hawthorne complained about the "damned mob of scribbling women" (*scribbling* was his favorite pejorative word for bad writing, and with surprising frequency he applied it to himself in politely modest self-deprecation in his letters) in 1855 indicates the staying power of the ladies' market—*Fanshawe* was published in 1828. Although this market stays indeed unto the present day (with all the astonishing changes of propriety), its most intense sentimentality was reached in the nineteenth century, completely encompassing the decades of Hawthorne's professional life.

5. So much commentary has been written on exactly this significance of "The Custom House" that I offer the point as a given and shall refrain from yet another demonstration.

6. Crowley's introduction provides an illuminating discussion of the prevalence of such terms.

7. Charles Wilkins Webber, "Hawthorne," *American Whig Review* 4 (Sept. 1846): 296–316, quoted in Crowley, pp. 126, 128, 129, 130, 131.

8. Samuel W. S. Dutton, "Nathaniel Hawthorne," *New Englander* 5 (Jan. 1847): 59–60, quoted in Crowley, p. 135.

9. Unsigned review, *Spectator* 25 (July 3, 1852): 637–38, quoted in Crowley, p. 244.

10. *Athenaeum* (July 10, 1852): 741–43, quoted in Crowley, pp. 245–46.

11. Anonymous, "Contemporary Literature of America," *Westminster Review* 58 (Oct. 1852): 592–98, quoted in Crowley, pp. 263–64.

12. *Brownson's Quarterly Review,* n.s., 6 (Oct. 1852): 561–64, quoted in Crowley, p. 267.

13. *Literary World* 11 (Sept. 25, 1852), 195–96, quoted in Crowley, p. 276.

14. Anonymous, "American Literature: Poe, Hawthorne," *Tait's Edinburgh Magazine* 22 (Jan. 1855): 33–41, quoted in Crowley, p. 309.

15. "Nathaniel Hawthorne," *Atlantic Monthly* 5 (May 1860): 614–22, quoted in Crowley, p. 341.

16. *North American Review* 99 (Oct. 1864): 539–57, quoted in Crowley, p. 418.

17. Park Benjamin in the *New England Magazine* 9 (Oct. 1835): 284–88, and again in the *American Monthly Magazine,* n.s., 2 (Oct. 1836): 405–7, quoted in Crowley, pp. 48, 50. A ranking with Irving in the 1830s was no mean praise, for the insistent cultural nationalism that intensely occupied the decades between the War of 1812 and the Mexican War often held up Irving, Bryant, and Cooper as the trinity of American literature, at least until Cooper's falling out with the American public.

18. Quoted in Crowley, p. 52.

19. "Tale Writing—Nathaniel Hawthorne," *Godey's Lady's Book* 35 (Nov. 1847): 252–56, quoted in Crowley, p. 141.

20. Mar. 13, 1821, in Julian Hawthorne, *Nathaniel Hawthorne and His Wife* (1884; facsimile reprint 1968, Hamden, Conn.), 1:107, 108. Also see Centenary *Works,* XV, 138–39.

21. *Ladies Magazine* 1 (Nov. 1828): 526–27, quoted in Crowley, p. 42.

22. *American Monthly Magazine* n.s., 5 (Mar. 1838): 281–83, quoted in Crowley, pp. 60–61, 63.

23. Anonymous, *Christian Examiner* 55 (Sept. 1852): 292–94, quoted in Crowley, p. 251. All italics mine.

24. Feb. 11, 1860, in J. T. Fields, *Yesterdays with Authors* (Boston, 1871), p. 87, quoted in Crowley, p. 514. Crowley suggests that this letter is an ironic commentary on Trollope: "Critics have always supposed that Hawthorne had been contrasting his own romances with Trollope's realism. It seems more likely that he was, with some bitterness, contrasting the romance with popular fiction which he could enjoy but could not altogether respect as serious literature" (p. 513). But the tone of the full letter does not support a charge of irony. I think that the more likely significance of the letter is the combination of wistful admiration—for the serious and successful working of a genre gratifying to ideological conservatism—with another sigh, like those in the prefaces, about lack of a popular following. Clearly, however, Crowley is correct in seeing that Hawthorne connects his own literary production with the unpopularity implicit in his charge of unreadability against himself.

25. "The Genius of Nathaniel Hawthorne," *North American Review* 274 (Sept. 1879): 203–22, quoted in Crowley, p. 515.

26. "Nathaniel Hawthorne," *Cornhill Magazine* 26 (Dec. 1872): 717–34, quoted in Crowley, pp. 496, 497, 498.

27. Anonymous, *The Times* (London, Apr. 7, 1860): 5, quoted in Crowley, pp. 329–30.

28. "Nathaniel Hawthorne," *Atlantic Monthly* 5 (May 1860): 614–22, quoted in Crowley, p. 346.

29. *Literary World* 8 (Apr. 26, 1851): 334–35, quoted in Crowley, p. 193.

30. "Nathaniel Hawthorne," *Southern Literary Messenger* 17 (June 1851): 344–49, quoted in Crowley, pp. 214, 216. My elisions are not intended to hide an example of confusion in terminology: although praising *The Scarlet Letter*'s actualities, Tuckerman refers to the book as a romance. Again, the terminology of the marketplace reveals tendencies, not absolute consistency.

31. Amory Dwight Mayo, "The Works of Nathaniel Hawthorne," *Universalist Quarterly* 8 (July 1851): 272–93, quoted in Crowley, p. 224.

32. "The Writings of Hawthorne," *Church Review* 3 (Jan. 1851): 489–511, quoted in Crowley, pp. 181–82. Italics mine.

33. *Brownson's Quarterly Review*, n.s., 5 (Oct. 1850): 528–32, quoted in Crowley, p. 179.

34. Wright Morris's discussion of Rockwell's art is brilliant and compelling: see *The Territory Ahead* (New York: Harcourt, Brace, 1957), pp. 113–29.

35. These observations are not necessarily a repudiation of populist art. Clearly, Rockwell's paintings are of great cultural significance, and, to keep the record honest, I love to look at them. They brilliantly take first place among the most entertaining and profound examples of the implications of verisimilitude and nostalgia.

36. *North American Review* 45 (July 1837): 59–73, quoted in Crowley, p. 58.

37. *Literary World* 7 (Aug. 17, 1850): 125–27, and (Aug. 24, 1850): 145–47, quoted in Crowley, pp. 119, 120.

38. *Pioneer* 1 (Jan. 1843): 41–42, quoted in Crowley, pp. 72–73.

39. *North American Review* 56 (Apr. 1842): 496–99, quoted in Crowley, p. 81.

40. *Boston Quarterly Review* 5 (Apr. 1842): 251–52, quoted in Crowley, p. 87.

41. *Antiintellectualism in American Life* (New York: Alfred Knopf, 1963).

42. I entered this idea in the first draft of this book, several years ago. But since then, this book has been begun, changed, and abandoned a dozen times as other, more immediate projects interfered. By the time I came to a complete draft, William Spengemann had published his splendid book, *The Forms of Autobiography* (New Haven: Yale University Press, 1980), and developed what I consequently must leave only adumbrated here. See especially Spengemann's discussion of *The Scarlet Letter* as autobiography, a stimulating and illuminating discussion of the first order.

43. Although Hawthorne thought that E. P. Whipple was his most instructive and cogent reader and commentator, Hutton's pieces contain in germ more

of the subtle and complex matters that concern modern critics than any other essays written in Hawthorne's lifetime. Hutton was co-editor of the *National Review* with Walter Bagehot. His major comprehensive piece on Hawthorne is "Nathaniel Hawthorne," *National Review* 11 (Oct. 1860): 453–81, quoted in Crowley, pp. 366–87; it is still well worth reading today.

44. In this connection, a useful and illuminating observation is the discussion of Hawthorne in Michael T. Gilmore's *The Middle Way* (New Brunswick, N.J.: Rutgers University Press, 1977).

45. "Nathaniel Hawthorne," *Spectator* 37 (July 18, 1864): 705–6, quoted in Crowley, pp. 407–8, 411–12.

46. *Graham's Magazine* 38 (May 1851): 467–68, quoted in Crowley, p. 198.

47. *Graham's Magazine* 41 (Sept. 1852): 333–34, quoted in Crowley, p. 255.

48. "Tale Writing—Nathaniel Hawthorne," *Godey's Lady's Book* 35 (Nov. 1847): 252–56, quoted in Crowley, p. 150.

49. Crowley, p. 6.

50. "The Works of Nathaniel Hawthorne," *Universalist Quarterly* 8 (July 1851): 272–93, quoted in Crowley, p. 222.

51. *North American Review* 41 (Apr. 1842): 496–99, quoted in Crowley, p. 82.

52. *Graham's Magazine* 20 (May 1842): 298–300, quoted in Crowley, p. 93.

53. *Athenaeum* (Aug. 23, 1845): 830–31, quoted in Crowley, pp. 95–96.

54. "Hawthorne," *American Whig Review* 4 (Sept. 1846): 296–316, quoted in Crowley, pp. 128, 131.

55. Arthur Cleveland Coxe, "The Writings of Hawthorne," *Church Review* 3 (Jan. 1851): 489–511, quoted in Crowley, pp. 182, 183.

56. *Graham's Magazine* 41 (Sept. 1852): 333–34, quoted in Crowley, p. 255.

57. "Nathaniel Hawthorne," *To-Day* 2 (Sept. 18, 1852): 177–83, quoted in Crowley, p. 278.

58. Anonymous, *Salem Gazette* 51 (Mar. 14, 1837): 2, quoted in Crowley, p. 53. Italics mine.

59. Anonymous, "American Novels," *North British Review* 20 (Nov. 1853): 81–99, quoted in Crowley, p. 301.

60. *Brownson's Quarterly Review*, n.s., 5 (Oct. 1850): 528–32, quoted in Crowley, pp. 175, 176, 178, 179.

61. "The Writings of Hawthorne," *Church Review* 3 (Jan. 1851): 489–511, quoted in Crowley, pp. 180, 182, 183.

62. Anonymous, *American Whig Review*, 16 (1852): 417–24, quoted in Crowley, pp. 267–68, 269.

A *Marble Faun* Context

I

Almost all commentators since the 1920s have noted consistently three aspects of *The Marble Faun* among the many that criticism has dwelt on. One is the wealth of guidebook details, much of it used as emblematic commentary on the action of the plot. The second is the fatuity of much of the dialogue and the inanity of some of the auctorial observations, such as those about nudity in art. The third is the problematic role of Hilda.

At least since F. O. Matthiessen's *American Renaissance*, there has been little disagreement about the general theme of the book, the felix culpa, and Hilda's role within it. All readers agree that the central idea is one in which Donatello's development shows that suprahistorical innocence is magically beautiful but inevitably evanescent, and that the effects of sin can lead to an anguished but ennobling understanding of isolation from and community within the magnetic chain of humanity.

Sin, isolation, and community are universals in human experience. Until one recognizes their reality in one's own life, and unless one participates in common human history, with all its substrata of our common condition, one is something less than fully human. But Hilda, putatively the moral arbiter of the Romance, refuses just such recognition and participation. In terms of the story's central idea, she becomes something quite different from Hawthorne's apparent intention: not a heroine, but a moral fungus, growing priggishly out of the disintegration of other people's lives. As an effect of nationalism, she is a force of *ideological* closure. Because of her representational function (she is

Innocence: respectable, Protestant, young America), it was difficult, if not impossible, for Hawthorne to do other than support her straight and narrow antithematic refusal to illustrate or endorse the utopian closure toward which the entire book moves.

Critical disagreements arise around these three points because it is puzzling to encounter pages offering guidebook materials apparently for the purposes of actuality rather than Romance; because it is disconcerting to encounter the examples of conversation (and not only those involving Hilda and Kenyon) that reflect the ideological conservatism of the ladies' literary marketplace morality rather than the morality of the tale itself; because it is risible to encounter the speculations suggesting that art is purified by discreet politeness and by clothing; and because it is a surprise to encounter Hilda's rocklike righteousness in opposition to the current of the book's theme. The encounters have led to various twentieth-century readings that seek to vindicate Hawthorne as an ironist, but it is more likely that the causes for surprise are not a function of literary irony. The political relationships of marketplace to author strongly suggest that the causes of critical puzzlement, disarray, amusement, and surprise reveal Hawthorne in the terrible actualities of his own context.

Writing in a foreign land, feeling displaced and out of direct contact with the American literary market, Hawthorne prefaced the book with his concern that during his years of absence his "small productions" had been "almost utterly overlooked" by "the great Eye of the Public." The capitalizations perhaps are humorous, but their presence reveals Hawthorne's consciousness of the concept. It is useful to remember that *The Marble Faun* was written long after Hawthorne had been established as America's leading writer with a reputation to defend; and that he wrote the book, preparatory to his return home, at least in part as a deliberate attempt to reconsolidate his position by keeping his private eye on that public eye and moving back into the vision of the Great Public. His move back to America was in every way characteristic of his lifelong shuttling between privacy and success. Because of the immediacy of Hawthorne's Classicist sense of antiquity (all history is current in its sameness) after his long stay in Europe, no other of his books was written with a deeper sense of his utopian philosophy, and no other of his books was written with more of an expatriate's desire to give up "somewhere else" and belong to the world of "Salem." In Hawthorne's own words, *The Marble Faun* is a reentry:

Unquestionably . . . a Gentle, Kind, Benevolent, Indulgent, and most Beloved and Honoured Reader did once exist for me. . . . But is he extant now? In these many years, since he last heard from me, may he not . . . have withdrawn to the Paradise of Gentle Readers . . . ?

Therefore, I have little heart or confidence (especially writing, as I do, in a foreign land, and after a long, long absence from my own) to presume upon the existence of that friend of friends.[1]

Hawthorne's desire to belong was deeply bound up with *The Marble Faun.* As he wrote to W. D. Ticknor from Bath (April 6, 1860) after receiving favorable reviews of the book, "I have been much gratified by the kind feeling and generous praise contained in the notices you send me. After so long an absence and silence, I like to be praised too much. It sounds like a welcome back among my friends."[2] The artist-Hawthorne was the man of a conservative utopian vision, in which America, like all human enterprises, was subject to the same limitations that characterized the human story everywhere—the Classicist essence of his vision. The marketplace-Hawthorne was the man of a conservative ideological allegiance, in which the American enterprise was the realization of all millennialist hopes—the Romantic essence of his problem. *The Marble Faun* expressed the central conflicts of Hawthorne's life: American *ideological conservatism* was paradoxically a reflection of *utopian Romantic* assumptions about America; Hawthorne's Classicist *utopian conservatism* was paradoxically a *radical* contradiction of American ideological conservatism. The young Hawthorne's lasting choice to be a Romancer was a radical professional choice—both in his expression of Classicist utopian theme and in the context of proper vocation for a proper male in the young America of the 1820s and 1830s. Only through the veiling emblems afforded by his radical vocational choice could Hawthorne fully express his conservative utopian vision. In *The Marble Faun,* as in no other of his books, do the confrontations between the thematic conclusions of artist-Hawthorne and the psychological requirements of marketplace-Hawthorne become so palpable. Inner vision plus hunger for success equalled failure of nerve.

In his own mind, the materials of the story's setting—antiquity, the gloom of history in which are successively buried repetitive tiers of the cyclic rises and falls of nations—provided not only a delicious series of puissant emblems for his utopian conservatism, but also a means whereby he could identify himself with his American public through the setting's very foreignness. Hawthorne's first act, the preface, is to preserve his own association with an America of the sketch by dissociating his own "dear native land" from those very materials of Romance that, the story itself is to say, are universal: "Italy, as the site of . . . my Romance, was chiefly valuable to . . . me as affording a sort of poetic or fairy precinct, where actualities would not be so terribly insisted upon, as they are, and must needs be, in America." His uneasiness about actualities is at once subverted in his acquiescent *"and must needs be"* (so much like *"and for good reason"* in "The Artist of the Beautiful") and is declared in the same breath with which he offers thanks that American actualities are *not* those of the ancient history of all human-kind, for which Italy, and especially Rome, become the dominating emblems. "No author," he continues at once,

> without a trial, can conceive of the difficulty of writing a Romance about a country where there is *no shadow,* no antiquity, no mystery, no pictur-esque and *gloomy wrong,* nor anything but a *common-place prosperity,* in *broad and simple daylight,* as is happily the case with my dear native land. It will be very long, I *trust,* before romance-writers may find congenial and easily handled themes either in the annals of our stalwart Republic, or in any *characteristic and probable* events of our individual lives. Romance and poetry, like ivy, lichens, and wall-flowers, need Ruin to make them grow. (p. 3, italics mine)

Of course, one can say that the preface's celebration of America is ambiguous, but it is not easy to maintain that view when one considers that throughout the book Hilda and Kenyon, constantly identified as morally true *and* as American, echo the same sentiment. After their years of exile they both decide finally to go home only when "Ruin" has spoiled Europe for them and they long for "the broad and simple daylight" of the native scenes they recall with increasing nostalgia. At one point Kenyon is quite explicit about it:

> "You should go with me to my native country," observed the sculptor to Donatello. "In that fortunate land, each generation has only its own sins and sorrows to bear. Here, it seems as if all the weary and dreary Past were piled upon the back of the Present. If I were to lose my spirits in this country—if I were to suffer any heavy misfortune here—methinks it would be impossible to stand up against it, under such adverse influences!" (p. 302)

No longer an ahistorical faun, but a count, a flesh and blood man of human history and community, Donatello makes a reply that is Benito Cereno's reply to Amasa Delano, that is Hawthorne's reply to Hawthorne. " 'The sky itself is an old roof, now,' answered the Count; 'and, no doubt, the sins of mankind have made it gloomier than it used to be.' " Yet, as thematically appropriate as Donatello's reply is, Hawthorne does not leave the reader with Donatello's angle of perception. He gives the last word to Kenyon, whose perspective, though sympathetic, is, like Hilda's, always one of implicit condescension. " 'Oh, my poor Faun,' thought Kenyon to himself, 'how art thou changed!' " (p. 302). Narrative point of view becomes a political victim, as though in "Benito Cereno," in the exchange about hope, newness, memory, change, and the eradication of the past in the last interview between Captain Delano and Don Benito, Herman Melville, through tone and point of view, had given the obtuse American moral and intellectual superiority over the frighteningly enlightened Spaniard.

In the largest political effect upon point of view in *The Marble Faun*, at the conclusion Hawthorne places Hilda and Kenyon in the position of supreme perspective, overseeing all of Rome from the dome of St. Peter's. For their olympian view they stand atop a church they disclaim, commenting downward upon a human situation in which they have struggled to remain uninvolved. That they feel free from a tale in which they were very much involved, however, gives the lie to their independence and forfeits their moral claims—but it is precisely that independent height of superior moral perspective that Hawthorne bestows upon them. Their hands are clean, they say, and before they become too depressed by Rome to regain what Hawthorne referred to as Hilda's "equipoise," and before Kenyon finds it "impossible to stand up," these handwashing, touristic Pilates will head for the untainted green hills of "that fortunate land," America. Hawthorne sacrifices the integrity of narrative point of view to say to his marketplace that there are two histories: that of America and that of the rest of the world. "You see," he says in effect to his countrymen, "I agree that America is not *morbid* and I delight in the fact that it is *sunshine*, not gloom. Despite my expatriation, I am one of you. I am sure you will welcome me back because, just like Hilda and Kenyon, I am so happy to be coming home." Bound to the purpose of reidentifying Hawthorne as a *national* writer, *The Marble Faun* reveals point of view as but one instance of ideological conservatism counterattacking against utopian conservatism and vocational radicalism within the artwork.

Having made Hilda the pure representative of the American contrast with all other history, Hawthorne was stuck with the need to sanction her. (At one point he even wanted to call the book *St. Hilda's Shrine*!)[3] Therefore, authorial speculations often coincided with Hilda's ratifying what is in direct conflict (Hawthorne as Hilda) with the thematic energy of the book's action and characterization (Hawthorne as Miriam). But as a Dove-Phoebe-Sophia-America amalgam, it is Hilda whose imaginative superiority and moral infallibility Hawthorne declares and sustains. As F. I. Carpenter pointed out long ago,[4] American iconography continues a long European tradition of the sensuous and passionate dark lady and the pure and spiritual fair one. Hawthorne's typal identification of Hilda would have been unmistakable for his audience and within his own intentions, for the classic division between the sensuous dark woman and the blond avatar of purity was commonplace by the time Hawthorne came to the last novel he published in his lifetime. As the "fair-haired Saxon girl" (p. 56), a Protestant "daughter of the Puritans" and a "Christian girl," "this young American girl" (p. 54) is quickly associated by Hawthorne with heaven, goodness, trueness, and purity (chapter 6). Hawthorne shifts the scene to the white doves and the spotless white raiment of eminently white Hilda in her pure, airy, tower-top home—a shrine to the Virgin, with perspectives far above the common streets (pp. 51–61)—in clear and immediate contrast to the claustrophobic, dark chapters of subterranean suggestiveness (chapters 3 and 4) that associate Miriam with possible Jewishness, possible negritude, Italo-European cosmopolitanism, and Catholicism.[5]

Miriam shares with Hilda a supportive womanly goodness, but her paintings are dark, passionate, and filled with murder. Biblical and classical in content, they are proto-women's liberation in attitude, pictorializations of female rebellion against males. "Over and over again, there was the idea of woman, acting the part of a revengeful mischief towards man" (p. 44). Hilda's copies, on the other hand, are spiritualizing idealizations of art, and as type of the lady, Hilda is constantly associated with the most orthodox conceptions of purity and spirituality—"womanly goodness." Miriam is presented as warm, even hot, in her passionate nature and her womanliness. Hilda, more than once, is spoken of (admiringly) as chill purity in her virginal girlishness. Like Hester Prynne, Miriam is dark and scarlet, with her rich, ruby glow of jewelry. In sum, Miriam is everything that is the repressed, passional, subterranean reality beneath Victorian respectability, just as Hilda is everything that is that respectability's apotheosis in the optimistic features of American millennialistic certitudes. The phrases contrasting Miriam with the repeated characteristics of Hilda are marked. Miriam perhaps "was the daughter and heiress of a great Jewish banker, (an idea perhaps suggested by a certain rich Oriental character in her face)" (p. 22). In contrast to Hilda, with her fair complexion, blue eyes, and light brown hair, Miriam "had what was usually thought to be a Jewish aspect," "dark eyes," and "black, abundant hair, with none of the vulgar glossiness of other women's sable locks; if she were really of Jewish blood, then this was Jewish hair and a dark glory such as crowns no Christian maiden's head" (p. 48). For even more dramatic contrast with the pure Anglo-Saxon type of American, perhaps Miriam even had "one burning drop of African blood in her veins" (p. 23). Finally and inevitably, though it might appear that there "is Anglo-Saxon blood in her veins, one would say, and a right English accent on her tongue," nevertheless there is about Miriam "much that is not English breeding nor American" (p. 109). In literary convention, Miriam is a name reserved for Jewishness (as Henry James was to use it, for instance, in *The Tragic Muse*); St. Hilda, on the other hand, evokes very different associations. Although both women are presented as beautiful, discerning (differently), and good, there was absolutely no question about which type represented God's country.

In the conflicting representations of his utopian conservatism (Miriam, Donatello) and his ideological conservatism (Hilda, Kenyon), Hawthorne was faced with mutual annihilations. He ended his story before its ultimate conclusion. Nevertheless, because his utopian and ideological conservatisms tend to annihilate each other, Hawthorne produced not a fascinating, rich, ironical book, but a fascinating, rich, botched one. Because the actualities of history and setting in the book indicate the underlying utopian truth of America's indistinguishable oneness with all fallen humanity, the surface implication of distinctions made by eyes, hair, complexion, names, race, and national origin are lies. But insofar as Hawthorne had his personal eye on the great Eye of the Public, he could not be true! be true! to his Romance with total seriousness, which meant he could not be true to his own actualities. The paradox is that his unwillingness to make a full commitment to being a Romancer marred him as a *novelist,* and the result is what almost all readers have felt: a surfeit of actualities in *The Marble Faun* and a discontinuity between guidebook details that function emblematically and those that do not. The sense of discontinuity arises from conflicting sources of the book's details: there are those actualities that are generated for the Romance by the underlying utopia and those that are novelistically prompted by the sketch-ideologies of verisimilitude. Because the underlying utopia was the book's *truth* and Hawthorne presented the ideological details as though they were the book's truth, he lost his hold on both Romance and novel.

One exquisite moment in the book becomes paradigmatic of the problem of actualities. When the party of promenaders comes to the spot where Curtius and his horse had sunk, in their turn, into the detailed tiers of buried actuality, we confront a moment in which we hover over the abyss of all human history. That actuality has many possibilities. There is the possibility of the picturesque, the light and shadow and chiaroscuro of verisimilitude. The picturesque for the marketplace meant the heightened effect of travel. Travel books were an extremely popular commodity in Hawthorne's marketplace. They served to bring home news and adventure, together with education in history and geography, in an age when communication and transportation were still limited but had developed enough to stimulate sharply an appetite for the sights and experiences that only the tiniest fraction of the population would be able to enjoy first hand. Some bookmen, like Melville's English publisher, John Murray, would accept no fiction, but only true accounts of travel. The picturesque, the actual heightened in quaintness, strangeness, and beauty, was the true account most worthy of pictorialization—and, therefore, the most interesting to read. The guidebook details about Curtius are intriguingly picturesque.

But they are more than that. Though Kenyon may deny as a condition of America that the Past is "piled upon the back of the Present," the European paradigm of Curtius makes the past and present mutually inextricable: the Past swallows the Present, and the Present is piled upon the back of the Past. Through all the changes in the book's geography, setting is a metaphor for human history: contemporary streets and houses are intermixed with relics from the past, some still functional, some in ruins. Present events, like present architecture, share in and grow from the layered past that lies buried underneath current surfaces. The details of actuality are possibilities in verisimilitude for the travelogue-picturesque, and they are also imaginative possibilities for the international solidarity of universal human history. But it is the latter possibility that has been presented to Hilda, and with the unwittingly arrogant certainty of blithe American optimism, in an instant she repudiates the depths, turns the picturesque to conventional moral purpose, and placing her pure little lady-foot upon the surface covering of the abyss, skips across it in a breathtakingly virginal denial of history, fallibility, humanity, and *all* actualities. Standing on the very place where the chasm opened under Curtius and his horse, Kenyon proclaims the depths beneath them as prophetic of all the calamities of Rome ever since. Considering that chasm, Miriam fancies "that every person takes a peep into it in moments of gloom and despondency; that is to say, in moments of deepest insight." But, as for Hilda, why " 'Where is it then,' asked Hilda. 'I never peeped into it.' " To that abysmal ignorance of abysses, Miriam replies, "Wait, and it will open for you."

> The chasm was merely one of the orifices of that pit of blackness that lies beneath us, everywhere. The firmest substance of human happiness is but a thin crust spread over it, with just reality enough to bear up the illusive stage-scenery amid which we tread. It needs no earthquake to open the chasm. A footstep, a little heavier than ordinary, will serve; and we must step very daintily, not to break through the crust at any moment. By and by, we inevitably sink! (pp. 161–62)

To this summation of time and the inevitability of human frailty statisticated by every energy of the Romance's plot and imagery, Hilda airily replies, "It seems to me that there is no chasm, nor any hideous emptiness under our feet except what the evil within us digs. If there be such a chasm, let us bridge it over with good thoughts and deeds, and we shall tread safely to the other side" (p. 162). And—hop!—we daintily float over life. At this moment Hilda is the forerunner of every mindless Shirley Temple affirmation that F. Scott Fitzgerald was to caricature in the Daddy's Girl of *Tender Is the Night:*

> There she was—the school girl of a year ago, hair down her back and rippling out stiffly like the solid hair of a tanagra figure; there she was—*so* young and innocent—the product of her mother's loving care; there she was—embodying all the immaturity of the race, cutting a new cardboard paper doll to pass before its empty harlot's mind. . . .
>   Daddy's girl. Was it a 'itty-bitty bravekins' and did it suffer? Ooo-ooo-tweet, de tweetest thing, wasn't she dest too tweet?[6]

The particularly revealing aspect of the Curtius scene is that Hawthorne does not dwell on the momentary possibilities of the picturesque any longer than Hilda dwells upon the possibilities of the book's subsurface theme. At those moments when there is an ideological repudiation of the actualities as discomfiting signs of utopian vision, actualities are annihilated entirely: they have no place to *be*, either in theme or on the ideological surface. In order to accord lebensraum to the actualities of the picturesque, Hawthorne had to eschew the functions of his book's central idea. Chapters 16, 17, 23, and 32 are examples of the actualities nearly devoid of thematic idea. The disconnection from theme is of Hawthorne-Hilda's making, for the ideological refusal to accept the thematic implications allies Hilda with the reading audience. In providing the picturesque per se, as well as in authorially corroborating Hilda's value judgments, Hawthorne makes himself one with the audience as well. The inclusion of extrinsic verisimilitude, as in the four exemplary chapters just specified, does what the characterization of Hilda does: it tugs the narrative toward the purposes of the sketch. Consequently, the guidebook functions of the novel seem an intrusive surplus of actualities to many readers because *The Marble Faun* has two centers of gravity: Hawthorne supplied realistic travelogue details in trying to cater to the demands of his marketplace at the same time that—in the major thematic energy of the book—he was testing his imaginative metaphoric uses of the details against those values. He tried so very hard to have it both ways.

It is that schizoid quality of the book that makes humanly understandable but critically untenable Hawthorne's recoil from the demands for actualities as he insists upon the legitimacy of the Romance. In *The Marble Faun*, Hawthorne even had to add an epilogue so that the narrative could conclude with a coherent tying up of loose actualities. He grumbled about the necessity. What he said, in effect, in his letters as well as in his preface and epilogue, was this: the Romance is free from the actualities so terribly insisted upon, and therefore it should not be judged by the verisimilitude or narrative logic of the sketch or the novel. If the reader enters with me into my vision of the events, the events themselves are of lesser importance. Realistic explanation of events is secondary to the imaginative vision of their meaning.

The best known and most compelling instance of Hawthorne's assertion of Romance is his evocation of objects seen in the haunted verge of the mirror in the midnight room illuminated by firelight and moonlight, as presented in "The Custom House" sketch prefatory to *The Scarlet Letter*. But in *The Marble Faun* he makes the plea for utopian vision over ideological function, in a context in which he himself has created the novelistic expectations. No sensitive reader of *The Marble Faun* can come away from it without an awareness of the willing attentiveness with which Hawthorne supplied pictures, for the sake of those pictures, of the actual Rome and Italy. What the reviews of *The Blithedale Romance* had signalled—a confusion of foreground and background for hostile and friendly reviewers alike—remained the sign of the unresolved politics of Hawthorne's fiction.

Hawthorne's sense of his materials was superb: the actualities of history imaginatively turned into metaphoric emblems of and commentary upon the gnarled relationship of innocence and experience throughout all human life, in all places, and in all times up to and including the present American moment. It was not that his undertaking was impossible or self-contradictory, but it did demand a consistent dedication to his own utopian uses of actualities rather than to the ideology of the marketplace. Otherwise, the one is constantly in momentary counterattack upon the other. For instance, in his description of a stroll on the Pincian Hill (chapter 11), after offering several guidebook details, Hawthorne then proceeds toward the thematic center, which is the metaphoric use of the materials: "These details . . . are the solid framework of hills that shut in Rome and its wide surrounding Campagna; no land of dreams, but the broadest page of history, crowded so full of memorable events that one obliterates another, as if Time had crossed and re-crossed his own records till they grew illegible" (p. 101).

But in his utopian purposes, and as his preface insistently reveals, Hawthorne *is* devoting his book to the "land of dreams," which is the realm of metaphoric meaning, the truth into which fact is transformed by the haunted and haunting imagination. In fact, at the end of the book, when he feels compelled to explain Hilda's disappearance from her tower, Hawthorne complains that some readers are not content to leave such matters to the imagination and the fairy precincts of cloudland. Characteristically, in the stroll on the Pincian Hill his mind moves from the hard, factual "broad page" to the problematical, "illegible" inscriptions of meaning. The transcription of the records into emblems of meaning, of buried and reburied facts into generalized, universal essence, was the source of Hawthorne's creative strength, but the conflict between ideology of fact and utopia of meaning breaks the narrative into small moments of self-destruction. Insisting that his story is not to be approached through the perspectives of "the solid framework of . . . shut in . . . history," which is the raw material of his utopian Classicist closure, he constantly wishes to divorce the events, through which he leads the characters of his Romance, from the novelistic actualities that literally provide the very materials inevitable for his imagination to work upon. Realism can border too dangerously on what it will become later in the century: open confrontation with American nationalistic assumptions. So he adds immediately, "But, not to meddle with history—with which our narrative is no otherwise concerned, than that the very dust of Rome is historic, and inevitably settles on our pages, and mingles with our ink—we will return to our two friends, who were still leaning over the wall" (p. 101). Unless Hawthorne were to invent the impossibility of a settingless setting, of course his materials had to "*inevitably* settle" on his pages and "mingle with his ink," a matter to which he cannot reconcile himself and from which he shrinks behind his prefatory justification of Romance. Here he is reacting against those materials *as important for themselves,* as fulfillment of the picturesque. The guidebook verisimilitude is something "with which our narrative is no otherwise concerned": let us return to our two friends in the Romance, in which the utopian Classicism will be camouflaged in relative safety. The utopia and the marketplace are always unreconciled; here the utopia makes a foray against intrusion of incipient ideology in a quick syntactical raid. Hawthorne's characteristic strategy for such skirmishes is the parenthetical construction (in this case indicated by dashes), as we shall see more clearly in the narrator's relation to Hilda. These authorial intrusions, whether on behalf of the utopia or, as is much more often the case, on behalf of marketplace ideology, always undercut the narrative's own reality. The story, we are shown, is interruptable. Because Hawthorne fails to make his fiction committedly integral with the political impulse of its utopia, it remains victimized, of secondary importance to the conflict beyond it, and the fully serious response of the reader is imperilled. Hawthorne's vocational irresolution functions exactly as Henry James complained it did: it generates the impression that because the author will not commit his ultimate dedication to the fiction's own reality, neither need the reader.

The division of political values extends itself into the fatuity of some of the dialogue, such as the discussions about nudity in art. Hawthorne repudiates the effusions of the "scribbling women," and the narrator is grateful that Hilda recognized her relationship to high art, forsaking "pretty fancies of snow and moonlight; the counterpart in picture of so many feminine achievements in literature!" (p. 61). Nevertheless, even when Hawthorne discusses some of the artists he knew in Europe (p. 133), his rhetoric is the rhetoric of the puffs and sentimentalities in the popular reviews: "By his magic," he says, praising an artist's painting, "the moon throws her light far out of the picture, and the crimson of the summer-night absolutely glimmers on the beholder's face" (p. 133). So much does the idiom of the marketplace pervade Hawthorne's consciousness that he reproduces its ideological rhetoric when he offers art criticism, using a language inimical to his own shadowy theory that "Romance and poetry, like ivy, lichens, and wall-flowers, need Ruin to make them grow." Whatever distinction Hawthorne intended between Hilda and the scribbling women, Hilda epitomizes rather than opposes them, for she renounces Ruin and its truths, constantly insisting that, if anything, shadow and gloom *get in the way* of art. And the auctorial voice refuses to contradict Hilda's certitude. The artist's skills, says Hawthorne's voice,[7] must be mastered to create the "loftier merits" "of the better life." They "must be put so entirely under his control . . . that . . . you will be apt to fancy that the loftier merits of the picture were of your own dreaming, not of his creating. Like all revelations of the better life, the adequate perception of a great work of art demands a gifted simplicity of vision. In this, and in her self-surrender, and the depth and tenderness of her sympathy, had lain Hilda's remarkable power as a copyist of the Old Masters" (p. 335).

Hilda is the embodiment of a marketplace that insisted on moral uplift, betterment, sunshine, spirituality, religion, and moonlight prettiness. And it is precisely those sentiments with which Hawthorne agrees in the auctorial voice, calling paintings of nudes "impure pictures . . . from . . . impious hands" (p. 337). When he hints that the works of Raphael and other great masters display their own birthmark-connections with the lustful touch of mortality, he is careful to exempt Hilda from contamination. He becomes pious about his own piousness.

On the one hand, he scolds Raphael: "And who can trust the religious sentiment of Raphael, or receive any of his Virgins as Heaven-descended likenesses, after seeing, for example, the Fornarina of the Barberini palace, and feeling how sensual the artist must have been, to paint such a brazen trollop of his own accord, and lovingly! Would the Blessed Mary reveal herself to his spiritual vision, and favour him with sittings, alternately with that type of glowing earthliness, the Fornarina!" (p. 337). But Hawthorne cannot rest easy with the cultural impiety of attacking Raphael whom, moreover, he has identified as a recipient of Hilda's adulation. Immediately and lugubriously he retracts the impiety that is the expression of his solemnly respectable piousness and clears the path for St. Hilda:

> But no sooner have we given expression to this irreverent criticism, than a throng of spiritual faces looks reproachfully upon us. We see Cherubs, by Raphael, whose baby-innocence could only have been nursed in paradise; Angels, by Raphael, as innocent as they, but whose serene intelligence embraces both earthly and celestial things; Madonnas, by Raphael, on whose lips he has impressed a holy and delicate reserve, implying sanctity on earth, and into whose soft eyes he has thrown a light which he never could have imagined, except by raising his own eyes with a pure aspiration heavenward. We remember, too, that Divinest countenance in the Transfiguration, and withdraw all that we have said. (p. 338)

Having managed with this withdrawal to have it both ways—to be one with his audience in its purse-mouthed Victorian prudishness and to be one with his audience in an unremitting adoration of the Raphael-loving Hilda—Hawthorne proceeds directly to an exculpation of Hilda from any possibility of impiety. "Poor Hilda, however, in her gloomiest moments, was never guilty of the high-treason, suggested in the above remarks, against her beloved and honoured Raphael. She had a faculty (which, fortunately for themselves, pure women often have) of ignoring all moral blotches in a character that won her admiration. She purified the objects of her regard by the mere act of turning such spotless eyes upon them" (p. 338). In this ideologically pious gesture, Hawthorne turns a smile to his readers in parentheses that serve almost invariably and conservatively as a reinforcement of the marketplace conventionality in *The Marble Faun.* The unconscious politics of syntactic structure is validated in the many authorial concurrences with marketplace ideology that make Hilda the anchor of moral value in the book. It is not only Hilda who is like the three monkeys with paws on ears, eyes, and mouth. The political effect of the essentially parenthetical phrase, "suggested in the above remarks," is to distance Hawthorne from his own narration, leaving his participation in the opinions equivocal. Often Hawthorne's parenthetical style is sly, the punctuation offering an ambiguity that is not an expression of the complex moral profundity with which he is deservedly credited, but is a narratorial ablution a la Pilate. Hawthorne hastens to remove himself and with him, implicitly, his readers, from the possibly dark over- and undertones of art. But then, why acknowledge the un-American qualities of the paintings in the first place? Probably because for Hawthorne the power of art to energize the thematic force of his utopian vision is irresistible, and he is too steady a Classicist, too large a spirit, and too great an artist to ignore the dark tones. Then why withdraw the acknowledgment? Because the withdrawal is the counterattack of the ideological super-structure that, in Hilda and Kenyon, is given the palm and the laurel in defining what is true and good. The entire recantation is a prolonged parenthesis of counterattack by Hawthorne's marketplace conservatism in his nervously compulsive reversions to speculations about art. Within this context, Hawthorne's prudish and sometimes silly pronouncements are not inexplicably out of character. From the perspective of the late twentieth century, it is extremely tempting to see the recantation as highly ironic rhetoric, but if it is a piece of irony, it is inexpensive self-indulgence on Hawthorne's part. It is a disappointingly easy, private defiance hiding nonconfrontationally behind public rhetoric, for within the total context of the book, this pious prose does nothing but reconfirm Hilda as the unimpeachable source of moral value. And Hawthorne seems complacent about or unconscious of Hilda's reduction of morality to a particularly American version of Victorian respectability.

When first confronted with the charm of uninhibited, natural, ani-mal spontaneity, represented by Donatello, Hilda responds primly. " 'It perplexes me,' Hilda said thoughtfully, and shrinking a little; 'neither do I quite like to think about it' " (p. 13). She repudiates the morbid in the visit to the Catacomb of St. Calixtus and refuses to see any valuable meaning in it. " 'How dismal all this is!' said Hilda shuddering. 'I do not know why we came here, nor why we should stay a moment longer' " (p. 25).

In presenting this "partly ideal creature" (p. 63), Hawthorne identifies her as an "inhabitant of picture-land" (p. 63). Picture-land is America, for with "her light brown ringlets, her delicately tinged, but healthful cheek, her sensitive, intelligent, yet most feminine and kindly face," Hilda is a beauty of "our native New England style" (p. 63). In reserving for Hilda the innocent purity and goodness that loft her out of the common run of mortal history, Hawthorne identifies his New England lady by "the sunshine of her soul" (p. 63). Miriam's and Kenyon's

conversation about the statue of Cleopatra displays Hilda's "womanhood
... as of the ethereal type, and incompatible with any shadow of darkness or evil" (p. 128). Hawthorne's representative Dove, the American
Paraclete, occupies a suprahistorical place in human existence. "Hilda
is just as safe, in these evil streets of Rome, as her white doves, when
they fly downward from the tower-top, and run to-and-fro among the
horses' feet. There is a special Providence on purpose for Hilda, if for no
other human creature," says Miriam to Kenyon. " 'I religiously do believe
it,' rejoined the sculptor" (p. 180). The "white, shining purity of Hilda's
nature is a thing apart; and she is bound, by the undefiled material of
which God moulded her, to keep the severity which I, as well as you,
have recognized" (p. 287), says Kenyon, speaking a piece that has clear
authorial sanction. The establishment of Hilda as moral authority is
Hawthorne's central gesture of homage to his marketplace. As Hawthorne's
literary act of returning home, the book becomes resistant to its own
theme and imagery.

The book's images of height and depth establish a constant in the
theme. What is pure and divine is universal, but somehow detached,
above the immediacies of human suffering, like the light on the Bible
in "My Kinsman, Major Molineux." One must climb endless flights of
stairs to reach Hilda's shrine. Yet what is dark and subterranean is not
only easily encountered but also inevitable, a "Shadow" that trails us
from the depths no matter where we flee. It is a "Model" for what art
presents of what confronts us unexpectedly everywhere. The images of
buried tiers of Rome and Etruria, all containing signs of the same
human existence, like the metaphoric function of works of art and the
career of Donatello, all unite into a major motif: the pure, golden joy of
an ahistorical condition never has been a human reality and is not
now—the "Sunshine of Monte Beni," aptly named, will not travel, for
mysterious reasons that no one can discover as ultimate or reversible.
Like the mystery of Miriam's Shadow-Model, the presence of a darkly
fallen condition is insoluble but inescapable. It is the ubiquitous given.
For all but Hilda, there is no invincible high place.

Miriam lives in an apartment several flights of stairs above the street,
but she is also most deeply ensnared in all of the subterranean actualities that Hilda repudiates. The Tarpeian Rock, which affords a wide
prospect of Rome all before us, is a site where one man, the Model, is
hurled downward to his murder at the base—a sin from which his
murderer, Donatello, falls upward into his humanity. Donatello lives at
the very top of the tower of the edenically named high, good place,
Monte Beni. But his high place, darkened through time and sin, shel-
ters no doves; it is an owl's tower. And it was an ancient prison of a mad

monk, who recapitulates the presence of the Model: the ghost of the monk is said to abide there still. So does the ghost of Eden: a type of the serpent, a worm, inhabits the lush and lovely greenery at the top of the tower, and Donatello can only reenact the original fall. From the heights, like God casting down Lucifer and then humankind, Donatello drops the worm as he had dropped the reptilian Capuchin. In his rich and intricate interweaving of details in this, his most complex Romance, Hawthorne makes everything the ghost of everything else. The setting echoes a continuing reverberation of the events; the events recapitulate the setting; the drama of interaction is haunted by the characters, who are educated into its meanings. It is precisely because of Hawthorne's brilliant success in thematically creating his underlying utopian vision that Hilda and her aura become so intrusively alien to the book.

As he does with the rosebush and the weeds on opposite sides of the prison door in *The Scarlet Letter,* Hawthorne begins *The Marble Faun* with an image that suggests an inevitable intermixture of dove and serpent in even the most innocent human lives. We are introduced to the story with "a symbol (as apt, at this moment, as it was two thousand years ago) of the Human Soul, with its choice of Innocence or Evil close at hand, in the pretty figure of a child, clasping a dove to her bosom, but assaulted by a snake" (p. 5). "At this moment," as the utopian theme is stated, there is a parenthetical thrust against the ideological foe (there is no American immunity, because there is no new history in which the two-thousand-year-old image is not apt), for Hawthorne is preparing his essential extension from the image: Nature itself is caught in the same condition as the human soul. Existence itself is fallen. Hawthorne's first presentation of the subterranean Model is a picture of a type of Caliban in direct contrast to Donatello's Ariel. The Model implicitly has an old and weary history; Donatello is a child; they are both creatures of nature.

In the "Specter of the Catacombs" we meet the goatish satyr, not the innocent faun. "He was clad in a voluminous cloak, that seemed to be made of a buffalo's hide, and a pair of those goat-skin breeches, with the hair outward, which are still commonly worn by the peasants of the Roman Campagna. In this garb, they look like antique satyrs; and, in truth, the Specter of the Catacomb might have represented the last survivor of that vanished race, hiding himself in sepulchral gloom, and mourning over his lost life of woods and streams" (p. 30). Donatello, once out of his childhood, is to reenact that gloom and mourning for a lost life of nature. Donatello and the Model become ghosts of each other. The Specter, like the underground man, Memmius, like Aminadab in "The Birthmark," is a model of the effect of original sin: the lasting, ancient claim of the debasing, subterranean brute nature that shadows the human race even in the garb of clerical spirituality (there does not seem to be one unstained cleric in Hawthorne's fiction). Donatello might represent the pure and delightful spontaneity of the primal, innocent creature of nature not yet fallen. But Hawthorne makes sure to tell us that as all the forebears in Donatello's faunlike race grew old, they unexceptionably became coarse and brutish in their natural animality. The faun must eventually come into the ancestral legacy of the satyr. Like dove and serpent, Donatello and the Model are opposite extensions of each other. In the Model, Donatello senses his own fate, and he hates this version of his own identity on sight.

Donatello cannot be totally separate from the dark stranger, nor can the latter-day Memmius, a "creature to whom midnight would be more congenial than noonday," be totally separate from the light. The Shadow is the agent whereby the lost Miriam is led "first into the torch-light, thence into the sunshine" (p. 31). The lines from heaven, height, and light to hell, depth, and darkness characterize the careers of the five major characters and, in a further consideration, reveal the presence of the literary genres of Hawthorne's marketplace. The center of the theme is the point at which the lines intersect, the balance point of child, dove, and snake. To say child, dove, and snake is to say Donatello, Hilda, and the Model, which is to say that one of the central expectations of the book is that Hilda's line will merge, at least at one point, in event *and in theme,* with Donatello's and the Model's.

The Model emerges from subterranean darkness, and he ends up in the same enclosed blackness, buried in the farthest recesses of the catacombs beneath the Capuchin chapel. His line is unwaveringly horizontal at the lowest and darkest depths of Rome (history) and of the human soul (theme). There is no conflict between background (the materials of setting) and foreground (the meaning of the metaphors) in Hawthorne's presentation of the Capuchin-Shadow-Model. Similarly there is no thematic rupture, no discontinuity between materials and metaphor in Hawthorne's presentation of Donatello and Miriam. Donatello, temporarily the Model's opposite, is a creature of air, sunshine, and innocent nature unconnected with human history. Whether or not he has furry ears in terms of verisimilitude and the sketch, he most certainly does in terms of metaphor and the Romance. He begins his life in unspoiled nature and at the sunlit top of the Monte Beni tower of his childhood of delight. Beyond that childhood, his origins go back beyond memory to a moment in prehistory. But time began with the Fall. Once forced into the mixed actualities of human history and the human soul, Donatello descends into subterranean immurement and darkness in prison, in mind, and in heart. But at the end, through the education effected by the sin and everything associated with the Model, Donatello (just like the Model at the beginning) emerges from gloom and moves toward the light. Donatello's line is a great V, and bespeaks the victory of the felix culpa. He falls from prehistoric Eden into time and sin, and in the process rises from his gloom to the light of mature understanding, love, and repentance in what could be called a triumph. Unlike the Model, who suggests the line of redemption but who is damned to move only toward the physical, not the spiritual, light, Donatello fully enacts the essence of Hawthorne's Christian imagination, embracing both the Classicist closure of the Fall and the Romantic openness of Redemption.

Miriam's line is drawn with Donatello's. Travelling a somewhat similar path, Miriam is Donatello's spiritual as well as physical companion. Her past is a compound of hints: a great name on which some kind of shame has fallen. She emerges from her mysterious darkness into passionate flight from embroilment with the Shadow of her past, only to fall into the actual sin of complicity in murder. This dark nadir of her life results in a penance reminiscent of Hester Prynne's. In the final full honesty of her submission to the inescapably mixed nature of human life, she accepts the burden of serpent that mixes with the presence of dove in her soul. She stops fleeing the truth, and, like Donatello, through sin she begins to move in shadow toward an upward line of redemption. She, too, raven-haired Jewess, enacts the closure and the openness of Hawthorne's Christian perception. She is last seen in a low place, on the floor of the Pantheon, in a low posture, kneeling—beneath a ray that is a direct line to heaven. She is beneath "the great central Eye" of the open dome, through which divine light falls on her in the darkness. Her line is one of fall, then horizontal darkness, then further fall (the murder), and then, implicitly, a steady upward rise.

Donatello is only the temporary opposite of the Model: it is Hilda who is the real opposite. The Model's religious frenzy is the desperation of the damned, who feel that hell is the absence of God and who are crazed with a desire to regain a sense of divine presence; Hilda's religious certainty is the rigidity of the elect, who are burdened with a constant sense of divine presence. Hilda maintains a steady, horizontal line at the brightest and airiest regions overlooking history, except for one sharp and momentary dip—the murder. Hilda is last seen at the top of that very St. Peter's she has used as a spiritual outhouse, relieved of her burden, bathed in pure radiance, and about to take her leave for that America she has consistently represented. As the Model's line has been a straight horizontal at the very depths of human experience, Hilda's has paralleled it at the heights above experience.

Kenyon, reduced to a cipher by his adoration of (St.) Hilda, is merely an undulating line that oscillates between the ideal that Hilda represents and the dark lesson he learns from Donatello, Miriam, and the Model. Knowing the truth of the utopia represented by the suffering of the other characters, he nevertheless not only does not have the strength to oppose Hilda's myopic view of things, but also he yearns for her. He becomes the participant in the drama only to the extent that he is an active observer, but he maintains a constant cool aloofness that allows him to turn away the thematic truth when he turns Miriam away. That cool aloofness is precisely the defensive protection that allows him to maintain his allegiance to Hilda. Like his counterpart, Coverdale, in *The Blithedale Romance*, he opts not for the dark lady but for the conventional girl. Hawthorne directly presents himself as narrator to his readers, and his instrument is the parenthetical statement whereby he declares his oneness with the ideological demands of the national Hilda, who is to be taken to wife. Hawthorne expressing Hawthorne on the level of ideology straightforwardly asserts a self who belongs to the Phoebe-Dove world of his marketplace and nation. Hawthorne indirectly presents himself as character (Kenyon, Coverdale), and his instrument is the perhaps subconscious characterization of all his failures of nerve. Hawthorne expressing Hawthorne from the perspectives of his utopia creates a pusillanimous character who, in his defensive withdrawal, commits exactly the sin of the heart that Hawthorne so passionately devotes his books to preaching against. The active but uncommitted— and finally renounced—sympathies that never quite involve Kenyon in the thematic foreground are the political essence of the self-loathing that Hawthorne expresses in his statements of weariness with the Romance.

Hawthorne's imagination characteristically discovers the point at which the lines of all his characters, except Kenyon's, are intersected by participation in or juxtaposition to a crime. The narrative structure as setting and as scene (in the Jamesian sense of the word as the dynamic of interaction among characters juxtaposed in a particular way) freezes for an instant—the murder—that is a vertical line of intersection with the characters' lines at a single moment. As theme, the narrative broadens out from that point in the dramatization of the universal intermixture of damnation and redemption revealed by the effects of sin and the archetypal casting down, or Fall. Setting as well as Jamesian scene—verisimilitude and the picturesque as well as their metaphoric values—establish and validate the inescapable presence of subterranean experience. History and crime. The actualities of the guidebook details are very much there. But when one climbs up into Hilda's realm, one rises above the thereness of human experience: "Only the domes of churches ascend into the airy region, and hold up their golden crosses on a level with . . . Hilda's eyes; except that, out of the very heart of Rome, the column of Antoninus thrusts itself upward, with Saint Paul upon its summit, the sole human form that seems to have kept her company" (p. 53). As for the thematic structure that broadens out from the crime, Hilda removes herself from it. The apparent dip in her horizontal line of unwavering holiness is only that—apparent. For Hilda disclaims any connection with her act of witnessing. She repudiates Miriam and Donatello tearfully but totally and manages to claim a position of spiritual, inner disconnection from sin fully as much as she does a legalistic, outer disconnection. Therefore, the narrative, after the crime, has little room for Hilda once her disclaimer is complete, and, in fact, she disappears increasingly and then literally from the story. The structure of *The Marble Faun*, like its setting, its events, its Jamesian scene, and its resulting theme all combine to reveal that Hilda's line is an impossibility, for there are no actualities in the book validating unmixed angelic existence.

The marketplace vocabulary for literary genres constantly illuminates Hawthorne's dilemma of allegiances. Hilda is all that is sunshine and reflective of what the American society insisted its actualities were. The Model is all that is morbid, subjective, and shadow. Hilda is all that is sought in the novel and the sketch; the Model is all that is repudiated in the tale and the Romance. Given the context of *The Marble Faun*'s theme, Hilda's presence is vexing in the book in exactly the same way and proportion that, given the context of Hawthorne's utopia, the sketch is vexing in his Romance. The disruptive ideological power of literary genres makes Hilda profoundly correct in only one of her many assertions: her insistence upon dissociation from Miriam and Donatello. She does *not* belong in the Romance, and an examination of the book's materials reveals how intrusive and anomalous her presence is.

II

Miriam had insisted on the reality of the serpent and its terrible strength. She and Hilda disagree about Guido's picture of the triumph of the Archangel over the Fiend, for Miriam's dark experience tells her that angelic dove wings would be vehemently torn in the struggle. "The battle never was such child's play as Guido's dapper Archangel seems to have found it," says Miriam (p. 184). But in revering the untouched purity that Miriam rejects, Hilda discloses that the essential difference between the two is acknowledgment of the reality of experience. Hilda seeks to transcend the earthly impurity, passion, and sin that Miriam insists are inescapable and real. Hilda would avoid evil, and Miriam would confront it. In this consideration, Hilda stands contrary to the entire Hawthorne canon, for in denying the reality of humanity that Miriam affirms, Hilda fulfills the role that Hawthorne's fiction reserves for the perpetrator of the unforgivable sin. In direct contrast to Miriam's conception of what the painting ought to be in order to be true! be true!, Hilda thinks that the pained delicacy and unruffled neatness of archangel Michael in Guido's painting is "the most beautiful and divinest figure that mortal painter ever drew" (p. 139). And for exactly those reasons, " 'I have never been able,' said Miriam, 'to admire this picture nearly so much as Hilda does, in its moral and intellectual aspect. If it cost her more trouble to be good—if her soul were less white and pure—she would be a more competent critic of this picture, and would estimate it not half so high' " (pp. 183–84). As Miriam tells her, Hilda lives in a transcendent hermitage. "You breathe sweet air, above all the evil scents of Rome; and even so, in your maiden elevation, you dwell above our vanities and passions, our moral dust and mud, with the doves and the angels for your nearest neighbors" (p. 53). Kenyon ambivalently rejoices that "Hilda does not dwell in our mortal atmosphere; and, gentle and soft as she appears, it will be as difficult to win her heart, as to entice down a white bird from its sunny freedom in the sky. It is strange, with all her delicacy and fragility, the impression she makes of being utterly sufficient to herself!" (p. 121).

Because Hilda had involuntarily witnessed Miriam's and Donatello's crime, her world is unhinged. But not once does she worry about Miriam and Donatello: she immediately consigns them to the fate to which convention consigns the souls of sinners. Her only concern is whether she has managed to maintain herself in the state of white purity with which she came from the Hand of her Maker. She glances in the mirror as she sits beside her sketch of Beatrice Cenci, victimized innocence tainted by the inescapable evil around her. And Hilda "fancied—nor was it without horror—that Beatrice's expression, seen aside and vanishing in a moment, had been depicted in her own face. . . .

" 'Am I, too, stained with guilt?' thought the poor girl, hiding her face in her hands." The syntactical effect of ideology, "—nor was it without horror—," is a mild precursor to the parenthetical construction to which Hawthorne then turns. At this point, the clear answer to Hilda's question is, "Yes, everyone is. That's what it means to be human." But at this crucial point, at which Hawthorne, the Romance writer, should dramatize the need to be true! be true!, Hawthorne, a member of his own audience, rushes forward, arms thrown up in panic, in one of his most revealing interjections to his reader: "Not so, thank Heaven!" he exclaims (p. 205). It is as intense a moment of failing his art as Hawthorne ever reveals, as though he, of all writers, had never heard of the sin of the Pharisee.

For although Hilda is miserable when she thinks she has been touched by the "moral dust and mud" of the ground level where all the rest of humanity lives, Hawthorne allows her emotional and spiritual radiance as soon as she clears *herself* of any indirect participation in the crime. Having conveniently used the Catholic confessional to unburden herself, this very non-Catholic daughter of Puritans may now maintain her dainty conscience. Without any right to the confession, she has confessed what she has seen. Thereby she thinks she has shed any remnant of sin, and Hawthorne justifies for Hilda a curiously double standard: no one can accuse her of concealing evidence, aiding, or abetting. She has made her peace with the law. On the other hand, she has confessed in a place where she thinks the secret will remain a secret. No one can accuse her of betraying a friend. She has made her peace with the demands for "sister feeling." Her hands and robe are clean. With a blithe innocence that becomes moral monstrousness, she simply shifts her burden of concealment to another, a priest in a church she does not even acknowledge. And then, in the joy of relief, the Dove can say insouciantly to Kenyon, "Now I know how it is, that the Saints above are touched by the sorrows of distressed people on earth, and yet are never made wretched by them" (p. 364). Whatever, if any, ironic burnings Hawthorne might have felt inside, he continues to maintain an apparent unconsciousness of Hilda's blasphemous arrogance. He allows her the prideful consummation of her smug rectitude: having misused the confessional to scramble back up into her rarefied purity, the "child of New England" can kick away her ladder behind her. "I shall never go to the Confessional again," she asserts; and in any case, "it was the sin of others that drove me thither; not my own, though it almost seemed so" (p. 367).

One of the interesting aspects of Hilda is her adumbrative connection with twentieth-century types. Herself a type of the American Victorian lady, her need for spiritual deodorizers is a reflection of her society's assumptions about transcendent national identity. The association of Hilda with the Shrine of the Virgin is but one more example of the Protestant domestication of the Virgin. As the angel in the house, the medieval, European Mary-Mother-of-God is transformed into the bourgeois American Mary-the-Lady. It was inevitable that Hilda should fulfill her career, finally, not as a heroine of art, for that would be far too radical, but as the domestic ruling angel in Kenyon's house. One can see in Hilda a step in the development and definition of the American Mom of popular culture. Concerned in every advertisement with underarms, panty girdles, disinfectants, detergents, douches, deodorants, Mom fulfills her divine duties as the saintly center of the virginal American home. Otherwise errant, Dad is guided and civilized by her. She is the superimposition of the modern homemaker upon the lady, whose skeleton supports her latter day outlines. And although the new freedoms of post-1960s mores allow controlled candor and libido in the popular presentations of Mom's household, anything radically threatening to conventional gentility remains as unimaginable in her parlor or bedroom as pornography in a Norman Rockwell painting. When Donatello begins to learn truths that the lady will not admit into reality, or even into discussion, he says of Fra Angelico's pictures that "his angels look as if they had never taken a flight out of Heaven; and his Saints seem to have been born Saints, and always to have lived so." Kenyon at once sees in Donatello's criticism "the reason why Hilda so highly appreciates Fra Angelico's pictures" (p. 310). In art as in life as in the Rockwell vision of the American home, the Hilda-sense of a "higher allegiance" and a higher identity demands an unremitting idealization of everything in sight.

Hilda is, in fact, willing to deny friends and works of art at a moment's notice should they fall short of what she deems appropriate in remaining true to her idealization of woman as God's vessel of purity. In his justification of the lady, Hawthorne collaborates in an entire society's dehumanization of women: he has Miriam, Kenyon, and himself as narrator agree that Hilda's "womanhood is of the ethereal type, and incompatible with any shadow of darkness or evil" (p. 128). Just as she purifies the great masters in her copies, she dismisses the humanity of art in favor of an inflexible aesthetic-religious ideal by which she evaluates painting and sculpture. Surveying a sculpture of which she is not sure she approves, she observes, "Human happiness," is "evanescent . . . and beautiful art hardly less so! I do not love to think that this dull stone, merely by its massiveness, will last infinitely longer than any picture, in spite of the spiritual life that ought to give it immortality." "My poor little Hilda," replies Miriam, "would you sacrifice this great mortal consolation, which we derive from the transitoriness of all things—from the right of saying, in every conjuncture, 'This, too, will pass away'—would you give up this unspeakable boon, for the sake of making a picture eternal!" (p. 150).

But the kind of consideration Miriam advances is inapplicable to the Hilda who, moving away from her mirror to avoid any hint of kinship between herself and Beatrice Cenci, says of Beatrice, "Her doom is just!" "Oh, Hilda," replies Miriam, "your innocence is like a sharp steel sword. Your judgments are often terribly severe, though you seem all made up of gentleness and mercy" (p. 66).

Miriam's voice speaks for the Hawthorne-narrator who dramatizes his utopian allegiance in her and Donatello's story at the moment that he states his ideological purpose in the story of Hilda. Donatello and Miriam become the medium for the perceptions that cannot be sanctioned by Hilda. "It was perceptible," says the authorial voice,

> that Donatello had already had glimpses of strange and subtle matters in those dark caverns, *into which all men must descend,* if they would know anything *beneath the surface* and illusive pleasures of existence. And when they emerge, though dazzled and blinded by the first glare of daylight, they take truer and sadder views of life, forever afterwards . . . Donatello now showed a far *deeper* sense, and an intelligence that began to deal with *high* subjects. . . . He evinced, too, a more definite and nobler individuality, but developed out of pain and grief, and fearfully conscious of the pangs which had given it birth. *Every human life, if it ascends to truth or delves down to reality, must undergo a similar change . . .* [italics mine]. (p. 262)

"The only way," says Miriam to Hilda, "is to stare the ugly horror right in the face; never a sidelong glance, nor a half-look, for those are what show a frightful thing in its frightfullest aspect. Lean on me, dearest friend!" (p. 185).

Miriam is "a beautiful and attractive woman" of "natural language, generosity, kindliness, and native truth of character" (pp. 23–24). Her paintings reveal "a great scope of fancy" that can master "the indefinable something added, or taken away, which makes all the difference between sordid life and an earthly paradise. The feeling and sympathy in all of them were deep and true." Her work has "depth and force" and "profound significance" (p. 45). They are the products of a woman whose dark experiences have taught her that if "you cannot suffer deeply . . . you can but half enjoy" (p. 47). Unlike Hilda's, Miriam's concerns in adversity are not for herself, but for those she loves. The selflessness that arises from her suffering is in marked contrast to the severity of Hilda's selfish purity. Nevertheless, Hawthorne subordinates the dark foreigner to the Anglo-Saxon American. He has Kenyon insist that Hilda's untouched innocence must not be disturbed.

"I shall tell Hilda nothing that will give her pain," Kenyon tells Miriam. "I feel that she was right [in casting you out of her life]. You have a thousand admirable qualities . . . But the white, shining purity of Hilda's nature is a thing apart; and she is bound, by the undefiled material of which God moulded her, to keep that severity which I, as well as you, have recognized."

Incredibly, Hawthorne has Miriam, of all people, reply, "Oh, you are right! . . . I never questioned it" (p. 287). At moments like this, when the characters suddenly turn the theme and themselves upside down in their adoring haste to acknowledge Hilda's superiority, the book descends into a bathos that is a precursor of another avatar, the lady in girlhood. Hawthorne almost always calls Miriam a woman and Hilda a girl, an undiscriminatingly blanket assumption of innocence. It is a convention that developed from the ideological rhetoric of literature into the convention epitomized in Hollywood by Shirley Temple and the southern belle—the lady as Missy. She might be naughty, perverse, and willful, but always, we are to believe, lovable. Whatever the gap might be between her lovableness and the insistence that she is beloved, she always is miraculously immune to the trouble in which she is caught, even if it be of her own lovable making. The pickaninnies grin and adore Missy, shuffle and adore Missy, in an unspoken agreement that she, after all, is the idol of true values. These genre movies never have to explain why the darkies should be inferior to and yearn to be like Missy. In their assigned role the lesser folk are engaged in a conspiracy with the marketplace: in the contrast between themselves and Missy they illustrate a set of assumptions in which the narrative vehicle, and thereby the moviemakers, consolidate their oneness with the audience by saying that like white, white Hilda, we are all white here. Hawthorne operates within the unspoken—and probably mostly unconscious—assumption that his white Anglo-Saxon Protestant American audience, about whom and to whom he writes and among whom he takes his place, are the only folk who really matter.

Although it is facile and confuses the point to call Hawthorne a racist, Miriam's "burning drop of African blood" and her Jewishness are the literary ideological tics of racist conventions that long precede Hawthorne in designating character. For Hawthorne's time and place as well as for Hawthorne, the assignment of alien traits assumed to be inferior in their differentness, notwithstanding that those attributes might be enticingly exotic or stirringly heroic, signals the probability that we are not to invest our expectations of the true heroine in the character so designated, and must seek the real representative of true values and beliefs in the holder of the proper national characteristics. Neither consciously nor expressively bigoted, in his ideological purposes Hawthorne turned as though by social reflex to racist contexts to keep Miriam from running Hilda completely off the boards in his drama. A book about the historical and metaphysical oneness of all human beings demands a choice of heroine that will repudiate the sterile smugness of nationalistic and exclusivist arrogance as the basis for one's fitness to be the heroine. It also demands the disavowal of the implicit definitions that make aliens and inferiors synonymous. But as a shy, maidenly prototype of what her characteristics can develop into, in all her qualities Hilda is a premonitory illumination of how the nature of the cultural juncture between the antiseptic American Saint Mom and "inferiors" can extend into a psychological capacity for the enormities of slavery, xenophobia, racism, and the vicious nature of warfare against whatever varieties of others.

The ideology of literary characterization leaves Hawthorne not knowing quite what to do with Kenyon. On the one hand, Hawthorne ideologically presents Kenyon as a male (manly, American, acquainted with the actualities of the world); even as an artist he works in solid stone. Yet the same ideology insists that as patriot and gentleman (Anglo-Saxon, American, Christian, and respectable), despite his necessary male knowledge of history and human actualities (from which the lady must be shielded), he can be allowed to fall in love only with Hilda. Only with Hilda, that is, if he is to be the one in whom readers can invest their expectations of the hero or good lover. Consequently, Hawthorne's own utopian sympathies and wisdom, for whom Kenyon, the artist, is the occasional spokesman, must go a-stuttering or totally muted in the presence of Hilda. In sum, both Hawthorne and Kenyon must pledge their allegiance to what both know better than to believe. Denying a felix culpa as she considers good and bad, light and dark, celestial height and subterranean depth "through the clear, crystal medium of her own integrity," Hilda insists that "Never!" can these opposites intermingle to create the possibility of redemption through sin. "There is," she declares to Kenyon,

> only one right and one wrong; and I do not understand (and may God keep me from ever understanding) how two things so totally unlike can be mistaken for one another; nor how two mortal foes—as Right and Wrong surely are—can work together in the same deed. This is my faith; and I should be led astray, if you could persuade me to give it up."
>
> "Alas, for poor human nature, then!" said Kenyon sadly, and yet half-smiling at Hilda's unworldly and impracticable theory. "I always felt you, my dear friend, a terribly severe judge, and have been perplexed to conceive how such a tender sympathy could coexist with the remorselessness of a steel blade. You need no mercy, and therefore know not how to show any!"
>
> "That sounds like a bitter gibe," said Hilda, with the tears springing

into her eyes. "But I cannot help it. It does not alter my perception of the truth. If there be any such dreadful mixture of good and evil as you affirm (and which appears to me almost more shocking than pure evil), then the good is turned to poison, not the evil to wholesomeness."

The sculptor seemed disposed to say something more, but yielded to the gentle steadfastness with which Hilda declined to listen. (p. 384)

It would seem here that Kenyon is to play the standard role of the older and wiser male teacher to the pure maiden. In terms of the theme and the story's events, Kenyon is closer to the truth than Hilda. The author himself has termed Hilda's certitude an "unworldly and impracticable theory." One waits for Hilda to be educated. But whenever there is a direct confrontation with her, Hawthorne capitulates. Though he always seems "disposed to say something more," he resorts instead to the ideological parentheses that suggest divine sanction for Hilda's assertions. Kenyon, therefore, cannot play the role for which he is occasionally prepared, but instead must be taught by his ignorant pupil. In every instance he must adoringly abase himself in worshipful capitulation to Missy. When Hilda announces that she now knows how saints feel, she does so with a smarmy and immediate propriety: " 'Not that I profess to be a Saint, you know,' she added, smiling radiantly." And Kenyon makes the only adoring reply that Hawthorne can ideologically allow him: " 'Do you say you are no Saint!' answered Kenyon with a smile, though he felt that the tears stood in his eyes. 'You will still be Saint Hilda, whatever church may canonize you' " (p. 364).

Kenyon suggests that perhaps "Sin is . . . like Sorrow, merely an element of human education through which we struggle to a higher and purer state than we could otherwise have attained. Did Adam fall, that we might rise to a far loftier Paradise than his?" Here Kenyon touches the very heart of the book, raising the central question to which the lines of the other major characters dramatize clear assent and ascent. But the New England maiden cannot be allowed to turn against the very conventionalities she represents:

"Oh hush!" cried Hilda, shrinking from him with an expression of horror which wounded the poor, speculative sculptor to the soul. "This is terrible; and I could weep for you, if you indeed believe it. Do not you perceive what a mockery your creed makes, not only of all religious sentiment, but of moral law, and how it annuls and obliterates whatever precepts of Heaven are written deepest within us? You have shocked me beyond words!" (p. 460)

Hawthorne has written himself into a corner. Here there can be no further ambivalences or disguises, for he is squarely up against the book's conflict of utopia with ideology. Either he must give the palm to Hilda, or he must repudiate her. To repudiate her he must deliberately make all the potential irony explicit in revealing that everything Hilda stands for is Dracula hidden in a masquerade of Pollyanna. But he denies the irony and so denies his own utopia. Standing the book on its head in a moment that is nothing less than the climactic statement of his theme, Hawthorne has Kenyon's grovelling bring him safely back into the marketplace world of the Dove. "Forgive me, Hilda!" begs Kenyon. "*I never did believe it!* But the mind wanders wild and wide. . . . Were you my guide, my counsellor, my inmost friend, with that white wisdom which clothes you as a celestial garment, all would go well. *Oh, Hilda, guide me home!*" (p. 461, italics mine).

And home they go, to the One Good Place, that "fortunate land" on the millennial side of the Atlantic, of Rome's history, and of the Romance's dramatized human experience. There Hilda will be "herself enshrined and worshipped as a household Saint, in the light of her husband's fireside" (p. 461).

Hawthorne's losing struggle with Shirley Temple prefigures the function of America's Darling as the triumphant golden bitch in the works of so many American authors, most notably F. Scott Fitzgerald. In her vanquishing Kenyon with a word is the triumph of the mindless and irrational optimism witnessed in Daddy's Girl, to return to that example for a moment. We never break free from the national implications of Hilda's triumphant skipping over the place of Curtius's demise. The lineaments of the Rosemary Hoyt "ickle durl" emerge from beneath the surface differences of time and idiom: "Before her tiny fist the forces of lust and corruption rolled away; nay, the very march of destiny stopped; inevitable became evitable; syllogism, dialectic, all rationality fell away."[8] Hilda's optimistic denial of the reality of experience is a mindless reduction of human pain to do-it-yourself, quick-fix redemption. Making the inevitable evitable at the spot where Curtius was engulfed, Hilda makes her little preachment: "Every wrong thing makes the gulf deeper; every right one helps to fill it up. As the evil of Rome was far more than its good, the whole commonwealth finally sank into it, indeed, but of no original necessity" (p. 162).

This starlet with Victorian diction simply cannot hear the profound implications of the comic view and of classicist disillusion in Miriam's weary response: "Well Hilda, it came to the same thing at last" (p. 162).

Even when the ideological effects upon plot (Hilda cannot participate in the careers of sinners) necessitate that Hilda be removed and confined away from the action, Hawthorne will not subject her to the dark, claustral restrictions of experience, but must insist upon Hilda's "special providence." *No* closure can act upon her. In the original version of *The Marble Faun,* Hawthorne simply shied away altogether from the actualities of Hilda's disappearance, leaving it entirely mysterious. In the added epilogue, he grumbled about the literal-mindedness of readers who insisted upon the actualities and could not leave Hilda's absence to the imagination. But he had no right to his grudge because he was engaging in a cheat that was the result of all his other capitulations. Having indicated in the thematic use of setting as well as in the theme that one cannot be a living human being and not somehow suffer *descent,* and having removed Hilda from her tower, Hawthorne had no place to put her that was ideologically acceptable. After all, in Rome the very air one breathes in descent from the tower exudes disease. In the Pincian Garden "sits (drooping upon some marble bench, in the treacherous sunshine) the consumptive girl, whose friends have brought her, for cure, to a climate that instills poison into its very purest breath" (p. 100).

The parenthetical utopian observation confirms no unmixed state of sunshine. Any place except Hilda's tower of the Virgin's Shrine subjects her to subterraneanism, especially in any kind of imprisonment. But she has been taken from the tower. Consequently, at the point where he has to account for Hilda's captivity, Hawthorne chooses to leave actuality altogether and speculates about the airy translation of Hilda into a "Land of Picture." He used the justification of the Romance paradoxically as an escape from the kind of actualities his theme, made possible by Romance, demanded. Precisely at a point of enormous potential interest, the education of Hilda into humanity at last, Hawthorne claimed the license of the Romancer to remove her from actualities with whose ideological implications he could not cope:

> Whence she had come, or where she had been hidden, during this mysterious interval we can but imperfectly surmise, and do not mean at present, to make it a matter of formal explanation with the reader. It is better, perhaps, to fancy that she had been snatched away to a Land of Picture . . . to converse with the great departed Masters of the pencil, and behold the diviner works which they have painted in heavenly colors. Guido had shown her another portrait of Beatrice Cenci, done from the celestial life, in which that forlorn mystery of the earthly countenance was exchanged for a radiant joy. Perugino had allowed her a glimpse at his easel, on which she discerned what seemed a Woman's face, but so divine by the very depth and softness of its Womanhood, that a gush of happy tears blinded the maiden's eyes, before she had time to look. (p. 452)

And so on. And on. Placing Hilda with the painters of the ideal Woman of Heaven is Hawthorne's evasive way of not really removing

Hilda from the tower of the Virgin's Shrine at all. That Hawthorne's solution for the problems of plot reveal to the maiden the ideal Woman as the Pure Virgin exposes the source of Hilda's character. There is every reason to understand Hawthorne's instinct to remove Hilda from the story, but he had to return her to earth and Kenyon—in an impossibly uninterrupted state of unmixed sunshine. In the terms set up by the story itself, Hilda literally was too good to be true! be true! In the terms set up by the story, Hilda was too pure to live, and it was Hawthorne's weakness that he let her. By translating her *out* of the story's action into a totally idealized somewhere else, Hawthorne was able to restore Hilda to her own happy ending with her original qualities unimpaired, her faith in art restored, and, most dishonest of all, her point of view vindicated.

Hawthorne was so eager to make Hilda his paragon for his marketplace that he was sometimes led into factual error in the narrative. Identifying the sketch in the old portfolio as Guido's original study for the paintings in the Capuchin church (pp. 140–41), Hilda, Kenyon, and Donatello agree that the face of the devil is that of Miriam's Model, while Miriam disagrees. But by the time Miriam, Kenyon, and Donatello examine the painting (p. 183), Hawthorne seems to have forgotten the point at issue. He did not specify it directly, although it was precisely the kind of detail that should have been dwelt upon and that ordinarily he would have developed. Evidently, what he remembered in the act of composition was that one person was to have been right while all the others were wrong. The forgetful author switched his characters' roles, for what he remembered was that it was *Hilda* who was right in contradistinction to all the rest.

" 'But we were wrong, and Hilda was right, as you perceive,' said Miriam, directing . . . Kenyon's attention to the point on which their dispute, of the night before, had arisen. 'It is not easy to detect her astray, as regards any picture on which those clear, soft eyes of hers have ever rested' " (p. 183).

In itself the error is minor. But it is revelatory. In the psychology of Hawthorne's allegiances and intentions, one is safe in standing firm with the approved ideology. He was always aware that an intense act contrary to orthodox sanctions acutely isolates the self. "This perception," says the authorial voice, "of an infinite, shivering solitude, amid which we cannot come close enough to human beings to be warmed by them, and where they turn to cold, chilly shapes of mist, is one of the most forlorn results of any accident, misfortune, crime, or peculiarity of character, that puts an individual ajar with the world" (p. 113). But he was also aware of the proto-existentialist aspect of the intense act, seeing the paradox that isolation through the act of will creates a community of initiates:

> Their deed—the crime which Donatello wrought, and Miriam accepted on the instant—had wreathed itself, as she said, like a serpent, in inextricable links about both their souls, and drew them into one. It was closer than a marriage-bond. So intimate, in those first moments, was the union, that it seemed as if their new sympathy annihilated all other ties, and that they were released from the chain of humanity; a new sphere, a special law, had been created for them alone. The world could not come near them. (p. 174)

But for one important difference, this might be a passage from *La Condition Humaine.* The difference is that the truly existential perspective applauds the self-construction of new identity beginning from a zero base. But as the image of the serpent indicates, and given the comment that Hawthorne's total ouevre makes on "release from the chain of humanity," Hawthorne's more conventional Christian perspective creates a struggle for reentry into the chain of humanity by a newly forged identity, but one fashioned by the sympathies that arise from repentance and penance. The personal temperament that absolutely demands the closure of snug safety and warm belonging possibly was the deep engine that generated both Hawthorne's utopia and at the same time, paradoxically, his ideological capitulations. But psychobiography can be an unfair game. It is enough to suggest that Hawthorne's finest psychological insights always, in all his fiction, are those attaching to the effects and possibilities of aloneness. Yet, given the inevitability of aloneness, which permeates all of Hawthorne's work and might be said to be the central subject of all his fiction, and given the desperate struggle to rediscover community, which might be said to be the central theme of all his fiction, Hawthorne's writings demand that ultimate sympathy must be reserved for those who change. Human depth and richness, like lichens, romance, and poetry, need ruin to make them grow.

Hilda's unchanging line of character direction is but one more sign that conformity to ideological superstructures tends to create monotony. The portrait of Hilda is propaganda. It is as unchanging in characterization as the idealizations of workers or warriors as superheroes in the clichés of socialist realism in art. In asserting the relation of ruin to the growth of art and asserting at the same time that his own dear native land is a place of cheerful sunshine untouched by ruin, Hawthorne illuminates nationalism's creation of a coercive atmosphere of ideological conservatism inimical to art. But in championing Hilda, Hawthorne is saying not only that his native land is not a land of poetry but also that it is somehow right in those values that make it inhospitable to art. Yet Hawthorne champions art in appealing for the Romance, and to the extent that art is a questioning of ideological superstructures it is dissent. It lends itself to the politics of the underground in exactly the same way that the theme of *The Marble Faun* annihilates Hilda. The fascinating fracture in the book between the triumphant role of Hilda and the nature and function of Romance as Hawthorne's utopia presented it reveals how much Hawthorne *was* Norman Rockwell at the same time he felt expatriated from the marketplace that loved and demanded his sketches.

Hawthorne constantly reveals his own expatriation from Hilda. She emerges—not as a creation of deliberate artistic irony—against his conscious intentions as obtuse, narrow, smug, inflexible, juiceless, cold, and prelapsarian, which is to say, prehuman. In such conversations as those between Miriam and Kenyon about the sculpted hand of Hilda (pp. 120–22); between Miriam and Hilda about the chasm beneath our feet (pp. 161–62); between Kenyon and Hilda about Miriam's relation to the Model (pp. 108–9); between Miriam and Hilda about trust in God (pp. 166–67); between Kenyon and Donatello about Fra Angelico (p. 310); between Kenyon and Hilda about Hilda's rigid judgment (p. 384); in Hilda's closing the window to Miriam's pleading voice (p. 177); in almost every detail of chapter 23, the confrontation between Miriam and Hilda; and in far too many other instances to be dismissable, it becomes clear that Hawthorne has at least a partial awareness of what Hilda is and responds with distaste and fear. But in exactly that fear, in his Yankee embarrassment about his vocational calling, he could never really complete the act, necessary for him, of expatriation from "Salem," and all his declarations of independence are never followed through with total war. For all the ambiguities of the dissensions and demurrers that Hawthorne cannot help but reveal in the nature of his theme, Hilda does emerge unscathed, unchanged—and right in all things. To see Hilda as an instrument of conscious irony saves face for Hawthorne as an artist, and therefore it is a tempting critical gambit, but it is a simplistic reduction of the problem. The claim of irony is in its moment of fashion, but it glosses over the complexities of political significance in Hawthorne's fiction by explaining away all the rich tensions of self-annihilation in one easy meaning: Hawthorne was only kidding. But to say that, in order to dismiss the ideological overtones distasteful to modern critical readers, is merely the obverse of Hawthorne's saying that he was only kidding by dismissing in parentheses the thematic overtones distasteful to his marketplace. James's admonitions apply both ways.

Hilda is an American priss because deep in his own being, in part, so was Hawthorne. Hilda-like, he gives Miriam a New England Puritan conscience at a moment of intense joy—"the very exquisiteness of the enjoyment made her know that it ought to be a forbidden one" (p. 82)—and his utilization of Catholicism in *The Marble Faun* has made readers wince. Although he finds in the ancientness and commodiousness of the Catholic church a lavish setting for his expression of the utopia from which his theme grows, he goes out of his way before his audience to disclaim the very Catholicism he chooses to utilize. The disclaimers are not a product of the thematic demands of the Romance; even the sinful intrigues of the historical institution of the Catholic church are background materials that are in perfect harmony with Hawthorne's view of the truth about human life. Because the presence of the disclaimers is thematically inorganic, it becomes a series of ideological parentheses and, as such, as intrusive as, for example, the prim authorial rejection of nudity in art. The insertions between dashes speak volumes: " 'No, no, Miriam!' said Hilda, who had come joyfully forward to greet her friend. 'You must not call me a Catholic. A Christian girl—even a daughter of the Puritans—may surely pay honor to the idea of Divine Womanhood, without giving up the faith of her forefathers. But how kind you are to climb into my dove-cote!' " (p. 54).

One might wish to claim that this righteous double-talk is Hilda's, not Hawthorne's, but it is Hawthorne who arranges Hilda's conversations in chapters 39 and 40 to justify the propriety of Hilda's use of the confessional. Hawthorne indicates that Hilda is aware of what might appear to be the sinfulness of acting Catholic, but he does so only to give her Yankee absolution. "Hilda, do you ever pray to the Virgin, while you tend her shrine?" asks Miriam.

" 'Sometimes I have been moved to do so,' replied the Dove, blushing and lowering her eyes.—'She was a woman once. Do you think it would be wrong?' " And then in the authorial voice Hawthorne observes that if Hilda "knelt—if she prayed—if her oppressed heart besought the sympathy of Divine Womanhood, afar in bliss, but not remote, because forever humanized by the memory of mortal griefs—was Hilda to be blamed? It was not a Catholic, kneeling at an idolatrous shrine, but a child, lifting its tear-stained face to seek comfort from a Mother!" (p. 332).

The parenthetical justifications of Hilda reach their nadir at the moment she suspects that she might be morally delinquent in her repudiation of Miriam, for that is precisely the moment when Hawthorne is most baldly faced with the problem of prudential orthodoxy versus his theme. Therefore it is the moment when the ideological function of syntactical structure is revealed in its most blatantly direct moment of parenthetical propaganda: Hawthorne presents Hilda as "recurring to the delinquencies of which she fancied—(we say 'fancied' because we do not unhesitatingly adopt Hilda's present view, but rather suppose her misled by her feelings)—of which she fancied herself guilty toward her friend" (p. 386). Armored by both parentheses and dashes, the one time that Hawthorne pops in to say that Hilda might be wrong, he does so to say that she is wrong to think that she is wrong the one time that Hilda thinks she might be wrong. Because Hilda can do no wrong, the parentheses and dashes are especially eloquent in her brief flirtation with Catholicism. In the first sentence of chapter 44, which presents Kenyon's response to the discovery that the Virgin's lamp in Hilda's shrine had gone out, "Kenyon knew the sanctity which Hilda (faithful Protestant, and daughter of the Puritans, as the girl was) imputed to this shrine" (p. 399). And again, in Hilda's account of her detention by benevolent Catholics: " 'I was a prisoner in the Convent of the Sacre Coeur, in the Trinita de' Monti,' said she; 'but in such kindly custody of pious maidens, and watched over by such a dear old priest, that—had it not been for one or two disturbing recollections, and also because I am a daughter of the Puritans—I could willingly have dwelt there forever' " (p. 466).

Because, through Hilda's use of the Catholic church, Hawthorne had to present the emotional purgation it can offer, he had to allow Hilda to skirt dangerously close to appreciation in her conversation with Kenyon. But the conclusion of the conversation, although not structurally parenthetical in any way, functions the way Hawthorne's parenthetical structures do in proper ideological affirmation or reversal of the flow of idea. Hawthorne is careful to have Hilda conclude, "If its ministers were but a little more than human, above all error, pure from all iniquity, what a religion it would be!" Kenyon's conventionally anti-Catholic response completes Hawthorne's ideological repudiation of what he has presented: " 'I need not fear your perversion to the Catholic faith,' remarked Kenyon, 'if you are at all aware of the bitter sarcasm implied in your last observation' " (p. 368).

William Charvat had noted that "Hawthorne's style is essentially parenthetical, and that this characteristic reflects the basically essayistic generalizing, and speculative quality of his fiction. His parentheses give him the latitude and flexibility that this quality requires."9 Hawthorne's stylistic peculiarity, like the eighteenth- and nineteenth-century literary convention in which the author steps front and center to lecture his audience, does indeed change the mode from fiction to

essay. When Hawthorne's essay is in accord with the utopian conservatism of his theme, it tends not to be parenthetical in structure because it
does not disrupt the flow of idea. Ordinarily such essay shows up in
preachy dialogue or in Hawthorne's authorial musing, not in contradiction but in development of the implications of what has just been
presented in setting, action, or conversation. Directly authorial presentation of the utopia tends therefore to occupy a longer duration than the
momentary interjection. *The House of the Seven Gables* offers probably
the best example of Hawthorne's authorial utopian Classicist speculations in the set-piece viewing Judge Pyncheon dead in his chair.

But, given Hawthorne's utopian theme, when the authorial moment
is an expression of *ideological* conservatism, it disrupts the flow of idea,
a reactionary counterraid from the marketplace against the major direction of the fiction. As *The Marble Faun* amply indicates, because the
marketplace ideology is extrinsic to the utopian dramatization, the
ideology tends to be intrusive and noticeable. Artistically, it is nasty,
mean, poor, brutish, and short. It is usually parenthetical. Its frequency
indicates the constancy of Hawthorne's ideological acquiescence, and it
is that failure of nerve rather than "speculative quality" that forms the
parenthetical aspect of Hawthorne's style.

As for what Charvat referred to as "speculative quality," Hawthorne's
contemporary reviewers, like all modern readers, note the brooding
intelligence and quiet musing that plays about the work. As the parentheses mostly come from the ideology, the speculative quality comes
from the utopia. The snug, settled, fireside quality that was such a deep
need of Hawthorne's personality is a quality of establishment, of closure,
and is expressed in calm thoughtfulness rather than interjection. The
psychology of his utopian conservatism might be called the temperament of his style. Whether Hawthorne set his tale in New England or
Rome, the events of his narrative are toned by a constant authorial
stance of meditative speculation about history's repeated revelation of
human frailty. Hawthorne holds up the events of his stories and always
asks, in effect, the same question: "May we not make surmises about the
connections between these apparently novel and peculiar circumstances
and the universal nature of the human heart?" From that utopian
question he branches out into both dramatic and essayistic inquiries
into the psychological and moral functions of inevitable human limitations. He always creates the essential political dimension by concentrating upon the relationship of the community to the apparently isolating
revelations of sin that mark the individual. The Romantic polis is
impossible as long as mortals dwell in history rather than in heaven.
The combination of Hawthorne's temperament and politics creates a

characteristic energy of allegorical force in his works for precisely the reasons that he is interested not so much in the realistically rendered actualities as in the fundamental political philosophy he sees in them. From *that* all morals and emblems flow in his fiction. Given his utopian conservatism, he already knows the significance of all events in their revelation of the human heart: Classicist closure. This is to say that his tendency to structure his fiction as allegory, his tendency to work from idea to emblematic embodiment of it, is a function of the utopian foundation of his imagination. Artists do not simply pre-select arbitrarily their characteristic voices. Their lives and personalities go into the casting about that eventually results in the development of their signatures. Hawthorne's temperament led to his characteristic imaginative brooding upon what I have been calling the principle of closure. The musing tone of his fictions and his gravitational turn toward allegory are instrumental expressions of each other, equal expressions of his utopian conservatism and his choice of the Romance.

But within the idiosyncratic context of his temperament, Hawthorne's politics created for him a special problem in the dramatization of action. Action in itself may lead to many unanticipated consequences. As a process of discovery, it may open up new worlds as well as destroy the old, known one. But in the retrospective nature of Hawthorne's fiction, the harbored and snug quality of the prose bespeaks a man of households, not a wanderer. As "Wakefield" and the Miles Coverdale persona of *Blithedale* suggest, Hawthorne sought closure in the very act of newness and exploration. Granted, Hawthorne repudiates his Wake-fields, but the language depicting the comfortable retreat to the coal fire in one's chambers is too strongly evocative of a *desirably* comfortable cocooning to successfully fulfill the function of irony. The language and tone truly belong to closure:

> Let us now imagine Wakefield bidding adieu to his wife. It is the dusk of an October evening. His equipment is a drab great-coat, a hat covered with an oilcloth, top-boots, an umbrella in one hand and a small port-manteau in the other. . . . Go quietly to thy bed, foolish man; and, on the morrow, if thou wilt be wise, get thee home to good Mrs. Wakefield. . . . (IX, 132, 133).
>
> One evening, in the twentieth year since he vanished, Wakefield is taking a walk towards the dwelling which he still calls his own. It is a gusty night of autumn, with frequent showers that patter down upon the pavement and are gone before a man can put up his umbrella. . . . Wakefield discerns, through the parlor windows of the second floor, the red glow and the glimmer and fitful flash of a comfortable fire. On the ceiling appears a grotesque shadow of good Mrs. Wakefield . . . an admirable caricature,

which dances, almost too merrily for the shade of an elderly widow. At this instance a shower chances to fall, and is driven, by the unmannerly gust, full into Wakefield's face and bosom. He is quite penetrated with its autumnal chill. Shall we stand, wet and shivering here, when his own hearth has a good fire to warm him? (IX, 139)

Similarly, Miles Coverdale is introduced as he is about to enter his chamber. "Arriving at my room, I threw a lump of cannel coal upon the grate, lighted a cigar, and spent an hour in musings of every hue . . . and then I went to bed, after drinking a glass of particularly fine sherry" (III, 8). This is at the end of the first chapter of *The Blithedale Romance.* The beginning of the second chapter is Coverdale's first reminiscence of Blithedale as—a magnificent hearthside fire: "there can hardly flicker up again so cheery a blaze upon the hearth, as that which I remember, the next day, at Blithedale. It was a wood-fire, in the parlor of an old farm-house, on an April afternoon, but with the fitful gusts of a wintry snow-storm roaring in the chimney. Vividly does that fireside re-create itself, as I rake away the ashes from the embers in my memory, and blow them up with a sigh" (III, 9).

Miles Coverdale is to be equated with Hawthorne as little as the lawyer in "Bartleby the Scrivener" is to be equated with Melville. True, there are many scenes and moments of snug hearthside peace in Melville's short fiction. But in what one takes away from the language and situations in the novels and stories, one senses that Hawthorne quietly delights in cloistered enclosure (the lovely, brooding vision of the firelit, moonlit parlor in "The Custom House" introduction to *The Scarlet Letter* is perhaps the best example), as Melville delights in something quite else. Hawthorne's writings leave the impression of a writer who immerses himself in and voices the psychology of closure, the enclosed and quiet hearthside existence in which to be in touch with the common, domestic life, and yet to muse and exercise the imagination at the same time. A single example from a work of openness, with the language and action not of cozy, sequestered musing but of bursting forth, makes the point. Compare *Moby-Dick*'s rhetoric, tone, and action in Melville's "Lee Shore" presentation of the perpetually outward-bound Bulkington with that of the representative Hawthorne passage.

But as in landlessness alone resides the highest truth, shoreless, indefinite as God—so, better is it to perish in that howling infinite, than be ingloriously dashed upon the lee, even if that were safety! For worm-like, then, oh! who would craven crawl to land! Terrors of the terrible! is all this agony so vain? Take heart, take heart, O Bulkington! Bear thee grimly, demigod! Up from the spray of thy ocean perishing—straight up, leaps thy apotheosis!

The difference in feel of the two passages is the difference not only between Melville and Hawthorne but also between the language of the Romantic and symbolic imagination (exploratory openness of meaning), on the one hand, and the language of the Classicist and emblemizing imagination (essentially prefixed meaning), on the other. Hawthorne felt restive about his domesticated marketplace identity, and, if the contradictions and tensions in his fiction mean anything at all, he yearned somewhat for a heroic self of pioneering openness. Yet, in his psychology, in what might be termed the politics of his temperament, he recoiled from that identity and usually cast it in the role of evil as in "Young Goodman Brown," "The Birthmark," and "Rappaccini's Daughter." Hawthorne the Romancer wanted the Romantic considerably less than he wanted the fireside. Openness frightened Hawthorne, and he shrank from it, which probably marked the politics of whatever psychological and social specifics occasioned his break from Melville. The irony is that the world remembers Hawthorne's pronouncement that Melville could not rest comfortably either in his belief or his unbelief, whereas it was the cooler and settled Hawthorne who, in effect, walked off to his death in a weariness of contradictions, stifled in the successful society to which he finally successfully belonged. The irony is that Hawthorne died in the act of setting out.

The essentially Romantic character, like Bulkington, cannot rest long on the lee shore, within the cozy and sequestered confines of established life. He seeks the fluid medium, not stasis. He is a pioneer in search of the new. Hawthorne preferred the snug contemplation of the past. For him actions were new illustrations of what mankind already had experienced. The substance they afforded him for storytelling was not, therefore, adventure, but their effects on personality and the relationship between the community and the self. In most cases in Hawthorne's fiction, the dramatic motivating act either has taken place before the story begins, as in *The Scarlet Letter* (the adultery) and *The House of the Seven Gables* (Pyncheon's sin and Maule's curse), or it is condensed to an almost instantaneous moment, gone just as it begins, as in *The Marble Faun* (the murder of the Capuchin). *The Marble Faun* in the Centenary Edition is 467 pages long, and yet only four and one-half lines are given to the crucial act itself. And that is given in the blurred rush seen through the eyes of the observer, Hilda. In the act of opening a courtyard door, Hilda "was startled, midway, by the noise of a struggle within, beginning and ending all in one breathless instant. Along with it, or closely succeeding it, was a loud, fearful cry, which quivered upward through the air, and sank quivering downward to the earth" (p. 171). The action, upon which the entire story depends, and the one in which the lifelines of the major characters meet, is reduced to "one breathless instant." What Hawthorne writes next is a metaphor for the nature of all his work: "Then a silence! Poor Hilda had looked into the courtyard, and saw the whole quick passage of a deed, which took but little time to grave itself in the eternal adamant" (p. 171).

Action, while it occurs, is fluid, unfixed, explosive in possibilities of meaning. But Hawthorne is concerned with fixing it as immediately as possible. Like "eternal adamant" history is fixed in its implications for human meaning, action is fixed in its Classicist implications for human history, and it is with the fixed and adamantine idea behind the acts that the philosophically conservative Hawthorne is fascinated. For Ahab, all meaning is fixed and all existence is an idealist's allegory. But for Ishmael, all meaning is as relative and constantly unmade as the readings of the doubloon nailed on the mast. For Melville-Ishmael, the fluid medium leaves nothing but motion, nothing static, everything open. The constant forward motion is the constant discovery of new meaning in the act of making symbols. For Hawthorne, the fixed brooding is the constant discovery of old meaning in the act of making emblems. Not the motion of the act but the silence after the act is what is important for Hawthorne, for it is in that silence that there is the stopped time allowing perception and definition of the eternal adamant. Again, the set-piece on Jaffrey Pyncheon's death is the paradigm for Hawthorne's gift: he does not even show the act of dying, but circles it by seating Jaffrey and then reentering the room after the act has occurred, in stopped time and silence. The musing *is* the action; the action is the statement of the meaning of closure. In the presentation of the dramatic actions that generate the plots, Hawthorne's books are speculative acts of silence. They spend themselves in fixing the meanings that define the actions. Consequently, Hawthorne's books are not media of prospect, but of retrospect.

With the generative action finished in one breathless instant or finished before the book begins, action, like meaning, has been fixed in the past, and the spooling of mind is not a process of discovery but of rediscovery. The consequent events we see in process, therefore, are already fixed. When present action is in a fluid state in which intensity existentially makes identity, there is not so much the force of precedent as there is infinite possibility of new action. But when present action is fixed as consequences of meanings inherent in the primal act, they are already chosen—nothing unforeseen can be in their place. Instead of struggling with the messy fluidity of discovery, Hawthorne controls events by subjecting them to idea before the book began, or at least after only a breathless instant. He does not have to enter the openness of discovering new worlds; what he does have to do is to invent bodies and events to march in a known world supplied by his utopian imagination. The Classicist point of view, seeing the narrowness of human options, seeks fixed values. Once Hawthorne gets action, which is to say unpredictable fluidity, out of the way, and fixes its reality in the past, the narrowness of human choices becomes a dramatic given in the narrative present. Paradoxically, the narrowness liberates Hawthorne for the full play of his conservative retrospection, which is the dramatization of his utopia. His Hesters and Dimmesdales never do, never can, get away to a new country, nor his Mr. Hoopers remove their veils. With the exclusion of fluid openness, Hawthorne is free to devote his attention to the "eternal adamant" of the Classicist idea for which his characters and their actions become prefixed emblems. Their lives are illustrations of what already has been established as universal moral law. The distance between what Hawthorne sees in his ideational foreknowledge and what his characters see in their own present actions in process is the dimension of motion and discovery in Hawthorne's work. Hawthorne allows his readers to see that dimension explicitly in the essayistic constructions of his authorial brooding and ironically in his parenthetical punctuations.

Hawthorne fills the distance between what he knows and what his characters see with the workings of the characters' psyches and therein lies his greatness. As the characters flutter in the eternal and adamantine grip of *what has always been since the Fall,* the readers, like some of the characters, come to understand the established moral lesson that Hawthorne had already derived from his Classicism before he invented his characters. His notebooks indicate again and again how his stories derive from a person or object or event that vibrates for Hawthorne with overtones of closure. For this reason, Hawthorne's endings often contain what amount to extended parentheses, statements of ideological counterattack against a preestablished utopia with which Hawthorne could not rest comfortably in his marketplace.

Consequently his endings tend to be truncations or tacked-on denials of everything that has gone before. As last words, they reveal the strength of the conflict between the energies of openness and closure and, thereby, take their similarity to endings in the larger development of American literature. Hawthorne's endings are significant not only as indications of his own conflicts but also as premonitions of the continuing effects of an American literary paradox: the assumptions of openness became a fixed ideological closure in American political allegiances. The tensions between dissent and nationalistic pieties continued to intensify from the Civil War onward, and a brief look at some representative endings reveals how lasting are the contexts with which Hawthorne began the struggle.

NOTES

1. Centenary *Works*, IV, 2. All further references to *The Marble Faun* are to this text and are indicated by parentheses in the body of the text. In citing this edition, however, I change spellings to current standard American English and leave the occasional instances of anachronism or error in the wording to the purisms of the Centenary Edition.

2. Centenary *Letters, 1857–1864*, XVIII, 262.

3. Hawthorne to Ticknor and Fields, Dec. 1, 1859, Ms. Berg Collection, New York Public Library: "A New York trade periodical, *The Bookseller's Medium and Publisher's Advertiser*, 2 (February 1, 1860), 223, announced the forthcoming book under this title." Claude M. Simpson, "Introduction," Centenary *Works*, IV, xxvi, n. 22.

4. "Puritans Preferred Blondes: The Heroines of Melville and Hawthorne," *New England Quarterly* 9 (June 1936): 253–72.

5. I am indebted to John Seelye for a suggestion that I cannot follow up because it would necessitate another chapter or, perhaps, another book on comparative uses of the light and dark ladies in American literature. But the suggestion is very appropriate to the discussion and is rich enough to warrant quoting here. In his letter, Seelye begins with the

> division early established by de Stael in *Corinne*, a text wherein the dark, sensuous woman is associated with artistic expression (and personal freedom) and the blond with social convention (and marriage), a conflict in which the dark woman is doomed. Inspired by Scott's *Ivanhoe*, Cooper employs the same division to miscegenetic ends. Most importantly, Hawthorne makes what would seem to be an open allusion to *Corinne* when he has Hester stand exposed upon a platform in the marketplace, a silent symbol of "art," where de Stael's heroine, in a comparable scene, is a vocal one. Rome celebrates that which Salem represses. That Hester stands in the *marketplace*, that her art is eventually one of compromise with societal (moral) demands, suggests that Hawthorne was well aware of the *Corinne* tradition, and adapted it to his own autobiographical uses.
> ... Melville's *Pierre* provides a very useful parallel text to *The Marble Faun*, with quite different conclusions. That is, Melville employs the same division between dark and light ladies, but with antithetical results. The marketplace is again the crux upon which the plot turns, in a double sense, Melville writing a book he claimed would be popular about a writer writing a book bound to fail, in effect thereby guaranteeing that his

own novel would also fail, for just the reasons carefully avoided by Hawthorne in *The Marble Faun*. A third vector is provided by Longfellow's *Kavanagh*, the ur-text in both regards, being a popular novel that actually violated the marketplace canon by giving the victory to the passionate lady, leaving the pale one to loiter wanly and die. . . . Melville set himself against the considerations of the marketplace, providing a radical "left" to the centrist position occupied by Hawthorne and the far right occupied by such as Willis and G. W. Curtis and their cohort of "scribbling" sentimentalists.

6. *Three Novels of F. Scott Fitzgerald,* ed. Malcolm Cowley (New York: Charles Scribner's Sons, 1953), p. 130.

7. Even though identifying the author with or as the narrative voice is today an act of heresy tantamount to committing critical suicide, it is an identification I insist on making in this discussion of *The Marble Faun*. Hawthorne lived in a time well before our critical and narratorial sophistications demanded every kind of supersubtlety in discussing narrative voice. The narrator in *The Marble Faun,* as in most of Hawthorne's fiction (the first-person narrator of *The Blithedale Romance* is a clear exception), was taken by his reading public as Hawthorne. Hawthorne knew that the first-person intrusions as well as the non–first-person observations of the authorial voice would be read as his own. Hawthorne spoke to his readers as directly in his interpolations as in his prefaces, and he knew he was doing so. Whatever the subtle and complex differences between the Hawthorne who sat down at his writing desk and the Hawthorne who stood up from it, Hawthorne's literary age, conventions, milieu, practice, and voice made the statements of the author the statements of Hawthorne. The metaphysics of difference between any person as a reality and as a fiction are a given for every human's life and to that extent are beside the point here. Insofar as there actually was a Nathaniel Hawthorne, whatever that entity, that is what I refer to as "Hawthorne" and that is what Hawthorne's literary marketplace read—and Hawthorne knew it read—when it read authorial observations. And that is what Hawthorne wrote from—and knew he wrote from—when he wrote those observations for others to read.

8. *Tender Is the Night,* p. 130.

9. Quoted by Fredson Bowers, "Textual Introduction," Centenary *Works,* IV, lxxvi–lxxvii, n. 33.

5

An Endings Context

Real people are presumably more multidimensional than whatever literary use may be made of them, and in real life Sophia (Dove) Peabody had qualities beyond the restrictive closure functions she represents as a metaphor in occasional references to her in this study. She was not literally Hilda. Yet the metaphor to which she is limited here has, like all metaphors, its own useful truth. It is close to the facts of her relation to Hawthorne's fiction. She favored the sunshiny conclusions that reflected the combination of Victorian conventionality and sentimentalized Romantic optimism so characteristic of the rhetoric and events of nineteenth-century American fiction. Her tastes were representative of everything that urged Hawthorne toward an ending for *The Marble Faun* in which the conclusion of the fiction became one with the closure ordained in Hilda's triumph. In a profound and central way, Sophia was to Hawthorne what Hilda was to Kenyon. Both Doves represented belonging. Sophia could never really pull Hawthorne into the polite but fervent enthusiasms she entertained for Transcendentalism. For all that he made his try at Brook Farm, Hawthorne could never quite share the sense of belonging that Sophia had within the Emersonian circle. Similarly, within the non-Transcendentalist precincts of received society, be it Concord, Salem, or Boston, Sophia was one of those who belonged, as Hawthorne never quite felt he did. Whether his late marriage and his tendency toward reclusiveness were a result of life with a strange mother and a possessive sister, especially in the years in "the chamber under the eaves" in Salem, is a question moot and useless. Certainly, as a youngster Hawthorne had seemed social enough in the bosom of his mother's family, the Mannings, and at Bowdoin College. And as a normal, social creature in the world, he functioned cheerfully and politely enough. Yet somehow Sophia was a member of society, and within himself, temperamentally, Hawthorne remained the outsider, looking on. If one of them were to be representative of the literary marketplace's audience, it would be the wife, not the writer.

When one thinks of attitudes toward the American experience in the works of Cooper, Melville, Stowe, James, Twain, Wharton, Fitzgerald, Steinbeck, Faulkner, Bellow, and Mailer, to list but few, one becomes aware of a precariously balanced wedding between the writer and that experience. In its actualities the writers find the materials for fiction and recoil scornfully from the Romantic certitudes they yearn toward, both in nostalgia and expectation. In each case, the currents generated by the poles of estrangement and belonging seem to be the electricity of American literature. One thinks of F. Scott Fitzgerald's golden girls as aspects and versions of the intricate complexity of mutual love, repudiation, fascination, and destruction that characterized Fitzgerald's relationship with his America and his Zelda. And although compared to the Fitzgeralds, the Hawthornes enjoyed a marriage of serene and loving gentleness, the resistance and repudiation were there when it came to Hawthorne's writing. "The conclusion that a lover cannot enter the precinct of the artist" was not foreign to the Hawthornes, as Arlin Turner pointed out:

> [Hawthorne]... had warned [Sophia]...during their courtship that he had depths which not even she could plumb. She wrote her mother on September 3, 1843, "No two minds were ever more completely different and individual than Mr. Hawthorne's and mine. It would be impossible to have intercourse with one another, if our minds ran into one another...."
> He said many times that Sophia was his best critic, but as a rule she read, or he read to her, a finished manuscript, for it was his habit to guard his creativity against even her criticism.[1]

The contradictions between the perceptions of the writer and his wife might have been no stronger than the agreements, but they probably were stronger than Turner suggests—definable essentially as differences between a dissenter's utopia and a belonger's conformities. To refer to Sophia as a metaphor, in order not to impose the injustices of oversimplification upon the real woman, one might say that Sophia *was* the marketplace in Hawthorne's relationship to his vocation. He knew what would be agreeable to her and what would not, just as he wrote *The House of the Seven Gables,* with its sunshiny conclusion, for her, to offset the darkness of *The Scarlet Letter,* with its shadowed ending.

Sophia was pleased by *The House of the Seven Gables* above anything else he wrote.

The contradictions between Hawthorne's and Sophia's perceptions are the contradictions between many of Hawthorne's works and their endings. They are the contradictions between Hawthorne's utopia and the ideologies of his marketplace. The endings often are not so much a matter of thematic rest as of rhetorical rest—the kind of cadence and words that signal to the reader that this is "The End." The endings often bring matters to a tactical closure attuned to the pleasure and expectations of the marketplace rather than to the problems raised within the fiction. In all the endings, whatever private, internal, self-readjustments are going on, what is in the foreground almost always is the business of selves struggling toward intercourse with the public state. It is a business of acceptance and belonging. For all of the commerce of inner self with inner self, the concluding freight of Hawthorne's endings concerns emergence into a public identity.

In what is arguably the most problematical of Hawthorne's books, *The Blithedale Romance*, Zenobia—the will of the heart, the passions—is dead, and Hollingsworth—the will of the intellect—is identified by his continuing isolated loneliness. It is and is not a mistake to draw equations between Coverdale and Hawthorne. It would be misleading and foolish to make a one-to-one equation between the two, but there are too many teasing similarities between the two outsider-observers—with their preference for the girl, whose complexions and sensibilities are those of Hilda, rather than the woman, whose complexion and sensibilities were those of Miriam—to ignore Hawthorne's affinities with his dramatized creature. It is seductively easy to use our sophistication about unreliable narrators to brush aside the ways in which, in part, Coverdale is Hawthorne's presentation and condemnation of aspects of himself. If Coverdale, in his vacillations between secluded observation and active participation, were to make a snug nest with a snug wife in snug society, it would be with the conventional Priscilla. Although Priscilla is not as dramatically clear an example as Hilda, she, too, in the fiction she inhabits, reveals the same kind of Hawthornian ambivalences that are exposed in an examination of *The Marble Faun*. Is she anemic wimp or sensitive angel? Is Coverdale a cold, pusillanimous fool or a man of insight? One can argue either and both, which is less important than a recognition of the political significance of the Hawthornian ambiguities that clothe the relation of the private to the public self. Priscilla does not quite guide Coverdale home as Hilda does Kenyon, but we are left with the assumption that she *could* have and with the certainty that she is the only guide left on stage: "As [Priscilla and

Hollingsworth] approached me . . . the powerfully built man showed a . . . childlike, or childish, tendency to press close, and closer still, to the side of the slender woman whose arm was within his. In Priscilla's manner there was a protective and watchful quality as if she felt herself the guardian of her companion, but, likewise, a deep, submissive, unquestioning reverence, and also a veiled happiness in her fair and quiet countenance" (III, 242). More important, we are left with the implication that if she had been Coverdale's nurse and guide, we then would enter (as with Hilda and Kenyon) the right, the good, the appropriately social domestic identity. The ending, implying as it does the proclamation of Sophia-Hilda-Priscilla as true guide, makes the life and death of Zenobia seem irrelevant. Yet, as in the case of Miriam, it is in Zenobia that Hawthorne invests the greatest interest and sympathy.

As Hawthorne ends his Romance, he gives Coverdale a revelatory auctorial function, speaking that aspect of Hawthorne that welcomes openness by repudiating the marketplace identification of women as ladies who are the trembling angels in the house: "It is nonsense, and a miserable wrong—the result, like so many others, of masculine egotism— that the success or failure of women's existence should be made to depend wholly on the affections, *and on one species of affection;* while man has such a multitude of other chances, that this seems but an incident. For its own sake, if it will do no more, the world should throw open all its avenues to the passport of a woman's bleeding heart" (III, 241, italics mine). The appeal is not to an ideal of independent women with all avenues open to them, a concept not congenial to the respectable gentility of the sentimental Victorianism that could envision women's rights only within a context of what was supposed as essentially female, a "bleeding heart." Hawthorne is not confronting and challenging the mores of the marketplace here. In fact, only two sentences later, Coverdale continues with this: "But a character, so simply constituted as . . . [Priscilla's], *has room only for a single predominant affection"* (italics mine), which in this case is precisely the "one species of affection" to which Coverdale had just alluded. It is just that single predominant species of affection that gives Priscilla the tremulous lady's Hilda-like iron core of strength: "No other feelings can touch the heart's inmost core, nor do it any deadly mischief. Thus, while we see that such a being responds to every breeze, with tremulous vibration, and imagine that she must be shattered by the first rude blast, we find her retaining her equilibrium amid shocks that might have overthrown many a sturdier frame. So with Priscilla!" (III, 241–42).

Once again, as he comes to his ending, Hawthorne counterattacks himself. That part of him that courageously engaged in vocational radicalism could sympathize imaginatively, though not temperamentally, with the passional and political openness of a Zenobian Romantic. But there was that other part of him in which his utopian Classicism and the ideology of the marketplace coincided in the evaluation of the lady of the house. The nationalistic Victorianism of the marketplace saw the angel as the emblem of domestic tranquillity and goodness in the society of sunshine. As William Dean Howells was to declare so famously, the smiling aspects of life are the more truly American. Case *closed.* And within his utopian depths, for Hawthorne, domestic peace and order, assimilated into Victorian ideals of decency as morality, were the emblems of ordered limitation within the common life, happy signs of necessary Classicist decorum presided over by the tremulous angel of steel.

When Priscilla covertly warns Coverdale away from the ruined Hollingsworth in the book's closing action, she is totally the female victim identified as "the result . . . of masculine egotism." She has Hollingsworth exactly where she wants him, imprisoned in her "woman's bleeding heart" and entirely dependent upon her "deep, submissive, unquestioning reverence." Identified by and with the ideologies of the marketplace, Priscilla becomes the sign and agent of closure, caging herself in total dedication to Hollingsworth through the same values with which she incarcerates him as her ward. *The Marble Faun* was Miriam's and Donatello's book, but Hilda and Kenyon inherited the stage and the narrative commitments demanded by an ending. *The Blithedale Romance* was Zenobia's book, but Priscilla inherits the stage at the ending. And in the final commitment and confession of the Coverdale who is not and who is Hawthorne, the closing words of the fiction are, "I—I myself—was in love—with—PRISCILLA!" (III, 247). The punctuation clearly is intended to convey Coverdale's moment "to blush, and turn away my face," but perhaps it is not merely annoyingly clever to suggest that the hesitations of the dashes suggest a moment in which, like the dashes and parentheses in *The Marble Faun,* the punctuation itself is political.

The Blithedale Romance is too problematical to allow us to conclude with certainty that Hawthorne was giving way to the potentially happy ending, but if he was, he had the wrong one. The entire weight of the book rests on the premise out of which Zenobia was created: if there is to be any redemption at all, it will come through the frank avowal of the full-hearted (bleeding or otherwise) strength and passion that defines Zenobia as the truly human woman within this fiction. If redemption is impossible, then the happy ending in any guise is probably a bow to the marketplace. If redemption is possible, ushering it in via the wispy and conventional femininity of Priscilla as sentimental heroine most certainly is a bow to the marketplace. In either case, the implications of the ending are ideologically rhetorical and conventional, a tentative counterattack against the forces Hawthorne at once feared and unleashed as the truth. Passion that disquieted his respectable society was like his Classicist utopia: it suggested subterranean truths that threatened the ideologies of the status quo. The creation of Zenobia reflected Zenobia's earlier sister, Hester, her later sister, Miriam, and the relationship to society of the passional similarities between the three women.[2]

Although Hester Prynne lived apart until her death, her public acknowledgment of sin led not only to her soul's redemption but also to *a publicly approved identity.* The A came to stand in people's memories for Able or Angel. It is interesting that even here, in the appropriate balance between apartheid and integration at the conclusion of Hawthorne's most successfully sustained long fiction, the proper state of the soul is signalled at least in part by a belonging place in society. Thematically, it is fitting that Dimmesdale must make a public confession of his private guilt before there can be any resolution to the action—but the public does not quite know what to make of it. Chillingworth earns hell through the unpardonable sin of keeping secret, for private purposes of intellect and vengeance, the universal condition of sin in which he and Dimmesdale, like all humans, inevitably participate. He thereby lost a sympathy of the heart, but presumably, nevertheless, the public state accorded him a funeral of honor. The problem is this: a resolution, similar to the ending of the *Oresteia* in Greek tragedy, is abstractly possible for Hawthorne's theme. Once the public state is educated into the true source of human oneness and sympathy, the good polis will replace the Erinyes with the Eumenides. But to suggest this as the true conclusion of Hawthorne's fiction is impossible for two reasons. One is that the utopia that insists upon sympathy through the inevitable oneness in the fallen state of all humans insists also, therefore, on the impossibility of the New World. The other is that the essence of Hawthorne's utopia stands in direct challenge to every aspect of Romantic-nationalistic ideologies dear to his society and its literary marketplace. In effect, Hawthorne sets up allegorical scenes, in James's sense of "scene" as a dynamic setting of psyches, in order to indicate where the resolution of human sin lies; but, paradoxically, because the closure from his utopia provides him no source of happy ending, the only such source he has are the facile and inappropriate impositions derived from the ideologies of his marketplace.

It would be silly to insist that Hawthorne should have written different fictions. He did not believe in a redeemer New World or in an Old World redeemed, in the fashion of the *Oresteia,* by the events of his characters' lives. Therefore, that public world, dragged in by its values in the endings, becomes an unwelcome and inappropriate source of the problematical in Hawthorne's fiction. If we *are* to consider the primacy of public values after all, then was that public world, as presented, worth the characters' agonies? Again—there is that which makes Zenobia seem thrown away. Given the conditions of secret truth and public ideologies, would one wish integration with the public state of the Peter Hovendens or the officialdom of the nineteenth-century actualities of "The Custom House" or of the seventeenth-century world of *The Scarlet Letter?* Would one want to live in Hilda's house? Would one want to open an intercourse with those worlds, unreformed, unredeemed, and uneducated as they remain after all the shadow and the pain? The very extent to which these questions are extrinsic but made inescapable by the endings suggests the divided nature of those endings.

The intricacy of the problem is best seen at the end of Hawthorne's most fully realized work. Pearl cannot effect the kind of ending Hawthorne has her initiate. The inevitably continuing presence of sin in human time is one of the central insistences of *The Scarlet Letter.* In this fiction, sin implicitly goes back before recorded time. Hawthorne shows its present manifestation in the very opening scene, amidst descriptions of the prison door, the jail, the cemetery, the rosebush, and the weeds that suggest the ubiquitousness of sin in time as well as space. The imagery, noted by all commentators, suggests an inextricable intermixture of good and evil; that intermixture does away with the beadle's and the Puritan society's assumptions about the New World moral clearing in the wilderness, blessed as the exclusive "righteous of the Massachusetts." The sin is not isolated in present time, but goes back before the book opens, about ten months, when Dimmesdale and Hester fornicated. But that, of course, is itself intermediate. As Chillingworth admitted, the wrongs began before the fornication, rising in the travesty of marriage and nubile, voluptuous young womanhood, a travesty forced upon passionate young Hester by her wedding to the dry, ancient scholar. But once one begins to follow the track toward beginnings opened by Hawthorne, there is no stopping. Within the imagery, the events, and the narrative comments of *The Scarlet Letter,* Hawthorne invited his readers repeatedly to consider the moral and psychological shortcomings of the harshly legalistic and unsympathetic Puritan state, and one asks what there was in the Puritan reverence of its saints' learning that respected the kind of life led by Roger Prynne and sanctioned the sterile marriage he made. But extrinsic considerations of the nature of Puritanism lead to ecclesiastical history. Even without the materials of economic and political changes, church history alone leads back to the ecclesiastical abuses of power that led to the Puritan separatism within the Reformation movement. And that leads back to causes of the Reformation and abuses within the Catholic church. And that leads back to the reason for Christ's passion and death. And that leads back to a scarlet *A* for Adam. And that leads back to the inscrutable purposes of God's mind, in which all time is simultaneous, not linear. If a reader follows back extrinsically the trail opened by Hawthorne, one comes out at the same place betokened by the path Hawthorne blazed intrinsically within the fiction itself: in all time, sin exists as a condition of life. But this consideration forecloses the possibility of resolution into a sinless state. Hawthorne's genius was never more successful than when he astutely identified and dramatized the appropriate psychology of a child in Pearl's circumstances and merged that literal actuality with the thematic *idea* of Pearl. As idea, Pearl is spirit, sprite, elfin in passionate beauty and vivid pink: she is the reincarnation of what will be shown in scarlet in Hester's own passionate, proud, nature. As such, she becomes a metaphor for the concept of sin's continuity in Hawthorne's Classicist utopia. It is not the least of Hawthorne's acute strokes that in her probing, mischievous, repeated references to the scarlet letter, Pearl almost drives Hester to distraction as she asks when she will have her own embroidered *A.* Therein she signals the central problem that Hawthorne's utopia creates for his endings: there is no redeemed New Life free from the parenting sins of the past. What Dimmesdale tells Hester in their forest scene is the idea of "Earth's Holocaust," central to almost everything Hawthorne ever wrote—there is no place to run to. There is no New World. There is no happy ending.

But Hawthorne added a Romantic element to his Classicist utopia: the idea of universal and mystical sympathy. His utopia produced an ideology of suffering, very much like Christian suffering: through the dark lady's full confession of the secret heart comes the public statement of our universal condition. In that public statement of our shared identity lies whatever redemption and sympathy of heart and mind that humanity ever receives. And in fact, with Dimmesdale's public confession, which in its essence is the attempted demolition of the sinless identity that the public has assumed for him, Pearl is humanized. As many readers have noted, it is that act of parentage that makes Pearl fully a child of flesh and blood, with both mother and father, not a child half of air and elfin spirit. The act humanizes her, allows her to cry and to kiss, two highly emblematic actions of which she had hitherto seemed incapable. But Hawthorne's utopia predicates all human history on the assertion that the fact of being human is the fact of being limited, of being a participant in the human state of sinfulness. It should be no more possible for Pearl than for Hester to live happily ever after. But she does. It is an insoluble dilemma, and Hawthorne seems to recognize it as the instinctive storyteller by the simple expedient of transferring Pearl out of the story. Off she goes to a normal, happy, wealthy, married life with children, none of whom is a bastard, far away in a foreign land. And she never again exists in the action or geography of the story's known universe. What Hawthorne cannot resolve he removes from the scene.

The ending does not come from intrinsic resolution but from the extrinsic marketplace. The conventions of the Romance dictated an ending in which all participants get what they deserve, an ending in which the good sufferers are left to inherit the scene and live happily ever after. One defense for Hawthorne, albeit a weak one, is that literary forms carry their own conventions and those conventions carry literary force. It is not Hawthorne but the conventions speaking. But *The Scarlet Letter* does not end at the happy ending. After an entire and artistically successful Romance completely repudiating Chillingworth's way and partly repudiating Dimmesdale's way, and sympathetically celebrating Hester's way, Hawthorne reneges. The total force of the book argues the utopian vision of ubiquitous sin and of redemption through sympathy in sin. Only in the dark night of the soul, out of which the dark lady struggles, changing from a type of Lucifer in her fall and defiance at the beginning of the book to a type of Christ in her humble, loving raising of the fallen at the end of the book, can true human salvation be fashioned: from sin to love through the fallen dark woman representative of universally stained humanity. But then Hawthorne does not simply evade his problem with the removal of Pearl and allowing her the happy everafter. He also comes forward with a statement that drives straight from the heart of marketplace ideologies in direct denial of everything his own Romance had been saying:

> Earlier in life, Hester had vainly imagined that she herself might be the destined prophetess [of "a new truth" to "be revealed, in order to establish the whole relation between man and woman on a surer ground of mutual happiness"], but had long since recognized the impossibility that any mission of divine and mysterious truth should be confided to a woman stained with sin, bowed down with shame, or even burdened with a life-long sorrow. *The angel and apostle of the coming revelation must be a woman, indeed, but lofty, pure, and beautiful; and wise, moreover, not through dusky grief, but the ethereal medium of joy; and showing how sacred love should make us happy, by the truest test of a life successful to such an end!* (I, 263, italics mine)

The ending of *The Scarlet Letter* is evasive at every level. The passage above concludes the penultimate paragraph of the book, in which, except possibly for the last sentence, the statements belong to the third-person narrator—yes, *Hawthorne*—who is talking about Hester. But even if that last sentence is an exposition of Hester's belief, the syntactical and organizational contexts of the sentences in the paragraph make it difficult to assume that the statements are not those of the omniscient storyteller. Yet, the marketplace-Hawthorne, unable to rest with the triumph of his ideological acquiescence, is also the Classicist Hawthorne, who cannot let matters rest with the implicitly coming millennialistic triumph of a Romantic utopia. He slips away from either commitment: immediately following the penultimate paragraph, the very opening words of the first sentence of the final paragraph are, *"So said Hester Prynne"* (italics mine). A Hester Prynne blind to the meaning of her own history? A Hester Prynne suddenly prompted to speak for her reading audience? An expiatory gesture of philosophical guilt by Hester's creator? Whatever she is, she is a Hester Prynne designed to let Hawthorne speak his utopian mind, to cover that speaking with ideologically acceptable statement, to honor his Classicist closure, to offer his acquiescent Romantic openness, and to escape from the consequences of the contradictions as the fact of the ending (there *is* no more!) allows him to duck out. Whoever that "speaking" Hester Prynne is, at the moment of the ending she is the voice(s) of Hawthorne.

It is one thing to tack on an ending according to the literary conventions of the form one employs. That can be seen as "purely literary," a history of conventions. But it is quite another for the narrative voice to present itself directly as a persona of the author in a pronouncement of values, for that becomes a matter of political and therefore social identification. In effect, though he *tells* us it was Hester speaking, to the extent that the speaking was cast entirely in the narrator's voice, Hawthorne was presenting himself (himself, in this instance, entirely "led home" by Hilda) as a public persona as destructive of the fiction as Hilda's triumph was in *The Marble Faun*. The voice that exalts the lady in unstained white is the voice of the marketplace; it is the voice of Hilda, who says, "I am a poor, lonely girl, whom God has sent here in an evil world, and given her only a white robe, and bid her wear it back to Him, as white as when she put it on" (IV, 208). As in *The Marble Faun*, even in the masterpiece of *The Scarlet Letter*—after an entire drama insisting that only the spotted, the sinful, the *human*, admitting its fallen state and finding through suffering therein the deepest possibilities of sympathy, can lead us to our noblest identity—the stage is inherited by the unfallen spotless heroine of the marketplace's ideologies.

And now the voice of Hilda is Hawthorne's directly. Whether this final conclusion in *The Scarlet Letter* is Hawthorne's voice in resignation, in affirmative acquiescence, or in ideological piety one cannot assert. Probably it is all three, and in proportions no one will ever be able to specify. What remains, however, is the failure of nerve, even in a masterpiece, the voice of the one who would belong, unmaking in political rhetoric what he has painstakingly created in image, characterization, and event.

In *The House of the Seven Gables* Hawthorne more successfully works out the energies of his utopia in the ending. Here, in a narrative frame of family feud, he has the materials for the kind of resolution that his utopia both demands and denies. Yet even here, the same pattern of Hawthorne's other endings emerges: an unbased optimistic openness (the unspotted white lady someday will arrive and redeem us; Hilda and Kenyon will shake the Old World from them and live New World lives), which is the ironically conservative conformity to Romantically nationalistic assumptions, takes over at the end. In each case there is a version of a tacked-on conservative ideological triumph over the dissenting major theme of Classicist utopian dissent from the prevailing assumptions of the society and its marketplace. The essential irony of Hawthorne's vocational position was that the *Classicist* utopia was the source of his *radical* dissent. As in *The Marble Faun* and *The Scarlet Letter*, the central focus of *The House of the Seven Gables* is the inevitable and inescapable presentness of the past. As in other books, imagery (especially the presentations of the house itself), characterization, and event intrinsically shape the fiction toward that theme. Yet, at the end, there is the usual Hawthorne reversal, suggestive of the possibility of a clear, clean new life in which the past finally has been sloughed off. We leave the darkly frowning house of the seven gables for Jaffrey Pyncheon's solid, new mansion and enter a new life.

One may offer that it was not Hawthorne's intention to suggest a redeemed new life but a lightened extension of the old one: we take old Uncle Venner with us, keeping our hold on the village past; Hepzibah and Clifford, in their dotage, bring their ruined old lives with them; and, most of all, Jaffrey's new house is but a continuation of the old, sinful life, built, just like the original Pyncheon's new house of the seven gables, on crime and greed. Moreover, in his treatment of Holgrave's career, Hawthorne makes an explicit repudiation of Romantic openness. Up until the end, Holgrave had been a Romantic champion of unlimited open possibilities. In his theories of newness he sounded like a channel of the kind of ideas Sophia heard discussed in Transcendentalist circles. In his occupations he was a free and open rover, the jack of all trades who could do anything and make a new life anywhere. But when he comes into property, he explicitly becomes a conservative who abandons his Thoreau-like ideas of the busk in favor of accumulated wealth, stone houses, and solidly fixed lasting identities.

> "The country house is certainly a very fine one, so far as the plan goes," observed Holgrave. . . . "But I wonder that the late Judge—being so opulent, and with a reasonable prospect of transmitting his wealth to descendants of his own—should not have felt the propriety of embodying so excellent a piece of domestic architecture in stone, rather than in wood." . . .
>
> "Why," cried Phoebe . . . "how wonderfully your ideas are changed! A house of stone, indeed! It is but two or three weeks ago that you seemed to wish people to live in something as temporary and fragile as a bird's nest!"
>
> "Ah, Phoebe, I told you how it would be!" said the artist with a half-melancholy laugh. "You find me a conservative already! Little did I think ever to become one." (II, 314, 315)

These aspects of the ending argue for a consistency between Hawthorne's utopia and the ideology offered at the conclusion. But there are too many nuances working against the success of the consistency.

First, Phoebe's sunniness within the old house has demonstrated that the ancestral mansion can indeed be lightened by her cheery presence; there is no *need* to move once the marriage is a fact and Phoebe effectively becomes mistress of the house. Moreover, in the marriage between a child of Maule and a child of Pyncheon, Maule's curse finally is laid to rest. Hawthorne intrudes a bit of spectral byplay in which he clearly suggests that the continuations of Pyncheon's original sin and Maule's curse are now nullified: the wrongs perpetuated by Matthew Maule are lifted with Alice's spirit, which, accompanied by a tinkle from her ghostly harpsichord, wafts upward at the close of the book. All that is left of darkness and horror are Alice's posies, blossoming cheerfully on the roof. Historically, the hidden motivations for incremental injustices are finally brought out into the light of sunshine when Holgrave opens the dark, hidden recess that contains the now useless deed. The deed's crumbling, *inoperative* state becomes an emblem for the state of the curse and the continuum of sin, all summed up in the fact that Jaffrey Pyncheon and all he stands for in the family history are dead. The heritage from the past now is cleared—*all* of the wealth, for which Jaffrey lied, stole, caused the death of his uncle, and ruined Clifford, is legally and ethically merged in the marriage of the two warring families. These facts make the removal from the ancestral house seem thematically and emblematically not only supererogatory but inappropriate. The lightened and resolved extension of the old life should be lived in the house of the seven gables. But Hawthorne suggests that the removal is not so much an extension as a break, even to the suggestion of new life and new vigor in the regeneration of the chickens: "Very soon after their change of fortune, Clifford, Hepzibah, and little Phoebe, with the approval of the artist, concluded to remove from the dismal old House of the Seven Gables, and take up their abode, for the present, at the elegant country-seat of the late Judge Pyncheon. Chanticleer and his family had already been transported hither; where the two hens had forthwith begun an indefatigable process of egg-laying, with an evident design, as a matter of duty and conscience, to continue their illustrious breed *under better auspices than for a century past"* (II, 314, italics mine).

All of the nuances of narrative force lead to expectations of a brightly remodelled interior of the same old house; consequently, the move to Jaffrey's house, overriding that force, becomes intrusive and especially noticeable as a thematic factor. It is not insignificant that at this crucial point Hawthorne, whose imagination absolutely dwelt in ideas of the continuation of the past, says not one word about the similarities between the sin-based establishment of the old house and the sin-based establishment of the new one. He clearly wishes to focus attention upon newness, sweeping under the narrative rug the implications of his own making and then standing on the rug. Hawthorne almost forces one to contemplate the move to Jaffrey's house with which the book ends. When one asks, what is gained by the move? what is the purpose of the move? what is the *moral* difference between the two houses? The only response (which ignores the questions) comes not from within the Romance, but from the marketplace: to make it good is to make it new, and to make it new is to make it good, and we all live happily ever after.

To say that in *The House of the Seven Gables* the discrepancy between utopia and ideology in the ending is lessened by Holgrave's paean to conservatism is to say that appearances of merger in this case derive not from the art but from the politics. The politics of relationship between Hawthorne the artist and Hawthorne the husband-citizen are the politics of relationship between his utopia and his society's ideologies. Democrat that he was, nevertheless Hawthorne's instincts were conservative in the essence of his utopia. His society's insistence upon the Good New World's limitless prospects of wealth and upward mobility were Romantic openness ironically tuned to the materialistic ideologies of nationalistic conservatism. Consequently, Holgrave's renunciation of his previously Romantic utopia is a fitting conclusion arising from the book's theme. His expression of his utopian conservatism in terms of wealth and solidly established family identities, however, is a much more problematical conclusion stemming from ideological conservatism, a cross-transference between utopias and ideologies that has continued from Hawthorne's Era of Good Feelings to the present.

The political ideologies that have accompanied economic Romanticism have argued for maintenance of the established institutions of capitalism in a bourgeois society as the means whereby economic openness and continuing development may be perpetuated. Consequently, the self-image or stereotype of middle America has been that of the other-directed, law-abiding, church-going, hard-working member of a respectable community that honors traditions and insists upon decorum, restraint, and propriety, but in which, through ingenuity and self-directed energies, economic individualism gains the fruits of openness.[3]

But precisely because the arts and the humanities question the values that have become established, the valuative context for the intelligentsia, in which class literary artists are central, has been at almost direct odds with the ideologies of the majority culture. From the Civil War onward, the received self-image or stereotype of the American and the bourgeois American community has come under attack by historians, philosophers, and practitioners of various arts, especially the literary. That attack is at the center of expatriate American letters and of almost all serious American poetry and fiction, naturalistic or symbolist, following World War I. Conversely, the received image or stereotype of the artist and the intelligentsia from the perspective of the majority culture has been one in which respect for intellect and anything at all arcane has been heavily leavened by a sense of high culture as something alien, foolish, boring, and threatening. The stereotype of the intelligentsia features a perverse and flaccid eggheadedness unrealistically and radically opposed to everything that has made America great. Artists and intellectuals, when not seen as models for the vertical mobility of economic Romanticism, have been seen as immaturely silly and removed from a world of real makings and doings—Hawthorne's "terribly insisted upon actualities." When hard times begin and indulgence becomes difficult, the conservative culture tends to regard the intelligentsia and art (except as commodity for investment) as both radical and a luxury. Conversely, the intelligentsia and the artist tend to regard the conservative culture as antiintellectual and dehumanizing.

Within the American intelligentsia since the Civil War, economic Romanticism generally has been met with a critical reaction championing the restraint of the individual in favor of egalitarian social planning for the majority good. On the other hand, that same intelligentsia has resisted society's conservative majority pressure for conformity and allegiance. It has responded to Classicist ideologies with Romantic ideologies: defiant openness of the self, of experiment, of expression, and of freedom from restraint—the Left Bank of Paris and Greenwich Village after World War I. Perhaps the shifts of valuative context from Hawthorne's day to the present may be expressed summarily in this way, through the concept of the self in relation to the polis: from the radical perspective, the self, if left to its own promptings in *economic* expression, would be greedy, rapacious, ugly, and dangerous. The primacy of the self is not desirable, and the self should be restrained and educated into its responsibilities to the needs and desires of the total community at large. The radical utopia calls for Classicist ideologies of closure. On the other hand, from the same radical perspective, if left to its own promptings in *social* expression, the individual self would reveal natural instincts of creativity, fraternity, equality, and love and should be allowed to express itself in creative freedom from the restrictive pressures of the conformist community. The radical utopia calls for Romantic ideologies of openness.

From the conservative perspective, the self, if left to its own promptings in *economic* expression, would be creative, and its energies, even though motivated by atomistic selfishness, would, if left alone, balance out through the activity of a free market into the satisfaction of the needs and desires of the community. The primacy of the self is both desirable and necessary. The conservative utopia calls for Romantic ideologies of openness. On the other hand, from the same conservative perspective, if left to its own promptings in *social* expression, the individual self would godlessly and unpatriotically run wild in depraved experimentation and bohemian license, and should be restrained by social institutions; the self must be limited by its responsibilities and the decorous demands of the respectable community. The conservative utopia calls for Classicist ideologies of closure. In short, the intelligentsia and the dominant culture in America have contained within themselves a unifying contradiction of Romantic and Classicist energies, but in a mirror image opposition to each other that has tended to erupt as a conservative versus radical opposition.

In the late 1950s, partly as a countercultural response to the cold war as it had become enunciated in the Truman Doctrine of 1947, and partly as a countercultural response to the McCarthy years, the beatniks developed into the beat generation. The beat generation became, in Norman Mailer's terms, the hip generation, and the hip generation blended into the hippies of the 1960s. From the radical perspective, this development of counterculture was a legacy of objection to (and the strategic need to shock) bourgeois society in tactical behavior as in social thought. However, because so many in the dominant culture became threatened by American Vietnam policies, the fact that the draft and the war became the focus widened the counterculture into a broad nexus with the dominant marketplace. That the dominant culture perceived economic possibilities in marketing the artifacts of counter-culture led inevitably to a marketing of mannerisms and attitudes as well—the language of clothing and hairstyles is as cross-transferable as the verbal rhetoric of ideologies. Not only did expensive boutique clothing begin to simulate the faded, sweat-stained clothing of the hippies and the radically perceived real people of a romanticized work-ing class, but culture heroes of the status quo on television began to look and sound indistinguishable from radicalized dropouts from the domi-nant culture. The visible forms of radical naturalism became the com-mercial forms of dominant style. The primacy of the maverick self, a mass-market remake of a popularized and mythicized Henry Thoreau, became the essence of the nexus between the conservative and the radical, the Romantic and the Classicist, the intelligentsia and the dominant culture. Romantic radicalism both triumphed and lost in the facility with which it was absorbed into the dominant culture. The radical changed the look and manners of society, but the utopian politics of dissent was dissipated. The dominant culture both triumphed and lost in the ease with which it coopted dissent. It diffused and defused the utopian politics of dissent. But it dissolved its own accus-tomed conservative features, and with the change of features there was a disruption of the power of the conservative utopia. The surface features of hair and clothes, the self-expanding drugs, the change in sexual mores and language taboos, at first associated with radical dissent, very quickly blurred defined and predictable boundaries of behavior.

If from the radical perspective the newly dominant individualism was a tradition of dissent, from the conservative perspective it was a legacy of continuing assumptions about the nature of patriotic belief: "Don't Tread on Me" means that I am not to be restricted in my economic Romanticism or my right to own guns. The merger of *ideological features* changed both opponents, and in the 1970s and 1980s made the individual the center of all values. The radical hippie self-absorption in psychedelics and the Republican yuppie self-absorption in economic Romanticism were matched expressions of the same phenomenon, called, fittingly enough, the Me Generation. In his influential study, *The Triumph of the Therapeutic,* Philip Rieff has analyzed the absorption with self as what amounts to unanchored Romantic ideologies cut adrift from any utopia and bumping chaotically and unwittingly against all utopian visions of polis.[4] In sum, Hawthorne seized upon the

unpardonable sin, the amorally isolated ego's unsympathetic manipula-
tions ("Ethan Brand," of course, is the paradigm), to characterize the
universals he saw reflected in aspects of his society's energies. That sin,
for Hawthorne, continued to develop as a consequential expression of
an atomistic psychology that focused on the actualities of his society's
Romantic materialism. In a cogent summary of *The Triumph of the
Therapeutic,* Gerald Graff observed that Rieff "declares that the modern
esthetic ethos has become an expression of the 'therapeutic mode.' " The
essence of the therapeutic outlook, Graff continues,

> is the assumption that there are no objective ends or imperatives to which
> human beings can subordinate themselves. To speak of a self (or a
> community) as dedicated to some objectively "high" or "worthwhile"
> purpose, or indeed to speak of it as conforming its activity to "reality" is
> absurd. The self is liberated from preestablished determinants, yet this
> liberation is empty, since its free-floating constructions cannot locate
> their relations to anything real. This indulgent view of the self, which we
> seem now to concede ourselves as a kind of compensation for the many
> difficulties of modern urban existence, at once frees the individual from
> obligation and strands him without any way of measuring the "self
> fulfillment" he has been freed to pursue. Like the creative writer, the
> therapeutic individual (or collective) is encouraged to underrate the
> ability of his consciousness to take orders from external reality so as to
> understand and master it rationally. On the other hand, as a consolation,
> he is encouraged to overrate the power of his consciousness to remake the
> raw material of reality according to strictly subjective forms. This combi-
> nation of resignation and euphoria carries over into political thought, the
> man of power being understood in terms reminiscent of those which
> define the visionary poet: the power of both figures consists in the ability
> to get their self-created myths publicly accepted. The ordinary individual,
> lacking any hope of acquiring such power, is urged to cultivate the
> autonomy of his personal self as a kind of "performance," which is to say,
> to make a virtue of the necessity of his dispossession from substantial
> external goals.[5]

The triumph of the therapeutic was, in part, the detritus of a Romanticism whose utopia and ideologies had become dissociated, and, in part,
it was the attenuation of radical dissent.

Although probably it is neither possible nor profitable to try to
quantify historical percentages of radicals and conservatives among
American artists and humanists, it is clear that at least since the Civil
War a large proportion of the intelligentsia in the United States has
taken a leading part in the radically critical and Romantic questioning
of Classicist social values. The tension between conflicting ideologies

following World War I crystallized around the Palmer raids, the Sacco-Vanzetti trial, and the Soviet Union; in the 1930s around the Great Depression, the rise of fascism, and the Spanish Civil War; in the late 1940s and early 1950s around the onset of the cold war and Senator Joseph McCarthy; in the 1960s and early 1970s around Vietnam and the Watergate and impeachment hearings. Following World War II, as the G.I. Bill supported unprecedented numbers of Americans through higher education, the academy, and most centrally the humanities, became not only a real but also occasionally even a considerable force in national life, especially in the function of dissent. Joseph McCarthy and Spiro Agnew are too easily written off as merely bad jokes in the history of American politics. Within the political context of the tribalistic ideological closure that paradoxically arises in America from aspects of the universalist openness of the Romantic utopia, McCarthy's and Agnew's instincts were on target. Both men identified the enemy as neocortical freaks and attacked the eggheads as Reds. Agnew assailed the universities for subversion and un-American frivolousness. Less spectacular than McCarthy, Agnew was fully as significant, for in his simplistic political crudeness he recognized as a primary tactical base the conflict in the relationship of the intelligentsia to the dominant culture. He called for a marshalling of "the silent majority" (those favoring conformity to nationalistic ideology) and he singled out "permissiveness" (Romantic openness) as the *bête noire* of the age. It is as though he sensed in the Romantic primacy of the *social* self precisely the merger in which the counterculture and the dominant culture met each other and turned into acceptable social currency the surface modes of what to Agnew was the radical enemy.

An example from the twentieth century, Agnew typified the cross-transference between utopia and ideology that characterized Hawthorne and his readership. Agnew excoriated social, not economic permissiveness; political and social, not economic Romantic individualism. He inadvertently became the target of his own attacks when he championed rugged individualism, for he held power in a historical continuum in which the primacy of the self had come to locate both conservative and radical in "liberationist" and "libertarian" rhetoric, semiotic systems that dissolve the modal distinctions between one and one's opponent. Hawthorne's advantage was that his utopia was wholly Classicist. Political minds like Agnew's are divided between an economic Romantic utopia and a social Classicist utopia. Hawthorne shared in populist optimism to the extent that as a Democrat he belonged to the anticonservative party of his day, but the clear singleness of his utopia is emphasized by the salient quality of those moments in which he allows ideology to counterattack against the utopia. His divisions are between utopia and ideology, between idea and moments of narrative tactics that arise not from idea but from ideological rhetoric.

At the convergence of emphases on the self in the 1960s, economic and social Romanticism joined hands in attitudes that echo a long history of national ideologies advocating the individual. At the other end of the spectrum from Agnew, the hippy flower-child manifestations that set the style for liberationist Romantic selfhood offered a rhetoric devoid of the philosophical discipline and clarity that was the spine of individualism in Emerson's high Romanticism or in Jefferson's Deism. The ascendency of liberationist ideologies of the self in the late 1960s was the turning point, as is always the case when the rebellion becomes established, at which humanistic critical energy began to examine and question its own success. The late 1960s were marked by such phenomena as divergence between Herbert Marcuse and Norman Mailer and the emergence of Mailer's "left conservatism," as well as by puzzled and uneasy reappraisals of positions and allies by scores of radically leaning intellectuals. Beginning in the 1970s, increasing numbers of the intelligentsia began to announce correctives to a sloppily conceived Romantic lifestyle. Just as they earlier had challenged the dominant conservative values of economic Romanticism, so they began to engage in an increasingly Classicist critical questioning of a social Romanticism gone sour in drugs and "non-negotiable demands," on the one hand, and in a superficial victory of style in facile commercialization, on the other.

In its voracious exploitation of markets, the business culture seizes on all phenomena for their profitability. The omnivorous absorption is all but indiscriminate; the only really operative criterion of acceptability, despite all the pieties and posturings, is "the bottom line": what will currently sell and make money? Consequently, even those complexes of value that arise in radical opposition to the dominant culture become commodities salable to emerging populations of clamorously self-absorbed, self-seeking customers. Radical values quickly become radical chic; revulsion from technological capitalism becomes the salability of nostalgia as either camp or antiques; and anticapitalist intellectual movements quickly become showbiz kitsch. The voraciousness of the marketplace accommodates everything. Consequently, it dissolves traditions, fixed conventions, lasting values, lifestyles, ideas, positions, and oppositions, and, thus, in the process, bourgeois society itself. An advanced, modern consumer society like America is self-devouring in its own marketplace. The disconnection of our business culture from any guiding utopia is the self-consuming ultimate triumph of the marketplace, in which conservative bourgeois culture paradoxically is threatened with dissolution by its own successful commercialism rather than by the revolution of the proletariat. As the opportunism of the marketplace reflected the ascendancy of the unanchored self in the pop culture of tee-shirts, therapy cults, personality talkshows, and lifestyle philosophies from Leo Buscaglia to Jonathan Livingstone Seagull, increasing numbers of the intelligentsia on the left began to feel like displaced persons. The opposing selves of Hawthorne became reenacted in the continuing paradox within which Romantic and Classicist utopias beget opposing ideologies. As in cosmic and biological existence, so too, apparently in political existence: always, in all ways, openness and closure contain within themselves the inevitable births of each other.

The intellectual and emotional celebration of the individual from Jefferson through Whitman devolved into fashion and business. Overused and abused words like "sharing" and "love" (as well as such stylistic afterbirth as "personal interaction" and "people-oriented") reflect a triumph of the therapeutic in which personal happiness (have a nice day, happyface) quite distinct from utopia and polis is taken for granted as the ultimate or the highest or the most moral imperative of being; in which indulgence of the self is favored over responsibilities of the self; in which self-fulfillment becomes a rubric for almost any activity without any utopian examination of the nature of the self being fulfilled or of the fulfilling activity; and in which gratification of the self is assumed as a good without serious ethical examination of the context in which that gratification takes place. Fashionably naked feeling, crying, hugging, primal-screaming, and similar therapies are summed up in the mass media through solemn pronouncements about the health and beauty of "getting in touch with oneself" and loving oneself, in phrases like "let it all hang out" and "if it feels good, do it," and in popular songs like "I Gotta Be Me" and "I Did It MY Way." The language of pop culture is a vein of failed Romantic ideology, articulating easy valuations that debased Romantic theories into ideological expressions of atomistically self-hugging indulgence in the Me Generation. In extreme and even parodic exhibitionist form (the public disclosure of personal sin in the issue-oriented forum of daytime television talk-shows), we continue the contexts in which Hawthorne ambivalently chose his narrative strategies.

In sum, Hawthorne's Classicist resistance to the prevailing ideologies of his day is a summation and foreshadowing of the satiric and dissenting attitude of most serious American literature up to the present. It is in essence a resistance to the cultural effects signalled by and partly caused by facile conservative ideologies as the rhetoric of a misunderstood Romantic utopia. The resistance to nationalistic rhetoric, which to

Agnew's middle America is merely unpatriotic sin, is a matter in which style is the political expression of philosophical implications, a matter not of literary abstractions but of the way people lead and lose their lives. Hawthorne foresaw in a personal but profound way that the literary marketplace is a litmus for the development of the nation. The continuing literary resistance to conservative nationalistic ideologies is an awareness of the possibility of national devolution into shallow consciousness, facile declaration, and unexamined opportunism. Ironically it is, in part, a protest against the blithe national propensity to recognize conservative ideology and its rhetoric while refusing to recognize the Classicist closure of the conservative utopia. The literary awareness of national devolution has kept the makers of American letters on guard against the very Romantic impulsions that led them to their sense of national identity and to their pens in the first place. Romantic Thoreau repudiated the commercialistic optimism and progress of American common life even as he insisted upon infinity as the true definition of the common. Romantic Emerson repudiated any social consensus as a measurement of identity at the very moment he insisted upon the spiritual possibilities of cosmically total identity within the common life. Classicist Hawthorne championed the domestic common heart and life as he denied attainable transcendence beyond them. The makers of American letters have resisted an application of Romantic optimism to the *actualized* history of American society even as they define their resistances in the context of an America defined as the culminating emblem of progress toward millennium—and even as the nationalistic closure of conservative ideology therefore demands exactly the application the writers resist. For those who, like major writers, wrestle out a utopia and its relationship to ideologies, that relationship provides the politics of relationship with the marketplace. Beginnings and endings—especially endings—are the most dramatic placements in fiction. Endings carry within themselves, therefore, a great probability for revelation of the politics of relationship. As his major works suggest, Hawthorne revealed a relationship of both resistance and capitulation, in which the essentially Romantic openness of possibility is imposed upon the fiction by the conservative shibboleths of nationalistic optimism. In his shorter works, usually the closure of the Classicist utopia has the last word. Nevertheless, even the tales, no less than the major works, proffer endings that reveal a political tension.

In "The Maypole of Merrymount," for instance, "Jollity and gloom were contending for an empire" (IX, 54). Gloom wins, as it must in this story, for gloom is associated with the intrusions of grim responsibility and duty upon an apparently Edenic jollity, whose imagery reveals it to be a version of animal debasement in a primitive state of nature. This is another of Hawthorne's stories about the felix culpa, and, as in *The Marble Faun* and Donatello's rise from jollity to gloom, we are not to mourn over the lost paradise. But in the longer work, Hawthorne was able to dramatize Donatello's original jollity, his subsequent rise, and Miriam's increasingly mellowing humanity; consequently, we consent to and applaud the inevitable and just triumph of gloom. But, limited by the constraints of the shorter form, Hawthorne does not show the reader the development of nobility in Edith and Edgar. Nothing within the fiction shows us why—aside from the obvious fact of their youthful connubiality—Edith and Edgar were lord and lady of the May to begin with. Their conduct in the tale makes it unlikely that they were the community's pet representatives of wild or easy pleasure, but we have no way to know. Furthermore, Endicott's iron intrusion is so fully presented in its repressiveness that nothing within the fiction shows us why life in his world is less debased than or preferable to Merrymount. Consequently, it is jarring to switch with sudden completeness from Edgar and Edith's apparently total identification with Merrymount to their apparently total acceptance of Endicott's world. In this tale, the political effects of the marketplace are in concord with Hawthorne's utopia, but they prevent full development of the shorter form of fiction. Gloom wins, but, although the marketplace demanded a moral, gloom was not what it wanted. In its historical implications, the ending provides what the marketplace does want: the conclusion that all ended well in American history. But because the entire story prepares for the sad necessity of the felix culpa and does not present in dramatic action its redemptive force, the ending has little dramatic force. We are told that "as their flowery garland was wreathed of the brightest roses . . . so, in the tie that united them, were intertwined all the purest and best of their early joys" (IX, 67). But those were the joys garnered in a condition blasted by the triumphant Puritans. Nevertheless, the last sentence, ex machina, simply asserts that "they went heavenward, supporting each other along the difficult path which it was their lot to tread, and never wasted one regretful thought on the vanities of Merry Mount" (IX, 67). The ending clearly comes from what the marketplace wants to buy. Even though it accords with Hawthorne's subversive utopia, its patent chiaroscuro moralizing makes it acceptable. Consequently, precisely because it does harmonize with Hawthorne's utopia it reveals the extent to which the effects of the marketplace make the endings mechanical. The revelation provides an important critical approach to Hawthorne's fiction: when Hawthorne does not dramatize and develop his utopia— that is, when he does not dramatize the inevitability of human limitation and the necessity to be true! be true! openly about one's limited identity—his endings tend to become tacked-on gestures, conventions of the marketplace. What is needed is the *dramatization* of the moral function of Classicism, the dramatization of whatever redemption arises from the utopian recognition of closure. But when Hawthorne provides that final necessity, he concludes what the nationalistic market will not bear, and then his endings tend to become counterattacks against his dramatized conclusions. In the tales, his endings incline to stop short of utopian commitment. "Young Goodman Brown," like "The Minister's Black Veil" and several other of Hawthorne's most widely received tales, leaves the same tantalizing sense of the unfinished, and it serves as a representative example.

The ending of "Young Goodman Brown" seems to be like the ending of "My Kinsman, Major Molineux." In both tales, the shaken protagonist, a heretofore innocent young man, is left to face the experience of his initiation into the knowledge that Satan, the father of sin, has some powerful relationship to all human beings. But "My Kinsman, Major Molineux" ends exactly where it should, in a limbo of knowledge, as yet unapplied, that will merge Robin with society and that yet is existentially open to all possibilities but one. The auctorial "kindly gentleman" knows that the world's Robins may make their own way, but can never go home again to childhood's expectations of unlimited openness, that all adults must remain in a world where the devil lives.

"Young Goodman Brown," however, goes a step farther—and, therefore, not far enough. Brown makes a choice for the daylight world only, repudiating all traffic with the nighttime world that is as much an actuality of human life as is the daytime. We see the daylight public community only through Brown's increasingly astonished midnight disenchantment. But we see the nighttime side of human identity through our own eyes—it is the dramatic action before us. We see and hear the action directly through the narrative's dramatizations. Consequently, although we know that Hawthorne wants us to see that the God-fearing dayworld of public, cheerful sunlight and the Satanworshipping nightworld of dark secrets and hellfire-light are both realities of life, and that Brown is wrong in accepting only one truth, it is difficult for the reader to see why Brown is wrong: every dramatized event reveals the falseness of the sunlit identity. There is every reason to feel that faith is lost when Faith's pink ribbons actually appear on that bush. Therefore, Brown's last despairing cry of resistance—"Faith! Faith! . . . Look up to Heaven and resist the Wicked One!"—is at once a heroic affirmation of dayworld beliefs and the error of continuing to insist on one world only. He affirms what no longer supplies any reason for his faith. The tale clearly implies that the unrelieved gloom of Brown's righteous life, subsequent to his exposure to the nightworld truth, is neither healthy nor good nor based upon the complex mixture of *full* human truth. Because Brown admits no intercourse with the world of night, he opens no intercourse with the world of day. And the inability to open that intercourse was one of Hawthorne's greatest fears. Significantly, the man who isolates himself from common, fallen, human society is in the wrong. But the implication of that wrongness is unsupported dramatically within the tale itself. There is no experience within the tale to make the reader really repudiate Brown's righteously exclusivist conclusions, and one wishes for a few balancing scenes in which we could see Brown ironically committing the nighttime satanism of pride in a few rejections of the common life.

In the last paragraph of the tale, Hawthorne provides several quick concretions of Brown's choice: Brown could not attend church services without hearing an anthem of sin and fearing that the roof would collapse under divine wrath. He shrank from his townspeople, and he shrank from his wife. He scowled and muttered when his family knelt down to prayer at his own hearthside. He snatched the little child away from the presence of Goody Cloyse as she catechized the youngster. But the events of Brown's behavior are all stated, all asserted within the last paragraph as something listed rather than dramatically shown. All that follows from Brown's choice is appropriate: when Brown "had lived long, and was borne to his grave a hoary corpse . . . they carved no hopeful verse upon his tomb-stone; for his dying hour was gloom" (X, 90). What follows Brown's choice is thematically appropriate and dramatically underdeveloped. But what would be needed would be nothing less than vignettes of Brown's life, and without the dramatization the final paragraphs are marketplace tokens: here, reader, is your summary moral.

As an example of the short story, "My Kinsman, Major Molineux" is a more brilliantly successful act of form than is "Young Goodman Brown." The former centers fully on the folly of the expectations of innocence, and thereby confronts fully the folly of the American society's insistence on righteous exclusivism and unlimited openness: it wholly assumes in form the burden of its theme. "Young Goodman Brown" sweeps up those ideological implications into one paragraph, an exit paragraph. Thereby Hawthorne can present and leave, at one moment, the political problematics of his tale. "My Kinsman, Major Molineux" is a far more dangerous tale for Hawthorne than "Young Goodman Brown." But having committed himself to Brown's decision rather than, as in Robin's case, to the unformed beginning of a new life, Hawthorne committed himself to a developed dramatization of the choice. But had he recognized and honored that commitment, he would have been stuck with a risky development of social defiance, and that was neither his desire nor his purpose in "Young Goodman Brown": he wanted to focus, as in "My Kinsman, Major Molineux," on the initiation, and the author deserves his own choice. Yet Hawthorne chose to have Brown make the choice he made. The rushed and condensed nature of the ending reveals the extent to which Hawthorne was at once drawn toward a repudiation of the unexamined exclusivist Romantic elements of American ideological conservatism, and toward a desire to avoid that conflict even at the cost of the form in which he was writing. The politics that take for granted the assumptions of the marketplace affect literary form in an impression of incompleteness or misfit endings even in some of Hawthorne's best known and most widely admired short fictions.

As it should, given Hawthorne's utopia, closure wins out thematically in the short fictions, too, with a few exceptions such as "The Artist of the Beautiful." In many of the tales the utopia and the endings agree, their *dramatic* success limited not by thematic inconsistency but by the ideological force of the marketplace. But many of the tales disclose the same dismantling of theme generated by the endings of the long Romances. The last paragraph of one of Hawthorne's best tales, "The Gentle Boy," is out of keeping with everything but the demands of the marketplace:

> As if Ilbrahim's sweetness yet lingered round his ashes; as if his gentle spirit came down from heaven to teach his parent a true religion, her fierce and vindictive nature was softened by the same griefs which had once irritated it. When the course of years had made the features of the unobtrusive mourner familiar in the settlement, she became a subject of not deep, but general, interest; a being on whom the otherwise superfluous sympathies of all might be bestowed. Every one spoke of her with that degree of pity which it is pleasant to experience; every one was ready to do her the little kindnesses, which are not costly, yet manifest good will; and when at last she died, a long train of her once bitter persecutors followed her, with decent sadness and tears that were not painful, to her place by Ilbrahim's green and sunken grave. (IX, 105)

Hawthorne, after all, was neither foolish nor unsubtle in his genius: he did not advocate or believe in a clichéd resolution of the human dramas he presented. The bitter irony in the characterization of daylight "Salem" is inescapable in the ending of "The Gentle Boy": the sentimentally cheap and decent quality of the painless sympathy, kindnesses, and

tears offered Catherine indicate sardonically that the nighttime qualities of the daytime "true religion" that killed Ilbrahim are no less an
abiding truth than they were at the height of the mother's evangelical
frenzy. We do not see meaningful reclamation enacted as part of the
tale's events, and a question arises about where all the sweetness and
light came from except, possibly, fatigue. But this tale is not a case
history of fatigue. The pathos of the ending, the tacked-on statement
about the reclamation of Catherine, the community's acceptance of
Ilbrahim's "gentle spirit," are common to many of Hawthorne's endings,
including those of his masterpieces like *The Scarlet Letter.* We do not
see the communal, Eumenides-like reclamation effected in the reintegration of the sufferer and the community, but receive merely closing
statements that are the conventional conclusion that they all lived
happily ever after.

The point at issue here is not a demand that we should issue fiats
about fictions Hawthorne should have written instead of accepting
what he did write. Nor is it a demand that all his fictions should
dramatize the process of reclamation and reintegration into the daylight
world of the marketplace. Such demands are foolish and useless. The
point is the relationship between the nature of the endings, which enjoy
the most forceful position in fiction, and the force of idea and dramatization that have been developed in the full course of the fiction. It is a
question of the relationship of statement to dramatization in fiction,
and a question of the nature and source of the statement. The utopic
source is clear, for instance, in "The Great Carbuncle," one of the tales
antipodal to "The Artist of the Beautiful." In a tale that implicitly
denies the primacy of the ideal over the actual (and thus is at odds with
Transcendentalism, Christianity, and some of the implications of
Hawthorne's own prefaces), the narrator concludes that "it is affirmed,
that, from the hour when two mortals had shown themselves so simply
wise, as to reject a jewel which would have dimmed all earthly things,
its splendor waned" (IX, 165). But Hawthorne selects his examples in a
way that makes the definition of "earthly" the primary problem. Those
who sought the carbuncle did not, in fact, seek anything *unearthly* at
all. What they sought were different manifestations of earthly pride.
What Hawthorne intends in this tale would be better expressed in the
phrase "would have dimmed all *common* things," for it is exactly in the
acceptance of the common life that Hannah and Matthew win narrative
approval. In this tale, the concluding moralizing statement suggests
neither incompleteness nor division between utopia and statement.
There are no doublenesses in this tale, for what we have seen before us
in dramatized form is what we are supposed to reject: contempt for the

common life. Without the problem raised by "Young Goodman Brown," we do not have to see the daylight world of common actuality in action because we are given full view of what repudiation of it is like. It is not a matter of accepting two worlds, but only one. The tale suggests the nature of Hawthorne's concluding statements by revealing that in his less complex and, therefore, less interesting fictions, Hawthorne best avoids conflict between those concluding statements and either problems of completeness or problems of relationship between ending and idea. In sum, his richer works are multidimensional; his concluding statements are not.

In Hawthorne's short fiction, one of the most complex revelations of his awareness of the conflict between his utopia and nationalistic assumptions is provided by "Old Esther Dudley." Here the combination of prefatory statement and narrative event is explicit. In this one of the "Tales of the Province House," Governor Hancock is given the rhetoric of openness, which is identified entirely as American. As a representative of the revolutionary wave of the future, the governor turns to Esther, the keeper of the old royalist faith and observances, and tells her:

> Your life has been prolonged until the world has changed around you. You have treasured up all that time has rendered worthless—the principles, feelings, manners, modes of being and acting, which another generation has flung aside—and you are a symbol of the past. And I, and these around me—we represent a new race of men—living no longer in the past, scarcely in the present—but projecting our lives forward into the future. Ceasing to model ourselves on ancestral superstitions, it is our faith and principle to press onward, onward! . . . my fellow-citizens, onward—onward! We are no longer children of the Past! (IX, 301–2)

Within the context of Esther's pathetic plight, whereby Hawthorne successfully creates the reader's strong sympathy for the old lady, the tone of Hancock's speech is problematical at best. Nevertheless, separating himself from the Tory storyteller, who identifies with old Esther Dudley, Hawthorne, as retailer of the old Loyalist's tale, identifies himself with all that Hancock represents and thereby becomes one with his literary marketplace. It should not "be concealed," Hawthorne cautions the reader, referring to himself, "that the sentiment and tone of the affair may have undergone some slight or perchance more than slight, metamorphosis, in its transmission to the reader *through the medium of a thorough-going democrat*" (IX, 291, italics mine). And, indeed, the Hawthorne-reteller does also create sympathy for Hancock, making him a man of kind courtesy and sensibility as well as a champion of Romantic, democratic convictions of openness.

But one remains entangled in Hawthorne's retelling of the old Tory's tale, in which the Loyalist's strong sympathy for the old order is retained in the presentation of Esther. The frenetic quality that is allowed into Hancock's speech suggests some discomfort, or at least ambivalence, on Hawthorne's part, for the rhetoric of the newly dominant majority declares the antithesis of Hawthorne's utopian conservatism. Esther Dudley and the old Loyalist who tells the tale to Hawthorne-as-narrator oppose dissent, change, and newness. They represent a steadfastness of allegiance to the status quo. Yet those who belong were swept out of their belonging by the Revolution, and it is precisely the loss of belonging that generates Hawthorne's strongly sympathetic depiction of the old lady. And here Hawthorne's doubleness exists entirely *within* his utopian self: on the one hand that self sympathizes with those who do not believe in revolutionary change; yet by virtue of that sympathy, the temperament of Hawthorne's utopian self seeks belonging to the status quo. Yet, and again yet—the status quo has become one of commitment to ideological openness espousing a constantly revolutionary millennialistic progress. Consequently, Hawthorne's sympathies are divided, and in an unresolved conclusion of sympathies, he repudiates, for not belonging, the Esther he pities because she does not belong. He registers his uneasiness about dissent and separateness in a little statement about timely belonging: "Living so continually in her own circle of ideas, and never regulating her mind by a proper reference to present things, Esther Dudley appears to have grown partially crazed" (IX, 298). That, at least, is a result of *not* belonging within the society of the marketplace. The tale's unresolved spread of sympathies reveals Hawthorne's recognition of Old Esther Hawthorne and of his lecturing the creature.

Examples of the problem of endings proliferate easily, and a representative concluding example comes best, perhaps, from "The Procession of Life." Taking the opening paragraph as a single entity, we find within that one small unit a relationship of idea and ending that reveals Hawthorne's unwillingness to avow in statement the dissent implicit through the pictured or dramatized event. The narrator views the procession of life as an emblematic march; at the beginning his perspective is implicitly revolutionary, seeming to call for Romantic openness of new social vistas not allowed by any arrangement of the polis in history to date: "The grand difficulty" about the march of human beings under "the Chief Marshall," God,

> results from the invariably mistaken principles on which the deputy marshalls [rulers] seek to arrange this immense concourse of people. . . . Their scheme is ancient [precedents and precedence according to birth,

wealth, power, position], far beyond the memory of man or even the record of history, and has hitherto been very little modified by the innate sense of something wrong, and the dim perception of better methods, that have disquieted all the ages through which the procession has taken its march. Its members are classified by the merest external circumstances, and thus are more certain to be thrown out of their true positions than if no principle arrangement were attempted. (X, 207)

The implications of potential change suggest the revolution that will correct the errors of the ages by rearranging actualities. But Hawthorne's statement of conclusion is once again a matter of idea not supported by the event, denying the need or even the wisdom of upsetting the status quo: "When the mind has once accustomed itself to a proper arrangement of the Procession of Life, or a true classification of society, even though merely speculative, there is thenceforth a satisfaction which pretty well suffices for itself, without the aid of any actual reformation in the order of march" (X, 208). The world in the dusky mirror seen by moonlight and firelight *is* the rearrangement of the world, and, thus, the act of Romancing fulfills the dissent of his utopia without having to upset an acquiescent relationship with the status quo. The facile political evasion disclosed by the unsatisfactory dissociation between the force of theme and the statements of conclusion must have fed Hawthorne's sense of the emptiness and unreality of his vocation and the forms it took. As he said in "Feathertop," "At its present point of vivification, the scarecrow reminds me of some of the lukewarm and abortive characters, composed of heterogeneous materials, used for the thousandth time, and never worth using, with which romance writers (and myself, no doubt, among the rest) have so overpeopled the world of fiction" (X, 230). He knew his vocational and temperamental complexities well enough and remained unsatisfied with himself and with the politics of his literary forms.

Hawthorne remains one of America's most culturally significant exemplars of some of the results of the politics of "the two Americas." If Cooper was the first major American to embroil himself in those politics through essentially essayistic assault, Hawthorne was the first to reveal their relationship to the process of serious fiction. But he was by no means the last to indicate the continuing presence of millennial openness as a background against which closures in the world of the terrible actualities are enacted in American fiction.

When Ishmael is fished out of "the great shroud of the sea" by "the devious cruising Rachel," he is "but another orphan" in a cosmos whose very openness turned out to be the most frightening closure. But, like the voice of the ocean at the close of Stephen Crane's "The Open Boat," the last word of the story proper is given to the sea. Infinite openness is closed as a possibility of human life and identity. The tantalizing Romantic possibility of all possibility, drawing Ahab as it draws all Idealist visionaries, "rolled on as it rolled five thousand years ago." Period.

Henry James closed his novel devoted to the identification of *the* American in a mid-state action. In *The American,* the pointedly named Christopher Newman has learned by negative example all the closures of human potential. He had come to Europe with American expectations —a kind of millennial expectation of the best of everything to be opened to him and to be taken by him into a vaguely envisioned ideal new self to be formed by the best of art, architecture, music, literature, history, and "the most beautiful woman in the world." Because they apparently summed up everything he had come for, in their revelation of the immoral closures they effected in actuality, the DeBellegardes negatively teach Newman the moral superiority and possibilities of exquisite true form within his own American openness. And openness, by contrast, he certainly represented. In the various occupations to and from which he flowed in making money, in his rise through the ranks in the army, in his willingness to seek and be open to new experience (as the nervous Reverend Mr. Babcock, with his nice New England reticences, and the philistine Mr. Tristram, with his vulgar tastes, could not be), in his unwillingness to identify people and their prospects by their closed status from birth, and in his eager good humor, he was constructed by James as the equation by which to measure the moral ingredient in his search for form: America equals openness. Not only is Newman The American, but he comes from the farthest reaches of the Land of the Golden West; he is a gentleman from San Francisco. In facing the ending of his book, James came flat up against Hawthorne's problem, for presumably the new man, newly educated in the meanings of moral form, in the context of the golden land would represent the millennial society. But James knew that the vulgarian Mr. Tristram, with his American Club at one end of the spectrum, and the Puritan eunuch, the finicky Mr. Babcock, at the other end of the spectrum, represented the full reach of American actualities. To what America could he return Newman? Morally, Europe had been used up. The *idea* of America existed in *The* American, but it was not in the actual America. There is nowhere that Newman belongs but in the limbo between the two Americas, somewhat like that onlooker, Hawthorne himself. And that is exactly where the ending leaves him, on the eve of his departure, telling Mrs. Bread that he did not mean that he would stay forever but that he would stay away forever. To reenact the experience of Europe in terms of the American actualities that Newman knew so well how to manipulate would have been merely to extend what Newman was absenting himself from, just as surely as Tristram merely continued his former self with his totally American life in Paris. James was exquisitely right in ending his book with Newman's inability to retrieve the paper from the fire. His very placelessness is the culmination of his American idea of the possibility of total openness, which is the necessary background against which James completes Newman's education into actualities. His very placelessness is the recognition that the idea of America has never materialized into the good polis in which *the* American appropriately settles.

The ending of *The Adventures of Huckleberry Finn* has been so fully discussed by so many commentators that there is no need to do more than recall its own limbo: "I got to light out for the Territory ahead of the rest, because Aunt Sally she's going to adopt me and sivilize me, and I can't stand it. I been there before." Presumably that beckoning openness will afford the freedom and morality that "sivilization" has betrayed in exactly the same ways that the DeBellegardes have betrayed the supposed meaning and honor of their own names. But there is *no* human territory allowed by the book. Only when Jim and Huck are alone in the woods or on the river does openness seem possible, but unexceptionably, every human contact is one kind or another of closure. What kind of new territory could Twain supply, then? His nostalgic recoloring of what life on the Mississippi once had been is one answer, and a long description of nothing but woods and river would have been another—and tedious—answer. But in confronting the juncture of openness and closure in the two Americas, Twain left Huck exactly as James left Newman: poised for flight. *The state of motion* is the only state left for the expression of the idea of America, for there is no actualized God's New Country such as proclaimed by nationalistic ideology.

America's version of *Madame Bovary*, Kate Chopin's *The Awakening*, applies to women's possibilities the same juncture of closure and oceanic openness that characterized the ending of *Moby-Dick* and Crane's "The Open Boat." Edna Pontellier cannot find in the "terribly insisted upon actualities" the vision, the Romantic utopia of the possibilities of life, that fills her growing consciousness. Chopin, too, leaves her major character in motion, caught at a moment of transition between two worlds. Edna leaves behind her the world of closure, but swims to her death in the vastness of the totally open ocean. Like all serious American writers, Chopin has no actualized American millennium to dramatize; yet she finds the very essence of her materials in the millennialistic energies of American expectation, and that expectation is oceanic in psychological as well as material dimensions. The process of disillusion through actualities is a process that defines the nature of the illusion. And, like Kate Chopin's work, the fictions of other turn-of-the-century women writers (Edith Wharton most particularly comes to mind) make clear that the politics of the two Americas is a matter not only of gender but of national imagination.

As we move up in the twentieth century, if we deliberately choose a scattering of writers very unlike Hawthorne and very unlike each other in quality, materials, theme, and style, we may come to suspect that the relationship of endings to a national continuum lasts up to the present. A brief glimpse reveals a tension of openness and closure.

The suffocating endings of Fitzgerald's books, *The Great Gatsby* and *Tender Is the Night,* impart the same tensions. The last words of *The Great Gatsby* evoke a sense of an entire nation poised for flight, in motion between two states: the past, which is all the actualities to which the dreams have been debased but in which we had the youth to dream of transcendent futures, and the future, which is the continuation of the dream of endless openness: "But that's no matter—we will run faster and stretch our arms out farther, and one fine morning—

"So we beat on, boats against the current, borne back ceaselessly into the past." The ending of *Tender Is the Night,* with Dick Diver—once *the* American in every hopeful and millennialistic sense of Newman and Huck—dwindling into nonexistence in a dead country of terrible actualities "somewhere or other," is a dying fall into limbo, not into Hawthorne's American dream of "somewhere else." Fitzgerald, too, has been given such wide attention that no more need be said here about the endings, except to remark that his work maintains its perennial appeal in the gorgeous prose that in its nostalgic sense of loss signals— probably more than any other fiction except Twain's—the very essence of openness in the national imagination.

Saul Bellow ended *The Adventures of Augie March,* the Huckish book that in 1953 signalled a change from Bellow's Kafkan modishness to picaresque exuberance, with an image that is an acute condensation of the poised motion between two states. All of Augie's adventures teach the inevitability of closure, the necessity and inescapability of the actual. But the lesson is played out through Augie's imagination, which remains unquenchably open to newness and expectation. The concluding image sums up the continuing juxtaposition of a state of closure and the idea of the good new land of all possibility: "Columbus too thought he was a flop, probably, when they sent him back in chains. Which didn't prove there was no America." Similarly, the ending of *Humboldt's Gift* juxtaposes a hint of open rebirth, a spring flower, against the promise of final closure, a home for the aged. Fittingly, the closing scene is set in winter—breaking up.

> Menasha and I went toward the limousine. The side of his foot brushed away some of last autumn's leaves and he said, looking through his goggles, "What's this, Charlie, a spring flower?"
> "It is. I guess it's going to happen after all. On a warm day like this everything looks ten times deader."
> "So it's a little flower," Menasha said. . . . Here's another, but what do you suppose they're called, Charlie?"
> "Search me," I said. "I'm a city boy myself. They must be crocuses."[6]

In the imagery of this ending Bellow plays the idea of Citrine's endlessly discerning, helpless, initiated intelligence against the idea of Humboldt's crazy, depressive, and endlessly demanding expectation in the ways that Whitman played openness and closure into a coherent tension in sections five and six of "When Lilacs Last in the Dooryard Bloom'd":

> Over the breast of the spring . . .
>   and through old woods, where lately the violets
>   peep'd from the ground, spotting the gray debris . . .
> Passing the yellow-spear'd wheat, every grain from its
>   shroud in the dark-brown fields uprisen . . .
> Carrying a corpse to where it shall rest in the grave,
> Night and day journeys a coffin.
>
>   . . .
>
> Here, coffin that slowly passes,
>   I give you my sprig of lilac.

The crocus, like that lilac the sign of rebirth, is the recurring gift of openness inevitably bequeathed to the inevitability of closure. It is with the objectified, dramatized moment of seeing Humboldt's gift that Bellow ends his novel in a state of motion, a suspended moment between winter and spring, between closure and openness, but with the fusion of the two necessarily awaiting an America beyond the ending of the book.

Norman Mailer's first two books end in closure. In *The Naked and the Dead*, the "Hot Dog!" of Major Dalleson is the devolution of all dreams to an actuality of coarse bureaucratic mediocrity of the imagination and of life. Yet that vulgar deadliness is defined by the absolute nature of American wishes: General Cummings's expectation of total command in an exclusivist elitist world, Wilson's tumescent dreams of a vaginal universe, Croft's crazy sense of what it will mean to conquer the mountain and stand on the summit of Anopopei. In *Barbary Shore*,

Mikey Lovitt's amnesiac entrapment in blind history is summed up in the last sentence, an apocalyptic foreboding of final conflagration: "So the blind will lead the blind, and the deaf shout warnings to one another until their voices are lost."[7] But the closure into blindness and deafness is defined by the absolute, open dreams of the Good Society that once motivated MacLeod and Lanny. And in *An American Dream,* all the cancerous corruptions of society are the "terrible actualities" that give sharpness to the concluding image evoking a continuing dream of the existential ability to contact the eternal Marilyn-Monroe-in-the-Sky. In all three cases the endings take their continuity with the endings of *Moby-Dick, The American, The Adventures of Huckleberry Finn, The Awakening, The Great Gatsby,* and *Humboldt's Gift* in a state of motion, suspended to be looked at, with the relationship of expectation to *polis* unresolved, imminent, but undramatizable. America remains unfound.

More recently yet, Joan Didion concludes a novel about America with another version of the caught moment between two states. In using the events of America's adventure in southeast Asia, Didion, in her style, her characters, and events, soaks her book in cynical, satirical repudiation of everything that the "terrible actualities" of American commerce and politics (of all hues) have become. Nevertheless, the national portrait, ironically titled *Democracy,* does not end in a final triumph of closure. Annoyingly mannered and annoyingly turning into one more novel about a novelist writing a novel about writing a novel (Joan Didion names her narrator Joan Didion), nonetheless the book catches the impossibility of American experience culminating in a satisfactorily fixed state of being. Echoes of what James and Twain wrestled with reverberate in the last two pages of the book's ending:

> It has not been a novel I set out to write, nor . . . have I experienced the rush of narrative inevitability that usually propels a novel toward its end, the momentum that sets in as events overtake their shadows and the cards all fall in on one another and the options decrease to zero.
>
> Perhaps because nothing in this situation encourages the basic narrative assumption, which is that the past is prologue to the present, the options remain open here.
>
> Anything could happen.[8]

Sounding like Bellow's Augie March rather than like Fitzgerald's Nick Carraway, who wryly denies openness in his final ironic evocation of it, Joan Didion's Joan Didion uses the antepenultimate and penultimate sentences of her book to cling to an echo of the dream of the good polis: the major character, Inez Victor, has effected a version of lighting out for the territory ahead of the rest. The possibilities at the very end are left open. Inez "said that although she still considered herself an American national (an odd locution, but there it was) she would be in Kuala Lumpur until the last refugee was dispatched. Since Kuala Lumpur is not likely to dispatch its last refugee in Inez's or in my lifetime I would guess she means to stay on, but I have been surprised before."[9] The disillusion with America is complete. The character Didion has destroyed by lampoon the full spectrum of American politics and politicians, but Didion is not content with closure. At the very ending, in what amounts to a reverse utopian and ideological kinship with Hawthorne, Didion has Didion retrieve a force of openness. James, Twain, Chopin, Fitzgerald, Bellow, Mailer, Didion—it need not be these, for one could choose many American writers at random, having special fun with Ralph Waldo Ellison's *Invisible Man*—are as different as can be from one another, but they all have in common a juggling of openness and closure that, as was true of Hawthorne, is a means of dramatizing the moral and political significances of American expectation. Surely, this does not mean that American authors have not, do not, or cannot end their books in total closure (Melville's *The Confidence-Man*) or total openness (Thoreau's *Walden*). And surely this does not mean that writers other than Americans have not, do not, or cannot end their books in the caught moment, in the instant of stasis in which the moment of flight or separation reveals the interaction of openness and closure in process (William Shakespeare's *The Tempest*, André Malraux's *La Condition Humaine*). But except for thriller and detective fiction—and even in those categories, most serious works are not exceptions—it is very difficult to think of books that end with concerns other than those of openness or closure. Rather, the continuing attraction of very diverse American authors to the tension between the closing down of expectations and the announced dream-vision of the good place reveals the extent to which this particular *universal* theme is most intensely summed up in the *American* experience.

The political relationships of openness and closure in Hawthorne suggest that the very essence of American literature will continue to announce the considerations inherent in Hawthorne's "un-American" Classicist vision of the limitations of development. Hawthorne's longings and reservations were at the epicentral beginnings of the merger of American literature with universal human expressions of the tensions between hope and actuality. Later writers without his cast of temperament, and benefitting from what James and the moderns who followed him contributed to narrative points of view, learned to escape the kinds of flaws that reveal the cultural significance of Hawthorne's work. However, their themes and endings continue to indicate an American context of Romantic openness within the disillusions of Classicist closure. The literature of all nations plays with that juxtaposition, for it is the throb of the universe, including human biology (and once more I invite the reader who has not done so to scan the appendix). But the Romantic pressures of endlessly open expectation make that throb more noticeably central in American literature.

A pulse of openness and closure, which is the very cadence of the cosmos, is as inescapable in the conflicts of plot as in the functions of neurobiology. Hawthorne juggled the two Americas, the psychological and political energies of openness and closure, when he juggled his own selves, caught in pressures of utopia and ideology. He knew that he was juggling the differences between the idea of America and the actualities of American experience, but he could never summon up the final full commitment to his utopia in despite of the marketplace. For all the complexities of his interacting stances, Hawthorne generally leaves us with a perspective shared with Hilda and Kenyon atop St. Peter's. Yet, in his conscious and emblematic dissent from the ideologies of openness as well as in his inadvertent failings, Hawthorne courageously widened the boundaries of national letters. He announced in his own mixed way that the imaginative reconciliation of openness and closure, from their widest universal relevance to their finest political significances, from starbirth to parenthetical style and punctuation, is intensely and exquisitely for America—as in some inevitable measure for all nations—the lifebeat of its literature.

NOTES

1. *Nathaniel Hawthorne* (New York: Oxford University Press, 1980), pp. 162–63.

2. As I indicated in my acknowledgments and as has been clear at several points in my discussion, I owe a debt of prompting to Nina Baym, Ann Douglas, Ellen Moers, Jane Tompkins, and writers of several essays of feminist criticism. There are many who provide bright and controversial new insights into nineteenth-century American writing generally and Hawthorne in particular. Clearly, an account of criticism provided by feminist scholarship would demand a different book from the one I have written. Nevertheless, the one I have written owes a debt to some feminist perspectives, and I am happy to acknowledge it.

3. It is clear that neither shibboleth nor anathema has a one to one or even necessarily true connection to historical reality. For instance, apologists for capitalism use arguments of economic Romanticism as though they were describing a reality of the free individualist in a free *laissez-faire* marketplace rather

than one of federal legislation, budget policies, fiscal practices, monetary control, trade and product control, government contracts, bailouts, and golden parachutes. The monetarists who argue for trickle down policies often appeal to the *laissez-faire* myth of rational man in a free marketplace, whereas the very nature of monetarism is inextricably involved in government, both in tax policy and Federal Reserve edicts. Furthermore, if by bourgeois society we wish to suggest the middle-class gentilities, conformities, and respectabilities that are interwoven with class status and privilege, then we no longer can assume that capitalism and bourgeois society are necessarily economic and social facets of the same system. In many ways Soviet society is more middle class than American society in its Victorianisms, and, in fact, the voracious nature of American marketing dissolves fixed standards of value and behavior, helping to create the laid back bohemianism that used to be reserved for artists and radicals. The respectable bourgeois bemoans the new morality on television, in movies, and in public dress, language, and behavior. This essay is not the place to trace the phenomenon or the relationship between the new morality and the commercial bottom line. It is necessary here only to observe that ideological rhetoric has a force reflective of beliefs that move people in actuality, although the rhetoric itself does not reflect the complex and often contradictory nature of that actuality. Discontinuity between rhetoric and reality is the dangerous result: the political destruction of a deeply understood connection between utopia and ideology is the destruction of philosophically understood language—which is the ideological destruction of the necessary utopia. In this sense of the destruction of meaningful language, the debasement of art to the regnant values of depreciated popular culture is a path to totalitarianism. In their many reaches, the implications of the cultural significance of Hawthorne are, to say the least, critically important.

4. (New York: Harper and Row, 1966).

5. *Literature Against Itself: Literary Ideas in Modern Society* (Chicago: University of Chicago Press, 1979), pp. 17–18.

6. Saul Bellow, *Humboldt's Gift* (New York: Viking Press, 1975), p. 487.

7. (New York: Rinehart, 1951), p. 312.

8. (New York: Simon and Schuster, 1984), pp. 232–33.

9. *Democracy*, p. 234.

A Beginnings Context

It might seem an overstatement to claim the universal applicability of openness and closure to all existence, including the politics of narrative structures. The claim seems especially overgeneral when one considers that whatever cosmic forces one invokes, the world picture of Hawthorne's day is not the world picture of ours.

But humanists and artists, as well as scientists, work according to a world picture. Unlike the scientist, the humanist or artist might not be conscious of a world picture, but nonetheless it is very much there in the work. The literary critic might be no more aware of a world picture than the original artist, but the work of criticism demands more deliberate theorizing than the artist might care to undertake. Criticism is at once more plebeian and more didactically conscious than art. While lack of consciousness of a world picture might not necessarily hamper the critic in a job of applied criticism, such a picture consciously derived becomes an enlightening guide. In our time of abstruse scientific complexity, a comprehensible world picture for the nonscientist (and often for the scientist) is in a bewildering state of disrepair. Yet the disrepair of a coherent world picture in the late twentieth century not only would not preclude Hawthorne's imagination were he alive today, but also would feed it, for the very abstruseness of matter as currently perceived makes physicists sound like philosophers, theologians, and poets. And although Hawthorne's essentially Christian frame of reference was to be severely tried by the science of the late Victorian era and was to be, in effect, dissipated by the developments following Einsteinian relativity and quantum mechanics, still there is that in current scientific theory that would allow Hawthorne today the same basis for attempted coherence that humanists search for in a world picture that accommodates and justifies critical theory. In sum, it is important to try. Are there aspects of our own sense of the nature of existence that are applicable to Hawthorne's frame of reference and that contextualize it within a universal system? Contemporary science generates speculation that openness and closure *are* absolute conditions, and I attempt to illustrate here, however briefly, those initial and inclusive conditions as a cosmic enclosure within which critical praxis might illuminate Hawthorne's authorial conflicts. Those conditions are the beginning point for extending terms from a world picture to applied criticism.

In the lurch of the twentieth into the twenty-first century and the apparent inapplicability of Newtonian mechanics to problems of space, time, and energy, we have come to question what we take for granted about "the way things are." Some astrophysicists contemplate black holes in space as "wormholes" connecting our universe with others having different physical principles—universes in which things are not at all "the way things are." In the stunning swiftness of changes in scientific theories (and in the integrity of great scientific genius), our leading minds remain uncertain about "the way things are."

The royal contemporary paradigm for me is the career of Stephen Hawking, who probably is the most revered cosmologist of the twentieth century since Albert Einstein. He has spent his brilliant life in the study of cosmic singularities (points of zero diameter and infinitely curved space in which the laws of science apparently fail to hold, such as the supposed center of a black hole). Recently, in speculation about the universe at ground state (the lowest state of internal energy at which an individual, whether an atom or a galaxy, exists), Hawking, in the extreme of a wasting illness, has changed his mind about his previous conclusions and is thinking out new directions. "If the universe is not in the ground state, science cannot predict the universe. The rest is up to God," he muses.

" 'Quantum mechanics has to describe everything,' said Murray Gell-Mann of Caltech" to a 1987 workshop on quantum cosmology at the Fermi National Accelerator Laboratory, and "it became clear that by 'everything' he meant the work of historians and crime detectives [and literary commentators] and the songs of birds as well as the motions of galaxies. But he added: 'the questions are all murky and border on the philosophical.' " If the universe we can know is in the ground state, what falls into the black holes might pass through into other universes. If the universe we "know" is in "an energetically excited state," the "wormhole" connections possibly executed by black holes "provide channels by which information from outside the system may enter. 'God knows what this information is; we don't,' Hawking says." Gell-Mann argues that much of the information we get must be subjected to "decoherence" that sets aside some of the alien possibilities we think we know about "the way things are" in favor of the probabilities that belong to the universe we think we can know.[1] We live in a moment of scientific speculation in which it seems possible to throw any system of epistemology or ontology into doubt.

But within the realm of what we currently think we are able to know, and within the shifting uncertainties of new perspectives on energy and matter, the principles of openness and closure seem constant and—shall I say it?—absolute in their relationship. This appears to be true wherever we look, whether at raw cosmic force at the most elemental end of the spectrum of development or at biological being at the most advanced end. And it appears true whether we look at the macrocosmic or microcosmic aspects of either end.

At the macrocosmic elemental pole, if there were nothing but unlimited openness, could the cosmos contain an example of it, there would be only an eternal Big Bang: no star, but only constant dispersion of the ur-particles that would have made the star—if, indeed, there could be mass at all in uncoalesced open energy. In probable fact, the confirmation of what astronomers call "The Great Attractor," which coalesces the drift of galaxies, indicates that despite the smooth haze of background microradiation left from the birth of existence, the universe does convert the outward-bursting mode into vast, centered masses.[2] But, on the other hand, if there were nothing but unlimited closure, could the cosmos contain an example of it, there would be no process of collision and uniting of particles to begin with—if there could be mass at all in absolute condensation. Current theories of "false vacuums" include speculations about "wrinkles" in space that create condensations such as ten kilograms of matter to an "area" of 10^{-37} centimeters, whose consequent unimaginable heat and compaction is a density of pure energies that enact, in effect, the creation of matter in release. By themselves, as *absolutes*, openness and closure are nonexistence. Neither one could act alone, for it would have nothing to act on; the self-cancelling contradiction would not be. As separate, absolute states, openness and closure are not conceptual possibilities except as a totality of zero. As such, in any discussion of being, let alone value, they are physical and philosophical irrelevancies. The universe can offer no example of either as absolute state, for were there such a state there would be no universe.

But in being, the two principles are a paradox of mutually creating opposed forces, always acting together, as one sees that interaction in fictionalizing a star. First there is openness, a vast irruption of violent energies outward, creating changing and enlarging particles and thereby creating the conditions for counterbalancing closure as particles begin to combine. Gravitational force is created as condensation of cosmic plasma masses into density that attracts more matter into the growing form that finally becomes the nuclear engine of starbirth. Even on the most minute microlevel, that of the three generations of charged leptons, meutral leptons, and quarks that are the basic particles of all ordinary matter, or of the bosons that carry the four basic forces of the universe (electromagnetism, the strong force, the weak force, and gravity), there is mutual interaction of openness and closure.[3] On a somewhat less mysterious microcosmic level, in the birth of an individual star the phase of accretion itself is possibly another example of the relationship of openness and closure. As the growing mass of gravitationally accumulating matter draws down a heavier and heavier rain of particles from the surrounding dust and gas out of which stars are made, the increasing fury of stellar formation appears to set up a wind that blows away nearby dust and gas, thereby limiting the size of the accreting mass to an entity that balances into continuing existence. Attraction creates dispersion; closure creates openness. In the consequent balance, the fairly common size of stars like our sun is determined and controlled, resulting in masses that develop the fusion furnace that is the engine of solar life.[4] An engine of energies *released* in the *condensation*, the star burns away in a slowly diminishing balance between the openness of hurling itself into dispersions of radiant energies and particles of mass, and the closure of packing itself into more and more constraining density at the core. As it converts its hydrogen, it transforms its core into heavier and heavier elements, until iron is created. At that elemental point, closure can overbalance openness, and the star falls in upon itself in overwhelming density. Closure seems to win.

But when this happens, the intense compaction of mass and energy causes an explosion of incredible magnitude, and, as a nova, the star blows its shell into free space. Closure causes its opposite. Openness seems to win.

But when this happens, the outward bound matter furiously hurled into space becomes part of the gigantic clouds of matter, which collides and combines with itself and builds up new densities. Openness and closure create their opposites.

Current speculation about false vacuums hypothesizes the case. Presumably, space and matter do not stretch out in absolute smooth and regular distribution following dispersion from the Big Bang. Present examination of "walls" of galaxies suggests a "lumpy" universe, a clumping of galaxy clusters over vast time-distances, as though there have been clusters of bangs or clusters of condensation caused by gravity. In either case, at what we now conceive to be the farthest reaches of space-time, whether the context is that of the birth of the universe or the birth and death of a single star, the speculations and "facts" that we currently "know" bear out an absolute relationship of openness and closure.

Wherever we turn, the process is apparently inescapable. In the context of elemental, prebiological cosmic forces, just as openness and closure are suggested in both macrocosm (space-walls of galaxy clusters) and microcosm (single stars), so, too, the same holds true for phenomena within the most advanced biological context, the human neural system. For this system as macrocosm, Paul MacLean's controversial school of neurobiology postulates a human brain in which the "protoreptilian" brainstem, the limbic system, and the neocortex at once all reinforce and suppress each other. Protoreptilian activity of the most primitive part of the brain (which we share with birds and reptiles) represents the self-aggrandizement survival functions of fighting, fleeing, feeding, and mating. More recently developed in evolutionary time, the limbic system, an advanced brain that has developed around and beyond the brainstem, represents such emotional complexes as exaltation. (It contains the rhinencephalon, the "nose" control that creates the Proustian interwebbing of memory and associated feelings triggered by smell.) The newest and most advanced of all, the neocortex, which has developed around and beyond the limbic areas, represents a gamut from logic to altruism. For the purposes of derivations of value, one sees the three brain systems related in a rough hierarchy of ethics and intellect from the "lowest" to the "highest."

My extreme oversimplification muddles the state of understanding reached by neuroscientists, for the interfunctionings of the "three brains" are neuroanatomically much more complex and less sharply separated than this sketch indicates. Nevertheless, as a general indication of *interactions,* the concept of the triune brain serves as a revelation of openness and closure. A state of open expansion of any one aspect of the brain paradoxically would close the system: unbridled protoreptilian aggression would be death; unbridled limbic feeling would be madness; unbridled neocortical logic and abstraction could be a lack of self that would be suicide. The scheme as metaphor has rich and multiple possibilities of nuance for speculation about the significance of evolution and implications for and definitions of the good human being and the good polis. It is fertile ground for the concerns of literary theory and criticism, especially in the relations of literature to society and history.

Here it is sufficient to point out that consolidation and closure of power, paradoxically resulting in unchecked openness of one brain function, would be the end of the total organism. On the other hand, total and unceasing conflict between the brain functions would result in psychosis of such intensity, such conflict of body response, that the organism could not survive. In their mutual suppressions and reinforcements (as metaphor, evocative of a government of checks and balances), the parts of the triune brain preserve an integrated total organism in a balanced interaction of openness and closure. Recent investigations of molecular biology and psychopharmacology indicate how central to psychic health the *relationship* of neural transmitters is in the intricate balance of messages from part to part of the total neural system. The hyperpolarizing and depolarizing states of neurotransmission among the parts of the brain enact openness and closure on the levels of abstract logic, aesthetics, morality, and survival.[5]

Within the biological context, in microcosm, in the synaptic junctures of neurotransmission, the principles of openness and closure are apparently as absolute as in the macrocosm (the interfunctionings of the total neural system). In the gates of the synapses, at the infinitesimal distance of 250 nanometers between transmission site and receptor site, molecules of transmitter flow freely until their presence causes transmissions that close the gates, so to speak. Openness alone would result in stimulation that literally would shake the total organism to death. Closure alone would result in a stasis that would be a paralysis of all functions: death. At every mass, dimension, and level of existence, openness and closure beget each other and are the basis of what we suppose is the way things are.

Even the hypercomplex state of contemporary science offers a usable set of principles for the humanist. Openness contains the essence of a translation into Romanticism: change, outward expansion, newness of expression. Romanticism contains the essence of a translation into radicalism: rebellion against the status quo. Closure contains the essence of a translation into Classicism: stasis, order, precedent. Classicism contains the essence of a translation into conservatism: preservation of the status quo. Although Hawthorne's world picture was not ours, everything we see in ours reveals the same all-encompassing force of openness and closure that enacted the way things are in Hawthorne's universe of Newtonian mechanics, as expressed, for instance, in the openness and closure of Newton's laws of motion. Our Big Bang theoretics allow us explanatory assumptions in common with Hawthorne: our own world picture, understood as a process of openness and closure, is an inclusive context for the complexities of his texts. His ignorance of quarks and cosmic singularities diminishes in no way his awareness of the social manifestation and the political presence of the universal process of openness and closure, whose force he acknowledged in the dynamics of his American literary marketplace. Hawthorne was caught in the conflicts of Romanticism and Classicism, radicalism and conservatism, as they were enacted within himself and between himself and his marketplace. The politics of his relationship with his marketplace accounted for many of Hawthorne's literary strategies and characteristics. He, like all humans, responded to the rhythms of openness and closure, which are our circadian rhythms, our political rhythms, our psychological rhythms, the seasonal rhythms of the planet, the rhythms of the self and of all existence. Hawthorne's responses were literary, and in the politics of his American context he is a crucially significant example of the connections between space-walls of galaxies and the political significance of moments of punctuation.

NOTES

1. All of the quoted material as well as the definitions of singularities and ground state are taken from the late excellent science writer, Dietrich E. Thomsen, "In the Beginning Was Quantum Mechanics," *Science News* 131 (May 30, 1987), no.22: 346–47.

2. See Ivars Peterson, "The Source of a Great Attraction," *Science News* 137 (Jan. 27, 1990), no. 4: 60.

3. See Michael S. Chanowitz, "The Z Boson," *Science* 249 (July 6, 1990): 36–42. See also Ivars Peterson, "Beyond the Z," *Science News* 138 (Sept. 29, 1990), no. 13: 204–6.

4. See C. J. Lada and F. H. Shu, "The Formation of Sunlike Stars," *Science* 248 (May 4, 1990): 564–72.

5. Although the concept of the triune brain is disputed by several neuroscientists, the neuroanatomical designations of any particular school of neurobiology is less important for my purposes than the applications derivable therefrom for the humanities. A brief introduction for the nonspecialist is Constance Holden's "Paul MacLean and the Triune Brain," *Science* 204 (June 8, 1979): 1066–68. An old but useful and not entirely outmoded discussion of neurobiology for the interested layman is the special issue on the brain of *Scientific American* 241 (Sept. 1979). A useful introduction to research on the limbic system, emotion, and behavior, especially the function of the hippocampus, is R. L. Isaacson's *The Limbic System*, 2d ed. (New York: Plenum Press, 1982; orig. publ. 1974). Particularly pertinent for my purposes is chapter six in Isaacson, "The Graven Image, Lethe, and the Guru: The Triune Brain," pp. 219–43. Also extremely helpful but generally unavailable is Martha Wilson's *The Organization of the Brain and Behavior* (copyright by Martha Wilson, the University of Connecticut). Professor Wilson's study is "non-MacLeanian." For help and

guidance in a field in which the untrained lay reader is quickly lost, I am indebted to Professor Wilson for her generous collegial helpfulness and care, which is especially remarkable considering the reservations or modifications she held about some of the ways I had expressed concepts in our communications. See also P. D. MacLean, "The Triune Brain, Emotion, and Scientific Bias," in *The Neurosciences, Second Study Program*, ed. F. O. Schmitt (New York: Rockefeller University Press, 1970), pp. 336–49; and MacLean, "Cerebral Evolution and Emotional Processes," *Annals of the New York Academy of Sciences* 193 (1972): 137–49. An excellent non-MacLeanian presentation of brain functions for the lay reader is Robert Ornstein and Richard F. Thompson's *The Amazing Brain* (London: Chatto and Windus, 1985). It is interesting to note that like the cosmological physicists investigating the largest dimensions of our world picture, the neuroscientists, working in the smallest biological dimensions, also cannot rest with a finished picture, given our century's rate of discovery. The authors of *The Amazing Brain* have modified their own views since they copyrighted the text of their book in 1984.

Index

A Note on the Author

MILTON R. STERN is Distinguished Alumni Professor of English at the University of Connecticut. He is the author of *The Fine Hammered Steel of Herman Melville* and *The Golden Moment: The Novels of F. Scott Fitzgerald* and the editor or coeditor of numerous books, including *Adventures in American Literature* and the Penguin American Library edition of *The House of the Seven Gables*.